YOU CAN WRITE

Mary Ellen Grasso   Margaret Maney

Broward Community College

Winthrop Publishers, Inc., Cambridge, Massachusetts

Library of Congress Cataloging in Publication Data

Maney, Margaret.
    You can write.

    1. English language—Rhetoric. I. Grasso, Mary
Ellen, joint author. II. Title.
PE1408.M3394   808'.042   75–1421
ISBN 0–87626–976–5

Copyright © 1975 by Winthrop Publishers, Inc.
17 Dunster Street, Cambridge, Massachusetts 02138

10 9 8 7 6 5 4 3 2 1

CONTENTS

63375

STAGE 7   THE OUTLINE, 137

STAGE 8   DEFINITION, 167

STAGE 9   PROCESS ANALYSIS, 187

PART 2   FINDING AND USING INFORMATION: THE BASICS OF THE RESEARCH PAPER, 249

Part 1

THE WRITING PROCESS: SAYING WHAT YOU MEAN

GETTING STARTED

How many times have you said, "I know what I want to say, but I just can't seem to get it down on paper"? How often have you heard yourself say, when trying to explain something to another person, "Well, you know what I mean"? These short circuits in communications happen to everyone and are always frustrating. For example, consider the process of writing to a friend, preparing a committee report for an organization to which you belong, working up a campaign speech for a political candidate, or presenting a resumé of your background to apply for a job. As a person who has had little experience in writing or as one who has had to do some writing and has had difficulty expressing ideas, you may have found that a gap exists between the ideas you want to communicate and their final written presentation. Recognizing this gap is discouraging, but it is also the beginning of learning to write well.

You need to realize that writing is a skill, and like any other skill it can be learned in stages and steps. Suppose you want to play a musical instrument, learn a new sport, or take up a handicraft. Before you can play chord progressions on a guitar, you must learn to position your fingers on the frets. When you first go out on the tennis court, you learn to grip the racket properly before you can execute an effective serve. Similarly, if you take up macramé, you learn to tie the basic knots before you produce a belt, a purse, or a wall hanging. In the same way, you can learn to say what you mean when you write and to say it well. If you follow the stages and steps necessary to produce effective writing, just as you would work through the stages and steps of mastering an instrument, a sport, or a hobby, you CAN write.

STAGE 1

MASTERING WORDS

1. Recognizing Different Language Situations
2. Distinguishing Denotative and Connative Meaning
3. Recognizing How Bias Words Work
4. Recognizing Special Problems in Word Choice

STEP 1 **Recognizing Different Language Situations.** The first step in writing is to recognize the right word for the situation. Think for a moment about how you might talk during a job interview. Would you conclude the interview by saying, "O.K., this job looks like a good deal to me, and I'm sure that I can handle all these types I'll bump into"? Would you be likely to say, "I think I have enough experience to handle the various kinds of people I will be meeting on this job"? Or would you say, "I am an individual with background that would enable me to facilitate the interpersonal relationships necessary for this position"?

If you want the job you should use the second comment. The first might be used in everyday conversation with your friends, but the extreme informality of this response might indicate to a potential employer that you would be unable to adapt your language to a more formal situation. The third comment sounds false; the employer could infer from it that you are making a misguided attempt to appear educated and competent.

What different styles of language do you need to recognize to be an effective speaker and writer? First, you will need to distinguish standard from nonstandard English. Standard English refers to patterns of grammar and syntax widely accepted as preferred usage. Nonstandard English is any usage that doesn't follow these patterns. Standard English may be either **formal** or **informal,** depending upon the situation.

3

STANDARD ENGLISH

INFORMAL ENGLISH

You use informal English at home, in conversation with your friends, in the classroom, in informal business situations, and in writing personal letters. When you use informal English, you are fairly relaxed about word order and rules of grammar, you use contractions, and you use many colloquial expressions.

FORMAL ENGLISH

You use formal English in professional situations, in business transactions, in business letters, and in expository writing. When you use formal standard English, you pay careful attention to word order and rules of grammar, and you avoid contractions and colloquial expressions.

Just as you shift your other behavior according to the situation, you must become adept at shifting language gears in moving from informal to formal standard English. Some differences between informal and formal English are shown in the following paired expressions:

	INFORMAL	FORMAL
Contractions	We'll go to the concert.	We will go to the concert.
	The press isn't sure about the facts.	The press is not sure about the facts.
Word Order	Who are you going with?	With whom are you going?
	What are you going to panel the room with?	What type of paneling will you use for the room?
Agreement	Everyone has their complaints.	Everyone has his or her complaints.
Case	It's me.	It is I.
Split infinitive	The men want to quickly finish the job.	The men want to finish the job quickly.

	INFORMAL	FORMAL
Clipped words	phone	telephone
	TV	television
	ad	advertisement
	exam	examination
Colloquialisms	How come the concert was cancelled?	Why was the concert cancelled?
	You're mad at me.	You are angry with me.
	A lot of us are going.	Many of us are going.
	This bike is o.k.	This bicycle is satisfactory.

Because colloquialisms occur so often in informal English speech, you will find that it is hard to leave them out of your writing. The ones listed above will be obvious to you, but you will want to become aware of others which are frequently used but which are not suitable to formal standard English.

COLLOQUIAL	FORMAL
That's a *funny* thing to do.	That is a *peculiar* thing to do.
This model is *different than* the first one.	This model is *different from* the first one.
The plan is *identical to* the other.	The plan is *identical with* the other.
Herman *can't help but* be a joker.	Herman *cannot help* being a joker.
The vacation package is a *good deal.*	The vacation package is a *good arrangement.*
Stand *in back of* me.	Stand *behind* me.
The key must be *someplace* in the house.	The key must be *somewhere* in the house.
The *kids* were here today.	The *children* were here today.

COLLOQUIAL	FORMAL
I was *mighty happy* about my promotion.	I was *very happy* about my promotion.
How about going to dinner?	*Would* you like to go to dinner?
Try and go tonight.	*Try to go* tonight.
He *blamed it on* Herman.	He *blamed* Herman.
We'll leave *inside of* an hour.	We will leave *within* an hour.
The salesman didn't say *if* he would return.	The salesman did not say *whether* he would return.
That girl is *just* beautiful.	That girl is *very* beautiful.

NONSTANDARD ENGLISH

Nonstandard English is usage which does not conform to the patterns considered correct or standard by most well-educated people. The following expressions are examples of nonstandard English:

It don't matter to me.
I can't hardly wait to see that movie.
I seen that show on television before.
Herman done that on purpose.
Hand me that there magazine.
My sister could of done the dishes for me.
Leave me be.
We was afraid we wouldn't get there on time.
I got the book off of Tom.
Herman ain't there.
We could of gone to the game.
The teacher done everything she could to pass me.
He give me the wrong answer.
I should have stood in bed.
You could have went with me.
The shot won't hurt none.

SLANG

Slang is language which relies heavily on newly coined words or on existing words used in some special sense. It is unconventional language that may be vivid, grotesque, comic, or vulgar. Carl Sandburg characterized slang as "language that takes off its coat, spits on its hands, and goes to work."

One of the chief characteristics of slang is that it is short-lived. In the 1920s, for instance, anything wonderful was the *cat's meow,* the *berries,* or the *bee's knees.* In the 1970s it became *groovy, fantastic, far out,* or *outasight.* The 1920s expression *twenty-three skiddoo* translates in the 1970s to *let's split.* Slang often changes not just from decade to decade but from month to month; so if a person uses slang that is even slightly out-of-date, he is definitely not *cool.* The word *cool* itself illustrates the changing nature of slang. Anything meriting approval in the '50s and '60s was *hot;* now it's *cool.*

While most slang is short-lived, some slang words are so useful that they become a permanent part of our language. *Lousy,* for example, has been around for 250 years. *Booze, blab, cram, lily-livered, laughing stock, dame, clod, bloody,* and *wench* have been around over 400 years. Some other slang expressions which are now accepted as standard English are *okay* as a sign of approval, *hoax,* which in George Washington's day was slang for falsehood, and *blind date,* slang in the '20s, but now a standard expression.

Argot is slang, or code language, specific to a particular social group. *Gat, hit, contract, heist, moll,* and *fence* are all 1920s underworld argot. Jazz music is a particularly rich source of slang: *bop, dig, beat, groovy, hip, pad, gig,* and *dude* are just a few of the terms it has produced. In recent years the drug culture has expanded an already colorful argot that includes *grass, tea, maryjane, weed, acid, coke, snow, scag, uppers, downers, bag, hit, lid, busted, stoned, spaced, crash,* and *crash pad.*

Occupations, sports, and special interest groups all have their own slang, known as *jargon.* The term originally meant meaningless chatter, but *jargon* now refers to terms for objects, processes or operations, prices, and transactions understood by a particular group. A person associated with the theater, for instance, will refer to a stage hand as a *grip,* to the various curtains as *teasers, tormenters,* and *travellers,* and to two people talking at the same time as *overlap.* Much of the jargon of special groups eventually becomes a permanent part of the language. For instance, the general population understands what an aviator means by being *socked in, flying blind,* and *bailing out;* and what the short order cook means by a *BLT* and *one over easy;* what Armed Forces personnel mean by *gold brick, blockbuster, black market,* and *running afoul;* and what students mean by a *bull session, brainstorm, cribbing, cramming,* and *acing* an exam.

While slang enlivens the language and is widely accepted in everyday conversation, you should not rely too heavily on it. Using slang will make the transition from speaking to writing expository prose difficult, since slang is seldom acceptable in formal expository writing.

STEP 2   Distinguishing Denotative and Connotative Meaning.   Just as you need to distinguish formal from informal uses of language, you will need to recognize that words can carry two kinds of meanings, denotative and connotative. The **denotative** meaning of the word is the factual or dictionary meaning. The **connotative** meaning is the emotional or imaginative response to the word. The denotation of *mother,* for instance, is simply "female parent." The connotations of *mother* might be warmth, protection, consolation, good food, and cheerful surroundings for one person, and nagging, misunderstanding, and restriction for another. The denotative meaning of the word *red* is "the light primary of the long wave end of the spectrum." But *red* has many connotations: blood, war, anger (to see red), or joy (a red-letter day). Politically, it is associated with the red banner of revolution (red scare) and with communism, as in Red China.

Think about names of commercial establishments and names of products. They are often made up of words which taken individually have specific denotations. When used in association with the firm or the product, however, these same words carry certain connotations. Consider, for example, Singer's machine, *Touch and Sew.* Each word has a generally agreed on denotative meaning. Yet the image connoted by the combination is that of a machine which almost sews by itself. Or consider an air conditioning firm called *Engineered Air.* Once more, each word has a particular denotative meaning, but the name of the firm takes advantage of their combined connotations. The customer, seeing them together, gets the impression that his air conditioning problems will be handled by professionals, so the name connotes confidence.

Now read the following two descriptions of a hospitalized patient to see how denotation and connotation work in longer passages of writing. The source for these descriptions is unknown.

A SICK PATIENT

DENOTATIVE DESCRIPTION

A man of forty-five, unclothed above the waist, lay on a bed in the hospital. His skin was deeply jaundiced except over his palms and soles, where a red color predominated over the yellow. His extremities were thin generally, although the feet and ankles were swollen. The abdomen was distended with fluid, and its superficial veins were abnormally conspicuous. The hair was sparse in the axillae and absent on the chest. The breasts were unusually prominent for those of a man. The patient's breath smelled of alcohol. If an examiner pressed upon the right side of the abdomen at the margin of the ribs, he could feel a resistance revealing an enlarged, hard, but smooth liver. The aggregate of the patient's physical abnormalities, combined with his medical history of heavy drinking for twenty years, were diagnostic of advanced Laennec's cirrhosis of the liver.

CONNOTATIVE DESCRIPTION

On the white sheets of a hospital bed, a human ruin was sprawled; his spidery extremities extended like vines from his misshapen yellow body. He lay naked except for pajama bottoms that could not close across his bulging abdomen. The huge belly was striped longitudinally by distended, dark veins, and in its middle a navel protruded like a stubby thumb. The pathetic abdominal mountain sloped to meet a hairless, sunken, jaundiced chest. At the apex of this disaster was a small head, fitted on a skinny neck and topped with a tangle of hair that was unevenly brown and gray.

The face, of indeterminate age but vaguely suggesting a man past fifty, was freshly shaven, and the body was clean, thanks to the recent scrubbing applied ceremoniously by the orderlies against feeble protest. Only the stench of the man's breath, resembling rotten fruit, still lingered to remind one of the human derelict lurching from the barroom. The face that presented itself from the white pillow appeared one of defeat and resignation except for the yellow eyes. These revealed a piteous hope that some magic medicine could return him again to the delicious aroma of spilled beer, ragged cigars, and Woolworth perfume. The eyes seemed to long for the nostalgic sight of scarred mahogany bars littered with ash trays and steins, draped with elbows, and canopied by the grim, intent faces of debauchers; and the magic medicine would restore to his ears the amalgamated din of jukeboxes, pinball machines, shrill laughter, and loud, empty conversation.

EXERCISE 1-1   IDENTIFYING DENOTATIVE AND CONNOTATIVE MEANING

A. What was the writer's intention in the denotative description? In the connotative description?
B. Which words evoke a strong emotional response? Underline them.
C. What pictures are conveyed by each of the underlined words or phrases?

STEP 3   **Recognizing How Bias Words Work.**   Some words which have a denotative meaning may each carry very different connotations. Consider the word *smell,* the denotation of which is a sensation perceived by the olfactory sense. Synonyms of smell which have unfavorable connotations are *stink* and *stench;* synonyms with favorable connotations are *aroma, scent, perfume, fragrance,* and *bouquet.* Some of these words even connote masculinity or femininity: advertisements refer to the aroma of a cigar but to the fragrance or scent of perfume.

When certain connotations of a word are emphasized over others, the word is being used as a **bias word** in that context. An author can slant his writing by using bias words, by selecting an emotionally charged word over an emotionally neutral one. Depending on his intention, a writer uses favorable or unfavorable bias words. He does this by choosing one of a group of words with similar denotations but different connotations: e.g., *skinny, thin, slender; stubborn, strong-willed, resolute.* Or, he may choose from a group of words which all refer to one category of objects but which have different denotations *and* different connotations: *shack, house, cottage; nag, horse, thoroughbred.*

BIAS WORDS AND THE COMMERCIAL WORLD

Bias words are frequently used in the world around you; they can lead you to patronize an establishment, purchase a product, or make a judgment. Consider the implications of the following words or phrases used in advertising: Fastrack, Yard Guard, Right Guard, Virginia Slims, Love, Instamatic, and Hollywood bread. Then consider the importance of word choice in the following newspaper headlines: "Dropout Knew Penalty," "Wife-swapping Player Traded," "Puppet Government Cuts Off Service," "Bill Fights Contribution Loopholes," "Pro–Pay Raise Official 'Examining Conscience,'" "Southern Coalition to Fight Acupuncture," "Redneck Fuzz Taunt Peace Loving Hippies."

EXERCISE 1-2   SUPPLYING BIAS WORDS

A. For each of the neutral terms below, supply one or more synonyms with unfavorable connotations and then one or more with favorable connotations. Compare your lists with those of other students to determine whether you all agree on the connotations of the words substituted for each neutral term.

UNFAVORABLE	NEUTRAL	FAVORABLE
_____	overweight	_____
_____	car	_____
_____	lawyer	_____
_____	doctor	_____
_____	writer	_____
_____	freedom	_____
_____	a date	_____
_____	common	_____
_____	stomach	_____
_____	pride	_____
_____	girl	_____

B. Now supply as many favorable and unfavorable bias words as you can for *girl*. Consider the implications of each word you have supplied.

Name _____

Date _____

Section _____

EXERCISE 1-3   FINDING BIAS WORDS

Find four brand names, four names of establishments, and four captions of newspaper or magazine articles which contain words that are biased or words which in context are biased.

Brand names
    1.
    2.
    3.
    4.

Names of establishments
    1.
    2.
    3.
    4.

Headlines or news captions
    1.
    2.
    3.
    4.

EXERCISE 1-4   RECOGNIZING BIAS WORDS IN JOURNALISM

Read the editorial page of your local newspaper for several days. Find an editorial or a letter to the editor that you think contains more bias words than it does factual information. Clip the passage, underline the bias words, and bring it to class for discussion.

STEP 4   **Recognizing Special Problems in Word Choice.**   Now that you recognize the levels of language, the distinction between denotative and connotative language, and the use of bias words, you will need to consider several special problems that can interfere with communicating specific ideas and information.

EUPHEMISMS

In the interest of "proper" English, people sometimes substitute an indirect or vague expression for one thought to be offensive or too blunt. They may say *passed away* for died, *in a family way* for pregnant, *indisposed* for sick, *exceptional children* for the retarded, and *maintenance engineer* for janitor.

JARGON

In addition to the specialized language peculiar to an occupation or interest, there is a kind of general jargon characterized by wordiness or verbal fuzziness. Such expressions as *utilize* or *implement* for use, *individual* for person, *dialog* for discussion, *viable* for workable, *commence* for begin, *prior to* for before, *subsequent to* for after, *make inquiry regarding* for inquire, are all unnecessary, and will rarely be found in good writing. The word *concept* has become a catchall word used indiscriminately by many writers and by Madison Avenue in particular. It is substituted thoughtlessly for words with more specific meanings: organization, technique, notion, idea, definition, principle, trend, plan, arrangement. Three jargon word families are to be avoided at all costs; these are the families of *-wise, -type,* and *-oriented.* A writer who can't leave these jargon families alone could conceivably write a horror like this: "Executive-type employees are time-oriented because, moneywise, they have to be."

POMPOUS WORDS

Pompous words are first cousins to euphemisms and jargon. Immature or careless writers sometimes use them to give the impression that they are well bred or well read. As a result, they might write *elucidate* for explain, *repast* for meal, *elicit* for get, *remunerate* for pay, *commensurate with* for equal to, *penurious* for stingy, and *munificent* for generous.

UNNECESSARY REPETITION

Writers are often unaware that they are fogging their meaning by being redundant — that is, they are repeating an idea in another word, phrase, or sentence. Thus, you see such expressions as *each individual,* our *modern world of today, advance forward, consensus of opinion, descended down, refer back,* and *repeat again.*

TRITE EXPRESSIONS

If a phrase is repeated often it may lose its original freshness and become meaningless. These overused expressions, or clichés, should be avoided because they will no longer convey any information to the reader. Here are some common examples of the kind of language to avoid: *all in all, as luck would have it, depths of despair, easier said than done, few and far between, ignorance is bliss, meets the eye, method in his madness, when all is said and done, words fail to express, in the last analysis.*

GOBBLEDYGOOK

Involved, unclear, sometimes completely unintelligible language that combines several or all of the special problems just discussed is often called gobbledygook. Government workers, sociologists, psychologists, educators, lawyers, and armed forces personnel are particularly guilty of producing gobbledygook. An educator, for example, might say, "Students cannot facilitate basic information processing due to inability to manipulate extrinsic factors in the module situation." *Translation:* The students can't concentrate on the basic lecture because they are unable to screen out distractions in the classroom. A psychologist might report, "Analytic focus centered on eliciting response on parameters defined by subject group for opening roles that would generate behavior commensurate to group purpose." *Translation:* The leader asked the encounter group which role each person would play to accomplish the goals of the group.

OBJECTIVE AND SUBJECTIVE WRITING

Why all this attention to the use of words? You have seen that there are several kinds of writing and that the type of writing depends upon the writer's intention. The author of the denotative paragraph about the sick patient was probably an internist or a pathologist. His purpose was to report, as factually and as accurately as possible, the condition of a patient with acute cirrhosis of the liver. His intent, obviously, was to reach the understanding rather than the emotions of his reader. His tone was therefore **objective,** and he achieved this objective tone by the use of denotative language. His method was the logical presentation of medical data which could be objectively verified.

From this logical presentation of facts, the writer then drew his conclusion. This denotative passage, then, is an example of **expository writing.**

On the other hand, the second passage about the sick patient, full of connotative words and phrases, was probably written by a novelist. His purpose was to produce in the reader a feeling of horrified fascination at the physical deterioration of a human being. His intent was to reach his reader's emotions first. Some readers would no doubt respond with pity at the portrait of a life so wasted; others would react with scorn or revulsion at this picture of a skid row alcoholic. The writer's method was primarily pictorial rather than logical; his tone was **subjective,** and he achieved this subjective tone by his use of connotative language. Because of its subjective tone and the different emotional responses possible on the part of the reader, this passage is an example not of expository writing but of **fiction writing.**

The two types of writing differ in intent and therefore in word choice. The writer of fiction interprets human life or some aspect of it from his or her particular viewpoint — that is, subjectively. The expository writer tries to report more objectively. To do so, the expository writer considers four questions:

1. What is my particular point about this subject?
2. Who is my audience?
3. What do they need or want to know about this subject?
4. How can I best convey my point to my audience?

The expository writer then sets about listing facts, examples, and incidents; analyzing the subject by classifying information; defining terms; comparing and contrasting the subject with similar topics; and demonstrating causes and effects of the subject. In the following Stages you will learn how to use these methods to demonstrate your points, and then how to combine these methods in an interesting and well-written paper.

STAGE 2

INFERENCES AND FACTS

1. Recognizing Inferences
2. Recognizing Facts
3. Distinguishing Between Reports of Facts and Reports of Inferences
4. Finding Sources for Expository Writing

STEP 1   **Recognizing Inferences.**   Your first concern as an expository writer is to communicate specific information, rather than vague or general ideas. However, a special difficulty for you as a beginning writer is that most people speak in generalities. As an illustration, listen to a conversation among your friends at the cafeteria. You might hear remarks something like this:

"The food prices are *reasonable* and the portions are *large*." "But the atmosphere in here is *pretty depressing*." Or: "That instructor is *demanding,* but he does have a *knack* for making the class *really interesting*." Or: "You ought to vote for Tony for president of student government, he's a *great guy*."

Ask yourself what all of these remarks really mean. What specific information has been transmitted? For instance, what does your friend mean when he says that the atmosphere of the cafeteria is *depressing?* Ask him. He may answer that "It's *dreary*." Do you know yet *specifically* what he means? Not exactly. Ask him to explain further. Now he may tell you that "The walls are painted gray, the room is lit with bare sixty watt light bulbs, the only decorations are bulletin boards, and the windows are blocked out by the new wing under construction." Now you know what your friend meant by *dreary* and *depressing*.

Go back and examine all the other statements in the conversation. You will notice that every italicized word or phrase is an inference. An inference is an *opinion,* a *conclusion,* a *generalization,* a *preference,* a *prediction,* or a *vague statement.* An inference raises one or more of the following questions: *what? when? why? where? how? to what degree? under what conditions?*

STEP 2   **Recognizing Facts.**   When these questions are answered, they are answered with **facts.** Facts make up the evidence which explains, supports, corrects, or proves the **inference.** You can verify a fact with evidence obtained by sight, sound, smell, touch, measurement, and mathematical computation. An inference, then, is an **abstraction;** a fact is a **concrete statement.**

You will need practice in learning to recognize inference words and their location in a sentence. As an alert reader, you will soon recognize that the inference term can be one of several parts of speech (noun, verb, adjective, or adverb) and that it can appear in any part of a sentence (subject, subject or object complement, or modifier). Furthermore, you will see that there can be more than one inference term in a sentence. In addition, you will begin to notice the many unsupported inferences you find in textbooks, newspaper and magazine articles, television commentaries, and advertisements. The following sentences and explanations illustrate the various roles played by the inference terms, which are in italics.

> *Femininity* is an *asset* to any woman.
> > *Femininity* is a noun and it is the subject of the sentence.
> > *Asset* is a noun, but it is the subject complement in the sentence.

> Peggy Parks *really hates* eight o'clock classes.
> > *Really* is an adverb modifying the verb *hates.*
> > *Hates* is a verb.

> *Old* people are *often lonely* and *neglected.*
> > *Old* is an adjective modifying *people.*
> > *Often* is an adverb modifying *are.*
> > *Lonely* and *neglected* are adjectives used as subject complements.

The *redneck fuzz* are *always taunting* and *provoking* the *peace loving hippies* who are trying to enjoy nature in the *beautiful* park.

Redneck is an adjective modifying *fuzz.*

Fuzz is a noun and is the subject.

Always is an adverb modifying the verbs *taunting* and *provoking.*

Peace loving is an adjective modifying *hippies.*

Hippies is a noun and is the direct object.

Beautiful is an adjective modifying park.

It is possible for an entire sentence to be an inference even though none of the words in it can be identified as inference terms. Slogans, sayings, and propositions are in this category. Consider the following: a rolling stone gathers no moss; legalize pot; if guns were outlawed, only outlaws would have guns.

EXERCISE 2-1   RECOGNIZING INFERENCE TERMS

In each of the following sentences, underline the inference word or words, name the part of speech, and tell how the word functions.

Example: Tuition at an out-of-state college is *expensive*.

Expensive is an adjective. It is the subject complement.

1. Affluence often spoils children of the wealthy.

2. The number of reported child abuse cases in the United States is rising sharply every year.

3. Marshall Field's has the most comprehensive men's department of any store in Chicago.

4. Community colleges should be conveniently located for the majority of students in a county.

5. Well-trained paramedical students can always demand good salaries and attractive working conditions when they graduate.

EXERCISE 2-2 SUPPORTING INFERENCES WITH FACTS

Following are examples of seven kinds of inferences. Underline the inference term or terms and supply at least two facts to support the inference.

1. *Opinion*
   Paul Potter makes people feel comfortable.
   A. (Fact)
   B. (Fact)

2. *Conclusion*
   The cost of living is rising steadily.
   A. (Fact)
   B. (Fact)

3. *Generalization*
   Women are terrible drivers.
   A. (Fact)
   B. (Fact)

4. *Preference*
   I prefer movies in a theater to movies on television.
   A. (Fact)
   B. (Fact)

5. *Decision*
   I plan to become an oceanographer.
   A. (Fact)
   B. (Fact)

6. *Prediction*
   I will probably fail biology.
   A. (Fact)
   B. (Fact)

7. *Vague statement*
   Americans are always on the move.
   A. (Fact)
   B. (Fact)

EXERCISE 2-3 DISTINGUISHING INFERENCES FROM FACTS

In the blank to the left of each sentence put an **I** if the sentence is an inference and an **F** if the sentence is a fact.

_____ 1. Fat people are compulsive eaters.

_____ 2. Normal body temperature is 98.6 degrees Fahrenheit.

_____ 3. Normal body temperature is 96.8 degrees Fahrenheit.

_____ 4. A motor home is ready to go when you are.

_____ 5. Eighty percent of U.S. motor homes are built with a Chrysler Corporation chassis.

_____ 6. American motor home manufacturers prefer a chassis built by Chrysler Corporation.

_____ 7. America is an affluent nation.

_____ 8. It is a disgrace that in an affluent nation like America so many people live below the poverty level.

_____ 9. My children will never drink, swear, or smoke pot.

_____ 10. Some parents are stricter than other parents.

_____ 11. In 1972 there were 50,000 reported cases of child abuse.

_____ 12. The actual number of child abuse cases in the United States is much higher than 50,000.

_____ 13. Fractures and malnutrition are two signs of child abuse.

_____ 14. That discotheque was a shambles after the raid.

_____ 15. Phil will inherit his uncle's 1919 Stutz Bearcat.

_____ 16. Although news of the Watergate Affair broke before the election, it did not prevent Nixon's re-election as President in 1972.

_____ 17. What the world needs now is a little love.

_____ 18. Cryogenics is the science of freezing the human body at time of death for restoration to life at a future time.

_____ 19. If cryogenics is successfully developed, it will raise serious moral, social, and legal issues.

_____ 20. Cigarette smoking is harmful to your health.

STEP 3   Distinguishing Between Reports of Facts and Reports of Inferences. Often a statement indicates that the information came from another source. If a fact comes from another source, the statement is a **report of a fact.** If an inference comes from another source, the statement is a **report of an inference.** The following sentences are examples of these types of statements.

REPORTS OF FACTS

The emergency room doctor told me that I had a compound fracture of my arm.

A Congressional study on Medicare revealed that almost one million Americans are in twenty thousand nursing homes.

The cost of living index rose 2.2 percent in March, *according to* Time *magazine.*

University City, Missouri, has a population of 46,309, *reports the 1973* World Book Encyclopedia.

The marbelized tiles for the family room, *according to our contractor,* would cost fifty cents each.

REPORTS OF INFERENCES

The emergency room doctor told me that I had a severe injury of my arm.

A Congressional study on Medicare revealed that a large silent minority of Americans are in nursing homes.

The cost of living index rose sharply in March, *according to* Time *magazine.*

University City, Missouri, is a middle-sized town, *reports the 1973* World Book Encyclopedia.

The marbelized tiles for the family room, *according to our contractor,* are moderately priced.

You will notice that the indicators of reports of facts and reports of inferences are in italics. These indicators *(according to, said, revealed, stated, reported),* can come at the beginning, the middle, or the end of a sentence.

Name _____

Date _____

Section _____

EXERCISE 2-4   RECOGNIZING INFERENCES, FACTS, REPORTS OF FACTS, AND REPORTS OF INFERENCES

Identify the following statements according to the key:

  I   Inference
  F   Fact
  RF Report of Fact
  RI Report of Inference

_____ 1. The Olivetti typewriter has an unbeatably solid frame.

_____ 2. Older people should remain independent and active as long as possible.

_____ 3. There are seventy million people over forty years of age now residing in the United States.

_____ 4. In 1900, the average lifespan was forty years.

_____ 5. The Honda is a great road bike.

_____ 6. According to the United States Department of Health, Education and Welfare, hyperkinesis affects three of every one hundred children from all socioeconomic levels.

_____ 7. The hyperkinetic child is an overactive child.

_____ 8. Clearcutting is the practice of cutting all trees on a given stand of forest regardless of the age or size of the trees.

_____ 9. *Field and Stream* magazine claims that the logging companies are devastating our forests by the practice of clearcutting.

_____ 10. The United States has fewer than one million acres of virgin forest left.

_____ 11. In the past ten years shoplifting has become a popular form of rebellion for American youth.

_____ 12. According to the FBI, shoplifting increased 79 percent between 1968 and 1973.

_____ 13. Pam insists that her boyfriend Wally is a real tightwad.

_____ 14. The family that prays together stays together.

_____ 15. Florida's waterways have a serious pollution problem, according to the Environmental Protection Agency.

_____ 16. One form of river pollution in the Miami River is PCB, an industrial pollutant.

_____ 17. The *Journal of Learning Disabilities* reported that stimulant medications for hyperkinetic children are beneficial in only about one-half to two-thirds of the cases in which the drugs are used.

_____ 18. In the United States there is one doctor to care for every 650 people.

_____ 19. The shortage of nurses is due in part to the fact that new and more attractive careers are luring women away from the ages-old job of caring for the sick.

_____ 20. The former president of the AMA predicts that the doctor shortage will be over by 1980.

_____ 21. Cryogenics clients are stored in vacuum capsules in freezer vaults.

_____ 22. It's the real thing.

_____ 23. The Office of Child Development states that adoption of interracial children poses serious problems to both the child and the adoptive parents.

_____ 24. Professors at Columbia University School of Social Work stated in a recent survey that raising a child from infancy to age eighteen in a foster home in New York City costs $122,000 — four times what it costs natural parents to raise a child, $34,464.

_____ 25. Runaways are one-half misguided kids and one-half not caring parents.

EXERCISE 2-5   SUPPORTING INFERENCES WITH FACTS

Supply at least four facts for the following inferences. Include a few reports of facts. Indicate in the blank to the left of the number whether you have written a Fact (F) or Report of Fact (RF).

A. *Inference:* One look around suggests that the modern supermarket is much more than a food store.

_____ 1.

_____ 2.

_____ 3.

_____ 4.

B. *Inference:* Severio Tranfani, Manager of Penney's sporting goods department, demonstrated his willingness to help a customer.

_____ 1.

_____ 2.

_____ 3.

_____ 4.

C. *Inference:* Television commercials often use comic exaggeration as a method of getting their points across.

_____ 1.

_____ 2.

_____ 3.

_____ 4.

EXERCISE 2-6   SUPPLYING THE INFERENCE FOR A SERIES OF FACTS

Following are three groups of facts or reports of facts which support separate inferences. Write an inference for each group.

A. *Inference:* _____

_____

_____

1. Rick O'Donald refused to pith his frog.

2. His lab experiment leaked all over his $16 biology textbook, making it unreadable.

3. His term paper disappeared on the day it was due while he was turning in his moth collection.

4. He slept through the final exam and woke up as the instructor was collecting the blue books.

B. *Inference:* _____

_____

_____

1. The primary needs of the beginning scuba diver are mask, snorkel, and fins; this combination costs between $25 and $35.

2. As the novice advances, he is introduced to the buoyancy compensator, which costs $40.

3. After the scuba diver has satisfied the instructor's requirements, he finally gets to the galvanized steel air tanks, which cost $120.

4. Regulators, a separate but necessary item for underwater diving, range in price from $50 to $70.

C. *Inference:* _____

_____

_____

1. A bumper sticker that appeared at the onset of the energy crisis admonished the driver behind, "Don't be Fuelish."

2. Another sticker reads, "We can burn our wheat, let them eat their oil."

3. Several years ago a popular sticker suggested that "The family that prays together stays together."

4. Yet another type of bumper sticker can be seen warning following cars, "I brake for animals."

EXERCISE 2-7   SUPPLYING INFERENCES FOR A SERIES OF FACTS

So much for inferences drawn from personal experience. Now you can deal with the kinds of statements that you are likely to come across in your reading. Following are three groups of facts or reports of facts about social problems in America. Write an inference for each group.

A. *Inference:* _____

_____

_____

1. The West German Social Security System provides health care free for all citizens; the United States Social Security System provides partial health care for its citizens only when they reach retirement age.

2. The West German government contributes 15 percent of its budget to its Social Security program; the United States government contributes 4 percent of its budget to its Social Security program.

3. The over-sixty-five citizens in West Germany receive free prescription drugs and eyeglasses; the over-sixty-five citizens in the United States do not.

4. Should a West German citizen become disabled, the Social Security System pays his full salary from six weeks after disablement up to a full year.

5. A United States citizen who is disabled while employed receives only partial benefits.

B. *Inference:* _____

_____

_____

1. Environmentalists trying to clean up one of the country's polluted waterways, the Miami River, discovered that the water has turned an iron orange because of the rotting metal from derelict boats and decaying automobiles.

2. The Pollution Board reported that forty industrial drainage pipes added to the 100,000 gallons of raw sewage dumped into the river each day.

3. Volunteer observers reported that tourists and natives alike discard piles of rubbish and beer cans into the river.

4. The Geological Survey explained that industrial pollution of the river is caused by the dumping of such items as carbonless carbon paper, paint, brake fluid, electric transformers, ink dyes, and plasticizers.

C. *Inference:* _____

_____

_____

1. Single family foster care for children in New York City costs an average of $10.80 per day.

2. In a private agency-operated boarding home for foster children in New York City, the cost is $15.09 per day.

3. New York City allocates $20.52 per day for a child placed in a state-controlled group residence.

4. For foster care in a state institution, New York City allots $20.88 per child.

STEP 4   **Finding Sources for Expository Writing.**   You have met one of the crucial challenges of expository writing — distinguishing inferences from facts. You have supplied statistics, incidents, and specific examples to support inferences. You have also drawn inferences from the enumeration of statistics, incidents, and specific examples on a particular topic.

Now you will be meeting the second challenge of expository writing — recognizing and using sources for the content of your papers. Once you recognize the wealth of source material available to you, you will never have to say, "But I have nothing to write about."

PERSONAL EXPERIENCE

For your first papers in this course, you may use personal experience as a source. Personal experience gives a wide range of subject matter: hobbies, jobs, sports, school, travel, family, friends, cultural activities, organizations, and social life. Drawing on your personal experience involves participation, observation by looking and listening, conversation, and interviewing.

MEDIA

The sources from which you will draw for your later papers — especially research papers — come from the media. Here again you have many possibilities: newspapers, magazines, journals, books, and advertisements; television, radio, and movies.

In Exercise 2-6 you noticed that inferences were drawn from such personal experiences as observing another student in biology class, scuba diving, and reading bumper stickers. As you drew your inferences, you became aware that more than one inference might correctly be drawn from a given set of facts. For example, from the statistics about foster child care in New York, you might draw this inference: "The larger the institution, the greater the cost to the taxpayer of caring for a foster child in New York." Another inference, equally correct, might be: Of the four methods of caring for a foster child in New York, care in a private home is the least expensive.

As inferences vary somewhat in wording, the reporting of facts drawn from personal observation varies according to individual experience. For example, ask five people to give what they consider to be an accurate fact for each of the following inferences. Record and observe the variation in responses.

Inference 1:   A *moderately priced,* unfurnished two-bedroom apartment.

Inference 2:   A *satisfactory income* for a recent college graduate.

Inference 3:   A *reasonable curfew* for a college freshman living at home with her parents.

Why do the responses vary? In these instances, they vary because of relative circumstances. For example, the inference term *moderately priced* when applied to a two-bedroom unfurnished apartment depends on a number of circumstances: the number of people sharing the rent, the amount of income available, the area of the country, the size of the city or town, the particular location of the apartment in the city, the facilities and services available, and the size of the rooms in the apartment.

If the writer or speaker took into account all these points and explained them, you would understand what he means by *moderately priced* for that particular circumstance. Consider the variables that would enter into the response for the inference terms *satisfactory income* and *reasonable curfew.*

You are now aware of legitimate variables in the wording of inferences and in the reporting of facts. However, you may have noticed in the discussion of the inferences supplied for Exercises 2-6 and 2-7 that one or more people wrote inferences with which the rest of the class did not agree. These students drew inaccurate inferences either because they did not take all the facts into consideration or because they misinterpreted one or more of the given facts.

As you learn to distinguish between inferences and facts, you become more skillful at observing the world around you. You will also find that you will read more analytically.

At first, you may think that the objective facts that you need to support your inferences in expository writing are cold and impersonal. You may also think that accumulating these facts is not a very exciting activity. However, as you gather these facts, store them in your mental sourcebook, and reflect upon them, you begin to make relationships. These relationships will lead you to form accurate and therefore effective inferences. It is **your evaluation,** then, that gives an original view to the subject matter of objective writing and persuades your reader that what you have to say is worth reading or acting upon.

You have seen how you assemble facts one by one from the various sources available to you and how you draw your inferences from these facts. Working in a sequential manner, you transmit the experience or the information to your reader.

The photographer transmits experience, too. However, he is able to capture a number of facts at one time. Different but equally correct inferences can be drawn from a particular photograph. A writer using a photograph titles (captions) it according to his purpose, using either an inference or a fact.

PHOTOGRAPH 1.   (Photo by Steven Mays.)

Inference caption: "Two sentinels stand guard over the graves of our honored war dead as Memorial Day dawns on Evergreen Gardens."

Fact caption: "Memorial Day Scene: Flag and palm mark the entrance of the war memorial section at Evergreen Gardens."

Discuss the circumstances under which a writer might use each type of caption.

Name _____

Date _____

Section _____

EXERCISE 2-8 CAPTIONING PHOTOGRAPHS

Following are three photographs. First, write an inference caption; then write a fact caption. Be prepared to discuss the circumstances under which you as a writer would use this photo and the two types of captions.

PHOTOGRAPH 2. (Photo by Steven Mays.)

Inference caption:

Fact caption:

PHOTOGRAPH 3.   (Photo by Dave Patrick.)

Inference caption:

Fact caption:

PHOTOGRAPH 4.   (Photo by Dave Patrick.)

Inference caption:

Fact caption:

Now you are ready to see how inferences and facts work together in expository writing. Because the paragraph is the basic unit of expository writing, you will want to try out your inference/fact distinction skills first on a paragraph. Following are two paragraphs written by college freshmen. The assignment was to choose as a subject a person currently in the public eye. The first sentence of the paragraph was to contain an inference which indicated admiration for or disapproval of the person selected, and the inference was to be supported with a minimum of five facts or reports of facts.

Study the two paragraphs which follow to determine the success of each. The sentences in each paragraph are numbered for identification purposes so that you can complete Exercise 2-9 and 2-10.

JANE FONDA

(1) One person I feel should not be in the position she is in is Jane Fonda. (2) I cannot think of her as an actress of any worth, nor as the liberated woman she thinks she is. (3) She is overrated in every respect of her career and her personal life. (4) Jane Fonda's acting career, it seems, is only a following in her father's footsteps. (5) She does not appear to have any real talent of her own. (6) I believe the only thing which has brought her this far is her name. (7) It certainly couldn't be because of any great magnetic charm or entrancing personality. (8) The movies she has appeared in show no great public appeal, nor do they show any sign of improvement in her acting. (9) I think they are merely one more outlet for her to attempt to expose to the world the repression of the American woman, which I feel is uncalled for and unnecessary. (10) Femininity is a great asset to a famous woman, and to any woman, for that matter. (11) Jane's recent outspokenness on the matter of women's liberation seems to be a total farce. (12) I see it as a means to receive attention and as something to turn to when she does not meet the standards that people set for her. (13) It is always easy to say that the reason for one's

failure is because of the narrow-mindedness of others. (14) I do feel that Jane Fonda could improve her image if she tried and if she wanted to. (15) She should try to be herself, not a martyr. (16) A little honest hard work and a little less of her speeches and demonstrations would do a lot of good.

ROD McKUEN

(1) Rod McKuen is one of the most successful contemporary poet-song writers in the country today. (2) Part of this success can be attributed to the fact that he has worked as a laborer, an actor, a stunt man, a disk jockey, and a newspaper columnist; and, because of these experiences, he is able to relate everyday feeling with everyday language in his poetry. (3) According to television talk show host Dick Cavett, Rod McKuen is "the most understood poet in the world." (4) In fact, his first three books of poetry sold over two and one-half million copies. (5) In addition to his poetry, Mr. McKuen is the composer and lyricist of scores for four motion pictures: The Prime of Miss Jean Brodie; Joanna; Me, Natalie; and the first film based on the characters in Peanuts, A Boy Named Charlie Brown. (6) Variety magazine reports that Rod McKuen has recorded more than thirty-five albums of his own songs and that other artists have recorded more than nine hundred of Rod's compositions. (7) In all, eighty million records of his compositions have been sold. (8) By any standards in the entertainment world, Rod McKuen can be considered a success.

EXERCISE 2-9 CRITICIZING INFERENCES AND FACTS

The paragraph about Jane Fonda contains sixteen sentences. Label each of the sentences as Inference (I), Fact (F), Report of Fact (RF), or Report of Inference (RI). After you have labelled each sentence, be prepared to discuss the extent to which this paragraph fulfilled the assignment. Your instructor may also ask you to comment on the sentence structure in the paragraph.

1. _____
2. _____
3. _____
4. _____
5. _____
6. _____
7. _____
8. _____
9. _____
10. _____
11. _____
12. _____
13. _____
14. _____
15. _____
16. _____

EXERCISE 2-10

Identify the sentences in the paragraph about Rod McKuen exactly as you did for the one on Jane Fonda. Discuss the inferences and/or reports of inferences that occurred in the body of this paragraph. Did you think they were justified? If so, why do you think so? How do they relate to the inference in the first sentence? How do they relate to facts in the paragraph?

1. ————
2. ————
3. ————
4. ————
5. ————
6. ————
7. ————
8. ————

STAGE 3

THE PARAGRAPH

STEP 1 **Writing the Controlling Inference in the Topic Sentence.** The paragraph is the basic unit of expository writing. In the paragraph the writer develops a single unit of thought. He introduces this single unit in the controlling inference sentence, commonly known as the **topic sentence.** The topic sentence consists of two parts — the limited subject and the controlling inference. The controlling inference is the writer's opinion, conclusion, or evaluation of the subject; and it indicates the single unit of thought that will be developed. In the topic sentence the writer commits himself to supporting the controlling inference by supplying **proof details** in the form of facts, examples, or incidents. Usually the topic sentence appears at the beginning of a paragraph.

Your study of Stage 2 has made you aware that an inference statement always causes the listener or the reader to ask the question, "What makes you think so?" or "What do you mean by . . . ?" In the cafeteria conversation, for instance, the speaker asserted his opinion about the atmosphere when he used the controlling inference *depressing.* Pressed for specific information to illustrate what he meant by the term, he had to supply proof details. When a speaker or a writer supplies proof details for an inference, he is saying to his listener or to his reader, "These are the reasons I believe what I have asserted. You may not agree with my opinion, but now you understand why I formed it." A writer's proof details, in other words, are the **evidence.**

When you write the controlling inference sentence for a paragraph, you need to ask yourself five questions:

1. Is my subject worth discussing (or is it obvious or frivolous)?
2. Is my controlling inference a single unit of thought (or do I actually have more than one idea here)?
3. Why am I making this assertion (what is my purpose)?
4. Who is my audience (what are their backgrounds, their interests)?
5. What method can I use to illustrate my point (what kind of proof details will I use to back up my controlling inference)?

Here are two examples of topic sentences with workable controlling inferences. In each sentence, the controlling inference is italicized. A discussion follows each topic sentence.

Topic sentence: The student parking facilities on this campus are *inadequate.*

Discussion: Test this sentence against the five criteria for a workable topic sentence listed above.

1. Is my subject worth discussing?
   Yes, because students have time and money invested in college work and should not be inconvenienced.
2. What is the single unit of thought?
   The *inadequacy* of the parking facilities.
3. What is the purpose?
   To prove that the parking situation is bad.
4. Who is my audience?
   College officials and other students.
5. What kind of proof details will I use?
   Facts:
   A. Ratio of students to student parking spaces
   B. Ratio of faculty to faculty spaces
   C. Number of students on campus at prime time vs. number of spaces available at that time
   D. Distance of student lots to classrooms
   E. Condition of parking lots (three-fourths of spaces flooded during rains, last lots to be cleared after snowstorms)

Topic sentence: The American society considers overweight people *socially handicapped.*

Discussion: There are actually two inferences in this sentence because there are two phrases which raise the question, "What do you mean by . . . ?" These two phrases are *overweight people* and *socially handicapped.* For purposes of this paragraph, however, it is obvious that the writer wants to focus on the idea of people being socially handicapped. Therefore, this phrase is the controlling inference for which the writer will supply proof details. He can assume that his audience would generally agree about the meaning of the term *overweight,* because the condition can be determined by standardized height and weight charts.

POOR TOPIC SENTENCES

Some topic sentences that may at first glance appear to be workable cannot be properly developed in a paragraph. Two examples follow.

THE DOUBLE INFERENCE

Topic sentence: Some newspaper columnists often *slant* the news by *hiding and distorting* facts.

Discussion: The writer of this sentence cannot develop a single unit of thought because he has two controlling inferences, *hiding* and *distorting.* He would have to give examples to demonstrate how columnists hide news and how they distort facts. He has thus committed himself to supplying two different sets of proof details for two distinct methods of slanting the news. He has too much for a single paragraph.

THE VAGUE INFERENCE

Topic sentence: *War and Peace* is the *best* movie I have ever seen.

Discussion: *Best* in this sentence is an impossible inference to prove. First, the writer would have to take into consideration every movie he had ever seen. Next, he would have to discuss all the categories of movies, such as comedies, historical movies, love stories, adventure stories, and war movies. Finally, he would have to take into consideration the many criteria used in judging movies, such as acting, direction, screenplay, sound effects, or cinematography. The writer has set himself an impossible task and the sentence must be scrapped.

Name _____

Date _____

Section _____

EXERCISE 3-1   CRITICIZING THE CONTROLLING INFERENCE IN THE TOPIC SENTENCE

Underline the controlling inference in each statement. Then apply the five criteria for writing a topic sentence to determine how workable each statement is.

1. Scuba diving can be exciting but dangerous.
   (1) Subject worth discussing? Why?
   (2) Single unit of thought?
   (3) Purpose?
   (4) Audience?
   (5) Kind of proof details?
       Supply at least four if you can.

2. The pass/fail system of grading in open admission colleges has a number of advantages.
   (1) Subject worth discussing? Why?
   (2) Single unit of thought?
   (3) Purpose?
   (4) Audience?
   (5) Kind of proof details?
       Supply at least four if you can.

3. People's book buying habits often reveal their personalities.
   (1) Subject worth discussing? Why?
   (2) Single unit of thought?
   (3) Purpose?
   (4) Audience?
   (5) Kind of proof details?
       Supply at least four if you can.

STEP 2   Limiting the Subject in the Topic Sentence.   In addition to forming a workable controlling inference, you must make the subject of a topic sentence **specific.** While a paragraph seldom has fewer than four proof detail sentences, it is not usually longer than 250 words. Suppose, for example, that you were to write this topic sentence: "Television commercials this season often rely on exaggeration." You might think that the phrase *this season* limits your subject. But when you begin to jot down your ideas for proof details, you will realize that you would have at least a dozen commercials to explain by way of illustrating your controlling inference term *exaggeration.* You would do better to modify your subject even further. Your topic sentence then might read: "This season's television commercials for cleaning products often rely on exaggeration to make their point." You could then use five or six examples, drawing your proof detail examples from a wax product, a laundry detergent, a dishwasher liquid, a carpet cleaner, and a wall cleaner.

STEP 3   Recognizing Unsuitable Topic Sentences.   You are now aware of three problems in the topic sentence: (1) a double inference, (2) an inference too vague to support with proof details, (3) a topic that is not sufficiently limited. There are two other kinds of unsatisfactory topic sentences. One is the question. For example, "Will success spoil the Dolphins?" cannot function as a topic sentence even though the sentence does contain an inference word, *success.* There is no way to supply proof details for a future possibility because the proof details cannot be verified. On the other hand, some questions converted to statements can function as topic sentences. Consider the following question: "Can inner-city schools in Atlanta keep pace with our changing urban society?" There is an inference term here, *keep pace.* But the controlling inference in the topic sentence must be an assertion of your opinion, your conclusion, or your evaluation about a subject. Because this sentence is in the form of a question, there is no assertion. Revised to form a statement, the sentence would read, "Inner-city schools are having difficulty keeping pace with the changing urban society in Atlanta."

The last type of unsuitable topic sentence to be considered is the one stated in the form of a fact. It is sometimes called a **dead-end** topic sentence because once the fact is stated, the writer can't go anywhere with it insofar as proof details are concerned. Consider this statement: "Absenteeism has increased 100 percent in the auto industry over the past ten years." Revised to form a topic sentence suitable for further development, this statement would read: "Absenteeism has become a growing problem in the auto industry in the past decade."

In summation, then, a topic sentence can be unsuitable because of one or more of five problems:

1. A double inference
2. An inference too vague to support with proof details
3. An insufficiently limited topic
4. Topic sentence stated in the form of a question
5. Topic sentence stated in the form of a fact

EXERCISE 3-2 LIMITING THE SUBJECT IN THE TOPIC SENTENCE

In each of the sentences below, the subject is not specific enough to be developed in one paragraph. Revise the topic sentence so that the subject is sufficiently limited. As you do this, you may also see the need for further limiting the inference.

Example: Parents can be inconsistent.

Revision: My parents are inconsistent in their expectations about my choice of a career.

1. Elected public officials sometimes fail to carry out their campaign promises.
   Revision:

2. Just as the drug problem seems to be leveling off, people are finding new drugs to abuse.
   Revision:

3. The ocean will eventually supply new sources of food.
   Revision:

4. Part-time jobs can be very boring.
   Revision:

5. Many fields related to medicine are now open.
   Revision:

6. New kinds of marriage are appearing on the American scene.
   Revision:

7. Some mechanical tasks are frustrating.
   Revision:

8. Old traditions are not necessarily the best ones.
   Revision:

9. Americans love to travel.
   Revision:

10. Inflation is a world-wide problem.
    Revision:

EXERCISE 3-3   CHOOSING SUITABLE TOPIC SENTENCES

From each group below, select the sentence that would be suitable for a topic sentence and mark TS in the blank. Then refer to the list of topic sentence problems and identify by one of the preceding numbers the problem in each of the other two sentences (see p. 54).

Example:

_____5_____ A. A survey indicates that men favor women's rights organizations 44 percent to 39 percent, whereas women oppose them 42 percent to 40 percent.

_____TS_____ B. The New Feminism has already left its mark on the 1970s in the form of legislative changes affecting employment.

_____2,3_____ C. The American woman should be the happiest in history.

GROUP 1

_____·_____ A. Women Act to Control Health Care (WATCH) is a Chicago-based women's group concerned about institutional health care available for Chicago's unwed mothers on welfare.

_____ B. The Chicago Maternity Center is the only remaining institutional service in an urban area that assists women in delivering babies at home.

_____ C. WATCH is now taking an active role to insure that women in Chicago get the kind of health care they need.

GROUP 2

_____ A. Can the establishment of experimental schools for reluctant learners solve the dropout rate?

_____ B. The New York Schools Exchange, a clearinghouse for many "free schools," listed more than four hundred in 1972.

_____ C. Within the limits of its budget, the Ford Foundation is assisting public school experimental programs in Berkeley, California.

GROUP 3

_____ A. Visitors are astonished when they first meet these gentle tribespeople, the Tasadays.

_____ B. The Tasadays of Mindanao, our only link with the Stone Age, are a unique tribe.

_____ C. The wild yam is the staple food of the Tasadays, although a banquet might include such foods as fat grubs, tadpoles, frogs, and stalks from palm trunks.

GROUP 4

_____ A. Out of every one thousand couples married in 1972, 455 are destined to end in the divorce court.

_____ B. The divorce rate in the United States is the highest in the world.

_____ C. The premarital contract, stating commitments with regard to children, work, and property, may be one approach to lowering the divorce rate in the United States.

STEP 4   **Supplying Proof Details.**   Once you have worked out a topic sentence with a limited subject and a workable controlling inference, the next step is to support your controlling inference with **specific** and **relevant** facts or reports of facts. You will want to avoid two types of unsatisfactory proof details. The first type is the **irrelevant statement** — a fact that does not relate **directly** back to your controlling inference. This kind of statement is sometimes called a **detractor** because it does not directly support the controlling inference. Read the following topic sentence with its proof details, and decide whether all proof details are relevant.

Topic sentence: At the 1972 Olympics in Munich, Mark Spitz, swimmer for the American Olympic team, turned in a *record-setting performance.*

Proof details:

A. In the 1968 Olympic Games, Spitz hoped to win six gold medals.
B. In Munich, he won the 200 yard butterfly and anchored the 400 yard freestyle relay, both in world record time.
C. *Time* magazine quoted Spitz as saying that he swam because he wanted to be recognized as the best in the world.
D. Mark tied the record for gold medals of five set in 1920 by an Italian fencer.
E. During the 1972 Olympic Games, Mark won seven gold medals.
F. In Mexico, in 1968, Mark won only a silver and a bronze medal.
G. Mark trained hard for four years before going to the Olympics.

The writer of this paragraph got off the track with several proof details. Two of the sentences, A and F, are irrelevant because they do not refer to the subject of his paragraph, which is the 1972 Olympics. Two of the sentences, C and G, are irrelevant because they have nothing to do with the controlling inference. Only three statements, B, D, and E, support the controlling inference, *record-setting performance.* When the detractors are eliminated, the paragraph has too few proof details. The writer should have included the other records set by Spitz at the 1972 Olympics to support his controlling inference adequately.

The second type of unsatisfactory proof detail is the inclusion of another inference. Known as a **minor inference,** this kind of proof detail does relate to the controlling inference; but because it is another inference, it must have a fact attached to it to serve as a proof detail. Notice how the minor inference works in the following example.

Topic sentence: My landlord is charging excessive prices for his rental units.

Proof detail in the form of an inference:
   A. The rent for a one-room efficiency is *outrageous.*

Discussion:
   Outrageous is a minor inference. The writer can make this minor inference sentence serve as a proof detail sentence if he cites a specific instance or example that illustrates what he means by *outrageous.* He can incorporate a fact within the sentence, or he can follow the minor inference sentence with a fact sentence. Here are two possibilities for revision:

Fact incorporated in sentence: The rent for a one-room efficiency apartment, $300, is outrageous.

Minor inference sentence followed immediately by fact sentence: The rent for a one-room efficiency apartment is outrageous. My landlord charges $300.

Here is another example of how a minor inference sentence is revised so that it functions as a proof detail supporting the controlling inference.

Topic sentence:
   Alcohol was involved in the two-car accident at Twelfth and Pine Avenues.

Proof detail in the form of a minor inference sentence:
   The alcohol content in the blood of the girl driving the compact car was high.

Revision:
   The alcohol content in the blood of the girl driving the compact car was high — 15 percent.

EXERCISE 3-4   WORKING WITH PROOF DETAILS

Following are four topic sentences with the controlling inference in italics. Each topic sentence is followed by a minor inference sentence.

A. In the first blank, make the minor inference specific by attaching a fact or by writing another sentence of fact to follow the minor inference sentence.

B. In the second blank, supply a second proof detail sentence that is strictly relevant to the controlling inference in the topic sentence.

Example: Holiday Park is *dangerous* at night.

    A. Muggings are *on the increase.*

        Revision: Muggings there have increased by 27 percent in the past six months.

        Or

        Muggings are on the increase. In the past six months there was a 27 percent rise in reported cases.

    B. Second proof detail: Stretches of darkness up to two hundred feet exist because of the unrepaired walkway lights.

1. Community college work study programs offer students *valuable on-the-job experience* while they are still in college.

    A. They can *get practical experience* in their major field of study.

       Revision:

    B. Second proof detail sentence:

2. Rock music is finding *many new forms* in the Seventies.

    A. It often appears in *intriguing combinations* with older forms of music.
Revision:

    B. Second proof detail sentence:

3. My new motorcycle has been a *disappointment* to me.

    A. In the first place, maintenance costs have been *higher* than I had expected them to be.
Revision.

    B. Second proof detail sentence:

4. There is a *great shortage* of white babies available for adoption in the United States today.

    A. One of the causes of this shortage is *certain legislative changes.*
Revision:

    B. Second proof detail sentence:

Up to this point you have been examining proof details in isolated sentences to determine if the statements were relevant or irrelevant to the controlling inference in the topic sentence. You will need to develop your skill in criticizing proof details in paragraph form. Here is a paragraph written by a student involved with a civic theater group. The assignment was for the student to select as his subject his special field of interest and to construct a controlling inference sentence followed by at least five proof detail sentences to support the controlling inference. Read the paragraph and the discussion which follows it.

A WAY TO THE FOOTLIGHTS

(1) The amateur actor who wants to win a role in a play produced by a civic theater group must put a five-point plan in operation. (2) At some time in our lives, the suppressed Walter Mitty escapes into our consciousness and we imagine ourselves projected on a silver screen or parading before a Broadway audience. (3) Since the world of professional theater will remain only a dream to most people, an aspiring actor can fulfill his desire to act by trying out for a role in a local civic theater group. (4) He should first arrange his schedule to see if he can fit in rehearsal hours. (5) Then he needs to read the play. (6) He should select a character he might like to play; but while he is reading the play, he might keep in mind other jobs related to the production of the play. (7) For instance, if he doesn't win a role in the play, he might consider working on lights or stage props. (8) Much could be learned about stagecraft and costume design just by working with the technical crew. (9) In fact, he might decide that a career in the theater can be his and that his dream of working on Broadway can be fulfilled.

DISCUSSION

The topic sentence in this paragraph is very workable. The subject is clearly limited — the amateur who wants to win a part in a play produced by a civic theater group. The controlling inference is clear — the actor must put a five-point plan into operation. The writer's commitment is to state as clearly as possible what these five points are. In the paragraph, however, the writer has strayed far afield; only sentences four and five and half of sentence six have any relevance to the commitment of his controlling inference. If these two and a half sentences are the only relevant ones, then what do the others contribute? Sentence two might serve as an interesting opener for a longer paper. Here, however, it is not only another inference sentence, but one which has no relation to the five-point plan. At first glance, sentence three seems to be relevant; however, it, too, is an inference and is irrelevant because it concerns professional, not amateur theater. The writer could possibly combine the ideas from sentences two and three into his topic sentence in order to enlist interest in his paragraph. The topic sentence then would read like this:

```
    Since the world of professional theater
remains only a dream to most people, an aspiring
actor can fulfill his interest in the theater by
following a five-point plan for winning a role
in a play produced by a civic theater group.
```

The writer would then be ready for his direct proof details: (1) arranging his schedule, (2) reading the play, (3) selecting the character he wants to play. He got into trouble in sentence six because he wandered off into related jobs in amateur theater. Thus, the second half of sentence six together with sentences seven, eight, and nine are all detractors. The confused reader is still waiting for points four and five, but they never do materialize. As the paragraph stands, it fails to fulfill the commitment of the controlling inference, and the reader remains uninstructed. Following is a rewritten version of the paragraph.

A WAY TO THE FOOTLIGHTS

```
    Since the world of professional theater
remains only a dream to most people, an aspiring
actor can fulfill his interest in the theater by
following a five-point plan for winning a role
in a play produced by a civic theater group.
First, he should study the rehearsal schedule
set up by the director and the dates the play is
to be presented to make sure that he has enough
```

time to attend rehearsals and to be present at
all performances. Second, assuming that he has
already read the play, he should select the
character he thinks he would like to play.
Third, he should interpret the part and practice
it aloud so that he will read well for the
tryouts. In addition, he should be prepared to
read other parts. Fourth, he must come to the
tryout on time and be prepared to stay for the
duration, since he may be called again by the
director to read for another part or to read his
part with other characters. Fifth, he must be
willing to accept any role the director may ask
him to play. Although this five-point plan will
not guarantee him a part, it will certainly
improve his chances of winning a role.

EXERCISE 3-5   CRITICIZING PROOF DETAILS IN THE PARAGRAPH

Read the following paragraph and complete the exercise by putting an R in the blank if the sentence is relevant and an I if it is irrelevant.

A CHILD'S VIEW OF RELIGION

(1) Children's religious discussions can be very amusing to adults. (2) For example, when my four-year-old brother Steve was asked who brought gifts to the infant Jesus, he confidently replied, "The three wise guys." (3) Failing to understand that the words <u>sheep</u> and <u>lamb</u> were not always interchangeable, he came home from church services one Sunday and announced at dinner, "There are sheep living in heaven." (4) When my father questioned him, he discovered that Steve was referring to the Lamb of God. (5) On another occasion we overheard a discussion between Steve and his cousin Bennie, also four. (6) The boys had been studying the Book of Genesis in their Sunday School class, and their comments made it obvious that either their teacher did not speak plainly or the boys did not listen closely. (7) The boys discussed the golden <u>cat</u> that Aaron allowed the Israelites to make when Moses was up on the mountain, and then they earnestly wondered about the <u>deaf</u> angel that killed all the first-born in Egypt. (8) Some time later, Steve and Bennie decided that they would take turns leading the hymn singing. (9) My brother selected his favorite,

"Up From the Gravy a Nose," more commonly known
to the congregation as "Up From the Grave He
Arose." (10) Bennie, however, insisted on
"Bringing in the Cheese," his corruption of the
old hymn "Bringing in the Sheaves." (11) A
four-year-old's view of religion can provide
adults with a hilarious collection of verbal
misconceptions.

Topic sentence: (1) Children's religious discussions can be very
amusing to adults.

2. _____

3. _____

4. _____

5. _____

3. _____

4. _____

5. _____

6. _____

7. _____

8. _____

9. _____

10. _____

11. _____ (Summary sentence)

STEP 5   **Providing Transition.** Now that you know how proof details are enumerated to support the writer's controlling inference, you need to know how to connect these details to make your paragraph read smoothly. Writers refer to the relevance of proof details as **unity.** They refer to the way the details are connected as **coherence.** The connecting words and phrases that give coherence to the details of a paragraph are called **transitions.** There are several ways to achieve coherence in a paragraph:

1. Repetition of a key word.
2. Use of a synonym for a key word.
3. Use of a pronoun to refer to a noun used in the previous sentence.
4. Use of a transitional word or phrase.

In order to choose an appropriate transitional expression, you should ask, "What is the function of this transition?" For example, if you had a series of facts that you were adding up to prove a point, you could use such expressions as *also, another example, in addition,* and *furthermore,* to name only a few. The following chart lists transitional expressions according to their function.

TRANSITIONAL EXPRESSIONS

To Mark Addition: and, again, also, moreover, first, second, third, equally important, in addition, then too, furthermore

To Indicate Time: in the beginning, at the outset, at the start, first, next, then, before, during, while, at the same time, concurrently, again, subsequently, at last, finally

To Indicate Spatial Order: above, below, beyond, near, far from, over, under, in the distance, on top of, nearby, to the left, to the right, straight ahead, opposite to, behind, adjacent to, at right angles to, perpendicular to, parallel to, to the east, to the west, to the north, to the south, further away

To Indicate Comparison and Contrast: similar to, like, similarly, in a like manner, just as, identical to, likewise, but, or, nor, however, yet, on the other hand, in contrast, conversely, on the contrary, unlike

To Indicate Cause and Effect: therefore, as a result, accordingly, consequently, after, hence, thus, subsequently

To Indicate Conclusion: therefore, thus, then, in conclusion, last, consequently, as a result, in the last analysis, in summary, in other words, to conclude, to summarize

The paragraph below illustrates the various transitional devices a student used to link his proof details about a political candidate. The devices are underlined. Identification of the devices by number appears before each one: (1) repetition of a key word; (2) use of a synonym for a key word; (3) use of a pronoun to refer to a noun used in the previous sentence; (4) use of a transitional word or phrase.

ROBERT WEAVER FOR CONGRESS

Robert Weaver is a highly qualified Democratic candidate for the Tenth Congressional District. [4]First, [3]he has had two years of International Law at Yale University, and [3]he has earned a Bachelor of Arts and a Master of Arts degree. [4]In addition, [3]he assisted in the framework of the United States Government services as a diplomat for fifteen years with assignments in Europe, Asia, and Latin America. Two of this [2]candidate's diplomatic titles were Vice Consul and Attache. [4]Furthermore, [3]he was named twice for the Pulitzer Prize. [4]Not only has [3]he written three books on international relations and defense, [4]but [3]he is [4]also an editor for People to People in Washington, D.C., and has been syndicated by United Features in New York. [1]Mr. Weaver is bilingual; [3]this allows [3]him to communicate with both the Spanish and the English speaking citizens of this city. [3]He is [4]also a member of the Senate Subcommittee on International Security. [4]Therefore, because of his outstanding qualifications, [1]Mr. Weaver should be elected.

When you are working at providing transition, you could think of the paragraph as a folding fan. A fan has webbing. All of the parts are attached to a pivot so that the fan can open and be operated.

Look at the illustration of the paragrah "Weaver for Congress" on the opposite page. Just as the paragraph has the topic and the summary sentence to frame it, the fan has the end ribs which serve as anchors. The proof details of the paragraph are like the intermediate ribs of the fan. In a similar manner, the transitional devices link the details much like the webbing of the fan links the ribs. If the webbing is cut at any point on the fan, the fan will no longer function. Similarly, if the proof details are not linked together, the paragraph loses its coherence. Finally, the controlling inference functions in the paragraph much as the pivot functions on the fan: both control the entire operation.

Robert Weaver for Congress

Robert Weaver is a highly qualified Democrat Candidate for the Tenth Congressional District.

First

Two years International Law – Has B.A. and M.A.

In addition

Assisted U.S. as diplomat

Candidate's diplomatic titles

Served as Vice Consul and Attache

Furthermore

Nominated for Pulitzer Prize

Not only

Has written three books on international relations

But also

Editor of People to People – syndicated

Mr. Weaver

Bilingual

He also

Member of Senate Subcommittee on International Security

Therefore

Because of his outstanding qualifications Mr. Weaver should be elected.

Name _____

Date _____

Section _____

EXERCISE 3-6   RECOGNIZING TRANSITION

A. Underline the transitions in the following paragraph.
B. Identify the type of transition by number as in the preceding paragraph.

MINIATURE BILLBOARDS

Bumper stickers relate a variety of messages about subjects of concern to Americans. Every four years political slogans appear like banners on the backs of cars all over the country. In 1972, for example, "Re-elect the President" and "Vote Nixon" were a common sight. On the other hand, in 1973 after Watergate, bumper stickers appeared with such statements as "Impeach the President" and "Don't Blame Me, I Voted for McGovern." Religious messages are as popular as political slogans. These religious messages often express love: "Smile, God Loves You," "Honk If You Love Jesus," or "The Family That Prays Together, Stays Together." Some bumper stickers, however, are not so warm-hearted, particularly those that refer to people's driving habits. These stickers say, "Your horn works, do your brakes?" and "I may be slow, but I am ahead of you." Still another sticker warns, "If you can read this, you're driving too close." Then there are those drivers who proclaim their individual preferences with such stickers as, "I'm single and love it" and "Ride a Bike to Live; Live to Ride a Bike." Finally, the most common sticker on the subject of America in general asserts, "America, Love It or Leave It." Other stickers counter this slogan with, "America, Change It or Lose It." In a mobile America with millions of cars on the road, perhaps bumper stickers give more exposure to people's ideas than do billboards.

EXERCISE 3-7   PROVIDING TRANSITION

The following paragraph is reproduced exactly as it was written by a student except for the fact that his transitions have been removed. Rewrite the paragraph, entering transitions at appropriate places. Don't use any expression more than once. To keep up the suspense and unify the details, you should find nine places where you can insert transitions. After your class discusses the transitions supplied for the paragraph, your instructor may wish to give you the ones supplied by the student writer.

A FLIGHT TO REMEMBER

Our flight from South Carolina to Bermuda proved to be a harrowing experience. We lost radio communications with the control tower at Charleston Air Force Base forty minutes after takeoff. As we prepared to return to the airstrip, the right engine started to backfire and miss. The crew repaired the radio and advised the base of our problems. We got ready to return to Charleston. A loud bang occurred, and the right engine started smoking; however, no fire was visible. The pilot instructed us to prepare for an emergency landing. The engine quit and the aircraft began to lose altitude. Oil covered the engine cowling, and the smoke got thicker and blacker by the minute; but there still was not any sign of fire. The pilot advised us over the intercom that we were back over land and not in any immediate danger. The tension really mounted as we started our descent. After the plane had circled the field for ten minutes, the tires of the aircraft screeched when they hit the runway; and everyone smiled for the first time in two and a half hours.

STEP 6 **Writing the Summary Sentence.** The last sentence in a paragraph is usually the **summary sentence.** It signals your reader that you are coming to the end of the development of your single unit of thought. The summary sentence is often stated in the form of a conclusion which reasserts your controlling inference. In the paragraph "A Child's View of Religion," in Exercise 3-5, the writer's controlling inference was that children's religious discussions can be *amusing.* The writer provided enough convincing proof details to support this assertion and was thus entitled to summarize by stating that a four-year-old's view of religion can be a *hilarious collection of verbal misconceptions.*

STEP 7 **Writing a Title.** The last step in writing a paragraph is to pick an appropriate title. Keep in mind the four points for a title:

1. It should be short
2. It should reflect the subject of the paper
3. It should not be the topic sentence
4. It should catch the reader's attention

Here are a few titles that freshmen writers chose for their first fact enumeration paragraph:

TEDIOUS TROUBLESHOOTING, about finding a discrepancy in the automatic flight control system of a helicopter; HIGH IN THE SADDLE, a paragraph about John Wayne's career; TAKE ME OUT OF THE BALL GAME, by a Little League father; AND ON THE SEVENTH DAY, by a student working as a mother's helper six days a week; FLYING HIGH, by an amateur kite designer; WARRIOR ON ICE, about Gordy Howe, hockey player; DEATH VALLEY, a paragraph about a student's field trip to a funeral home; VANTASTIC, about campers.

WRITING SUGGESTION: THE PARAGRAPH

Your source material for your first writing assignment will be personal experience. Get your idea for a subject from one of the following suggestions; then, following the five steps of Stage 3, write a paragraph.

SUGGESTIONS

1. Select as your subject one person currently in the public eye. That person may be in sports, politics, law, medicine, theater, films, television, art, science, education, the Armed Forces, law enforcement, or social service. Explain in your paragraph why you admire or disapprove of this person.

2. Use as the basis for your subject one of the following: the most controversial, frightening, frustrating, humorous, or thought-provoking experience, observation, or idea that you have recently encountered.

3. Select one of the following topics: old people, college registrations, mass protest, television commercials, current music, teachers, a special place, bumper stickers, pop art, computers.

4. Use the following photograph as your subject. There are many possibilities for a controlling inference and many proof details that can be supplied.

Use the rating sheet on page 79 as a guide for writing your paragraph.

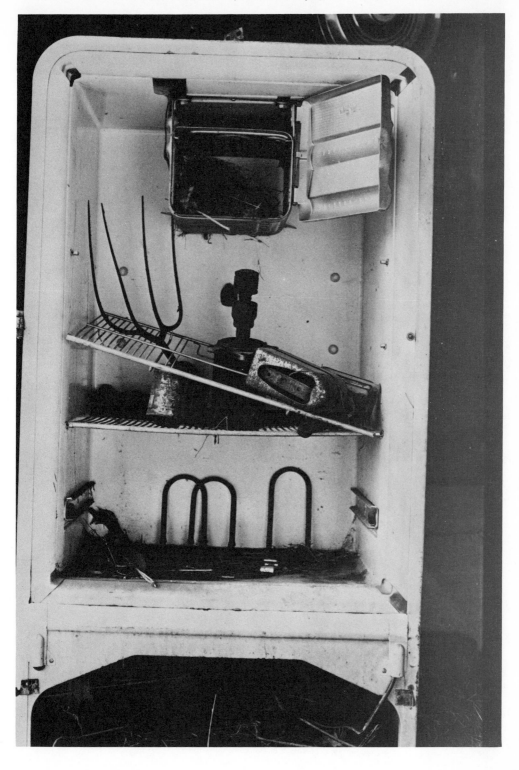

Name _____

Date _____

Section _____

PARAGRAPH RATING SHEET	Poor	Average	Good	Excellent

TOPIC SENTENCE

_____ Subject suitably limited
_____ Controlling inference

BODY

_____ Minimum five proof details
_____ All proof details relevant
_____ Any minor inference includes fact

TRANSITION

_____ Adequate number of transitions
_____ Transitions appropriate to function

SUMMARY SENTENCE

_____ Restates assertion of controlling
inference or
_____ Draws a logical conclusion from
proof details

TITLE

_____ Enlists reader interest
_____ Reflects subject of paragraph
_____ Short

MECHANICS

_____ Spelling
_____ Grammar
_____ Sentence structure
_____ Sentence variety
_____ Punctuation
_____ Manuscript form
_____ Title in capitals
_____ Proper margins
_____ Neatness
_____ Numbers properly written

LANGUAGE

_____ Appropriate language level
_____ Effective word choice

Name _____

Date _____

Section _____

PARAGRAPH RATING SHEET	Poor	Average	Good	Excellent

TOPIC SENTENCE

____ Subject suitably limited
____ Controlling inference

BODY

____ Minimum five proof details
____ All proof details relevant
____ Any minor inference includes fact

TRANSITION

____ Adequate number of transitions
____ Transitions appropriate to function

SUMMARY SENTENCE

____ Restates assertion of controlling
inference or
____ Draws a logical conclusion from
proof details

TITLE

____ Enlists reader interest
____ Reflects subject of paragraph
____ Short

MECHANICS

____ Spelling
____ Grammar
____ Sentence structure
____ Sentence variety
____ Punctuation
____ Manuscript form
____ Title in capitals
____ Proper margins
____ Neatness
____ Numbers properly written

LANGUAGE

____ Appropriate language level
____ Effective word choice

STAGE 4

REWRITING

1. Getting Your Paper Back
2. Understanding Correction Symbols

STEP 1 **Getting Your Paper Back.** When you hand in your first paper, you may say, "Well, I think I've done a good job." You followed all the steps for writing a paragraph, you worked hard to express yourself, and perhaps a friend or two looked at the paper and thought it was good. Now you have nothing to do but to wait for your paper to be returned with the grade on it.

You may find, however, that the paper is returned to you with a grade lower than the one you had expected and that the instructor has made comments and corrections. Your first reaction may be one of disappointment. Keep in mind, however, that a grade reflects three considerations:

1. Content (the quality of your ideas and how well you have developed them)
2. Method (the organization of the paper)
3. Mechanics (grammar, sentence structure, spelling, punctuation, manuscript form)

Working through the seven steps to paragraph writing, you learned how to form suitable inferences, how to support them with adequate proof details, and how to organize the details into a coherent paragraph. Now you need to combine these three skills with acceptable mechanics, because if the mechanics aren't correct the meaning will not be clear. Consider, for example, these sentences written by a student attempting to describe the scene on entering a discotheque: "Directly ahead is the bandstand with red and purple lights and five musicians lit up." He compounds the confusion by adding: "Going backwards by the bar, comfortable sofas welcome couples to the left and right." By the time the reader has had to deal with incapacitated musicians and animated sofas, he's not sure what scene he's in.

What may have happened here is that the student was so concerned with content and organization that he overlooked problems that occur in grammar, sentence structure, spelling, and word selection. Another problem may have been that when the student submitted his final draft, he did not proofread it carefully, or he submitted his first draft.

Even professional writers, although they are highly trained in all the communication skills, often write three or four drafts of a paper, and sometimes even of a letter, before they are satisfied. You too will need to rewrite. You will need to make at least two drafts before submitting any paper. Even with this rewriting, you may still overlook some points concerning content, organization, and mechanics. The time and effort your instructor takes in reading your paper and marking it is of no value unless you take the time to interpret those marks and comments and to make the necessary revisions. This effort on your part will help you to avoid making the same mistakes on your next papers.

STEP 2   **Understanding Correction Symbols.**   Here is the original and the revised version of a paragraph written by a student who selected as his subject "a special place." The original is shown with the instructor's correction symbols and comments. The student's revised version follows. First, read the original paragraph just for content and organization. Then read it again, and as you come to each correction symbol, refer to the correction symbol list in the **Mechanics Guide** to determine what that symbol means. If the explanation for the correction symbol is not clear to you or if you are not familiar with the particular problem indicated by the symbol, turn to the basic review sheets in the **Mechanics Guide.** These review sheets group the basic mechanical errors according to their types. You will notice that the symbol is not only defined, but that a sentence illustrating the particular type of error is given along with the correction for the error.

ORIGINAL PARAGRAPH WITH INSTRUCTOR CORRECTIONS

Title   WALKING ALONG LAS OLAS BOULEVARD IS INTERESTING

City? State?   Las Olas Boulevard is a delight to tourists
because of its many outstanding features. In
the background is the city's newest attraction,
The First National Bank Building, the first
skyscraper in this tropical city of low
buildings, it towers above the many small   *cs*
shops. Men's and women's boutiques showing the
latest fashions line the palm bordered
boulevard. Included with these are art   *ref*
galleries and import shops (with famous paintings) *mis pt*
and goods from countries throughout the world.
sp; abr.   Resturants, photo studios, travel bureaus, and *rep.*
card shops each individually styled yet woven   *fig. sp.*
together help to make this small shopping
center. Leaving the downtown area, the street   *dgl.*
sp.   widens to form two seperate lanes with palm   *Where did*
trees and flowers on each side. Large white   *the islands*
houses located on small islands (with private   *come from?*
mis. pt.   drives) are on one side of the street, while the
other side has small shops, motels, and
occasional fishing ramps. The water is beautiful *You didn't*
of what?   on both <u>sides</u> and large boats are often docked *mention*
what?   <u>nearby</u>. The street ends at the beach where high- *water earlier*
rise apartments stand overlooking the ocean.
This beach, with its white sugar sand, is the
irrel.   longest unbroken beach in the world. It is no
wonder that Las Olas Boulevard is a delight to
tourists.

*Your T.S. and proof of details are good. You need
to work on sentence structure and small mechanical
problems. Some confusion — how did you get
from the street to the islands and water?
Lead the reader in. Any other colorful details?
Summary sentence is exact repeat of T.S.
Write a new one.*

REVISED VERSION INCORPORATING INSTRUCTOR'S SUGGESTIONS

A TOURIST'S DELIGHT

Tourists visiting Ford Lauderdale, Florida, find Las Olas Boulevard a special attraction because of its many outstanding features. The tourist can start his walking tour at the beginning of East Las Olas Boulevard, using as a landmark the city's newest attraction, the First National Bank Building. Although this building is not directly on Las Olas, it towers above the palm-lined boulevard because it is the first skyscraper in this tropical city of low buildings. Walking along, the tourist passes men's and women's boutiques displaying the latest fashions in clothing and jewelry. In addition to the boutiques are small art galleries exhibiting paintings and sculptures by international and local artists. The tourist can also visit import shops with specialty goods from around the world. Restaurants, photography studios, travel bureaus, and patio shops complete the small but elegant shopping center along the boulevard. Although the buildings represent several architectural styles — Spanish, New Orleans, New England, and contemporary — they blend harmoniously to make a distinctive picture. Leaving the shopping area, the tourist crosses the bridge over the sparkling Intracoastal Waterway; there he can pause to look at the graceful white houses on the small Las Olas Isles and at the many handsome boats docked along their seawalls. The boulevard ends at the white sugar sand beach where high-rise apartments overlook the ocean. A walking tour of Las Olas Bouelvard is a must for a visitor to this city.

STAGE 5

FROM PART TO WHOLE

1. Looking at the Whole Theme
2. Looking at the Pattern for the Whole Theme
3. Considering the Word Count for a Theme

You have seen that the paragraph, the basic unit of exposition, develops a single unit of thought. You know that the purpose of expository writing is to explain an idea, an organization, a system, a process, or an object. These explanations frequently involve more than a single unit of thought. Suppose you were in a work/study program in hotel-motel management, and your assignment for the term was to serve as an assistant to the manager of the college cafeteria. Assume that student patronage of the cafeteria has declined 20 percent in the past two months and that the manager has asked you to conduct a survey and to submit a written explanation of your findings. You would obviously have to look into several areas — food, service, price, and atmosphere. Because you would draw a conclusion about each of these areas after completing your survey, your explanation would begin with **multiple inferences,** rather than with a single controlling inference. Based on your findings, your explanation might begin like this:

> Although the cafeteria prices are competitive, more students are going off campus to eat because the food *lacks variety,* the service is *poor,* and the atmosphere is *depressing.*

The manager would expect you to supply specific details to support each of your inferences because only then could he take steps to correct the problems. Because your report involves a number of units of thought, it would be written in several paragraphs. A multiparagraph paper is commonly referred to in a composition course as a **theme.**

THE THESIS STATEMENT

The multiple inference sentence for the theme is called the **thesis statement.** The thesis statement serves the same function for the theme as the topic sentence does for the paragraph. It lets the reader know what the limited subject is, what assertions the writer is making about the subject, and what proof details to expect. The thesis statement is more involved than the topic sentence because of the multiple inferences. Each inference in the thesis statement becomes the controlling inference in the topic sentence of each developmental paragraph. In the short theme (five hundred to eight hundred words), if you have three inferences in the thesis statement, you will have three developmental paragraphs. Each paragraph will give supporting details to illustrate, explain, describe, or prove the inference terms in the thesis statement. If it stands by itself, each developmental paragraph with its topic sentence, proof details, and summary sentence can be considered a one-paragraph theme. Taken together, however, these developmental paragraphs are unified and related to the thesis statement with the aid of transitional sentences or expressions, just as sentences within the paragraph are unified by transition. The concluding statement of a theme, which may consist of several sentences, summarizes the entire paper or draws a logical conclusion from the evidence presented. The concluding statement for the theme serves the same function as the summary sentence does for the paragraph.

STEP 1   **Looking at the Whole Theme.**   Here is a theme written by a student who decided to write more than a single paragraph about a person he admired. The theme is annotated in the margins so that you can see how the various parts work together. Notice that the paper begins with a lead-in statement. Its function is to interest the reader in the subject and to lead into the thesis statement. The thesis statement and the topic sentences are underlined; the inferences are underscored with a wavy line. Following the annotated theme is a diagram which shows the pattern of order for writing the theme.

JACQUES COUSTEAU

Many Americans might never have known of the French scientist Jacques Cousteau if it had not been for his documentary series <u>The Undersea World</u> <u>of</u> <u>Jacques Cousteau</u>. At first, television viewers were interested only in the subject matter of the film which introduced them to the undersea world Cousteau refers to as "inner space." But as they continued watching these documentaries, many viewers became interested not only in the subject matter, but also in the background of this unusual man. <u>Jacques Cousteau is to be admired because of his inventiveness, his contributions to marine science, and his dedication to his field.</u>

Of these admirable characteristics, <u>Cousteau's inventiveness has assisted him most in his desire to explore the new world of inner space</u>. First, the aqua-lung that he invented has proved to be a valuable piece of marine equipment for exploration of the undersea world because it enables underwater explorers to breathe without the assistance of air hoses from the surface. The aqua-lung, carried on the back of the diver, allows more freedom of movement than did the underwater devices of the past. With this aqua-lung and a water-tight camera, Cousteau has been able to explore ocean depths that had not previously been explored. He has also invented other types of marine equipment such as the mini-sub and personal diving equipment. In addition, he was the first to use underwater television to maintain contact between divers in the water and scientists aboard the ship and to use the bathyscaph which enabled him to make observations two miles below the surface of the sea. Cousteau's inventiveness has really made inner space a new frontier.

<u>Cousteau is to be admired not only for his inventiveness, but also for his many contributions to marine science</u>. Two of his books, <u>The Silent World</u>, written in 1953, and

Lead-in statement

Thesis statement

Transition topic sentence

Proof details

Summary sentence

Transition topic sentence

The Living Sea, written in 1963, described his experiences exploring the ocean depths and made millions aware of the importance of marine science in our modern world. He also made a film documentary on the Galapagos Islands and one of its inhabitants, the marine iguana, important to marine science because of its ability to slow down and even to stop its own *Proof* heart beat. Another film documentary explains *details* some of the behavioral characteristics of the sperm whale, such as its grouping and mating habits. The purpose of this documentary was to help prevent this mammal from becoming extinct. Other fascinating film documentaries produced by Cousteau which help to explain the undersea world are those on the sea otter, the bottle-nosed dolphin, octopi, and the ecology of *Summary* reefs around the world. The diversity of his *sentence* many contributions to marine science is an indication of why Cousteau is a leader in the field.

Transition Cousteau's inventiveness and his *topic* contributions to marine science are matched by *sentence* 3 his dedication to the field. For example, when all research money was diverted to armed defense during World War II, Cousteau continued his research using his own financial resources. Following World War II Cousteau, with the help of a financial backer, purchased a ship, the Calypso, to further his research. On some of *Proof* these voyages, the men have salvaged cargo from *details* sunken ships. Instead of merely selling the cargo, however, Cousteau carefully catalogs the various pieces of sunken treasure and notes the sea's effect on them. This operation in itself adds to historical knowledge. His *Summary* unselfish devotion to his field is an admirable *sentence* quality.

At a time in life when most men are retired, Jacques Cousteau, who is in his seventies, is still with his men, diving and researching. This scientist, physically and mentally active *Concluding* and still contributing to the marine world, is *statement* truly a man who deserves admiration.

STEP 2   Looking at the Pattern for the Whole Theme.

JACQUES COUSTEAU

Lead-in statement:
Thesis statement: Jacques Cousteau is to be admired because of his inventiveness, his contributions to marine science, and his dedication to his field.

Introductory paragraph (120 words)

Transition:

Topic sentence I. Inventiveness
A. Invented aqua-lung B. Invented mini-sub C. Invented other types of gear D. Used underwater TV E. Used bathyscaph
Summary sentence:

First developmental paragraph (170 words)

Transition:

Topic sentence II. Contributions to marine science
A. Wrote two books B. Produced documentary on Galapagos C. Produced documentary on sperm whale D. Made other documentaries
Summary sentence:

Second developmental paragraph (250 words)

Transition:

Topic sentence III. Dedication to his field

A. Used own money for research
B. Purchased ship for research
C. Voyaged to all parts of world
D. Catalogued salvaged cargo

Third developmental paragraph (115 words)

Summary sentence:

Transition:

Concluding statement: This scientist, physically and mentally active and still contributing to the marine world, is truly a man who deserves admiration.

Concluding paragraph (115 words)

STEP 3   Considering the Word Count for a Theme.   You will notice that the word count for each paragraph has been noted on the pattern for the theme. Expository themes for the first semester of English are usually between five hundred and eight hundred words. Thesis statements with three or more inferences cannot be adequately developed in fewer than five hundred words. The introductory paragraph for this length theme is brief; the conclusion is even briefer. The developmental paragraphs, however, known as the **body** of the paper, follow the regular principle of paragraph development — that is, each controlling inference seldom has fewer than four proof detail sentences to support it.

The diagram you have seen is only a basic pattern for expository writing. However, if you did nothing more than follow this pattern, you would have a well-organized, adequately-developed paper. Once you have mastered this basic pattern, you will be able to develop variations on it and to learn more sophisticated techniques of writing.

You have now seen the basic component of the theme, which is the paragraph, and the whole theme in pattern form. Stage 6 will show you how to limit a subject, how to develop a thesis statement by analyzing the subject, how to write a lead-in statement, and how to arrange the paragraphs of the paper to support the thesis.

STAGE 6

ANALYSIS: CLASSIFICATION AND DIVISION

STEP 1 **Analysis as a Method of Organizing Thought.** Analysis is a method of developing and organizing a subject by breaking it down into its parts. Through analysis, you convey to your reader a discovery about your subject. This breakdown helps to explain how the parts relate to each other and to the whole. There are two methods of analysis: **classification** and **division.**

Take a typical day in your life — a twenty-four hour period packed with a chaotic jumble of activities. You might have to grab breakfast, drop the dog by the veterinarian's for shots, research your sociology project, pick up the television from the repair shop so you can watch the documentary assigned for anthropology class, type up your process report for English class, give your friend a promised coaching session for tomorrow's mathematics test, put in at least two hours on your student workship, get a good meal tonight because you skimped last night, and get some sleep. You have so much to do that you haven't even found a half hour for fun.

Almost instinctively, you begin the first logical operation in any analysis; because to make sense out of your day, you must classify and divide all of your activities to give them some order. Classification means grouping; it means sorting and putting together items, activities, or ideas that have something in common. Thus, to plan your day, you start classifying what you must do according to types of activities: survival needs, studies, work, errands, and, hopefully, recreation. Then, in order to get a complete picture of what you must accomplish during the day, you divide each general activity into its component parts. This classification and division operation makes your day look something like this:

Survival
eating
sleeping

Studies
sociology research
English paper
math coaching
documentary

Errands
dog to vet
TV from repair shop

Workship
dittoes for debate coach
stencil for speech test

Recreation
concert at recreation center (?)

You may not do all of these things in sequence. However, in order to remember all of the things you must do and in order to save yourself time and energy, you need analysis to plan your day; without it you will conclude (and with good reason) that you should have stayed in bed.

Look at the way analysis works in another situation. Your college would not make sense without classification and division. College personnel, for instance, have to be classified by duties: administration, instructional personnel, non-instructional personnel, and maintenance staff. Each of these classes of employees is then subclassified, usually by the type of work each group does. Thus, non-instructional personnel breaks down into counselors, academic advisors, paraprofessionals, and clerical workers. Think about another instance where classification and division are necessary; you would have a hard time finding your way through the college catalogue if it were not classified according to major areas of instruction. A community college catalog, for example, usually classifies its areas of instruction as Business Administration, Communications, Fine Arts, Physical Education and Recreation, Mathematics and Science, Social Science, Pre-professional Programs, and Technical Education. Each major class of studies is then subclassified into separate subject areas. Communications, for example, comprises English, Speech, Reading, Foreign Languages, and Journalism. Each one of these subject areas is then further subclassified into courses by type. The two subclasses under English would be Composition and Literature and these areas are in turn subclassified. Literature may be divided into American literature, English literature, World literature, and special literature. These subclasses are finally divided into individual course offerings. American literature, for example, might be divided into American Literature before 1900, Contemporary American Literature, The American Short Story, The American Novel after 1920, or Modern American Poetry. When you stop to think about it, almost everything around you is classified and divided — stores, athletic teams, libraries, geographical areas — even your own home.

STEP 2   **Using Analysis for Subject Limitation.**   Just as fact enumeration is a way to support your inferences, analysis is a way of limiting and organizing expository writing. Assume that you are given as a possible subject for one of your first themes your home town or city. Analysis will help you with the first requirement of expository writing, suitable limitation of your subject. For example, you might make a quick analysis of your city or town in terms of areas classified on the basis of function. Your analysis would look like this:

AREAS OF TOWNS

Residential   Industrial   Commercial   Educational   Recreational

Since your first themes, however, are probably going to be only about five hundred words, you can quickly see by studying your analysis chart that you cannot handle all of these areas in a short paper. You must therefore think about limitation. Assume you are a business major. You focus on the commercial area of your town. You think about the office buildings, the various shopping centers; and then a picture of the new shopping mall that took three years to complete comes into your mind. You think about the "everything under one roof" concept of planned shopping centers as an improvement over the older, random growth types of shopping centers. At this point you decide that the subject for your paper will be shopping malls — a new concept in city planning. Your extended analysis chart would look like the diagram on page 94.

AREAS OF TOWNS

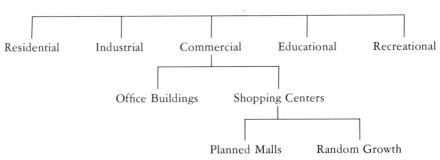

STEP 3   **Supplying Proof Details for the Subject.**   In order to determine what you are going to say about your limited subject, you now start a list of ideas (proof details). Your list might look something like this:

clothing stores	art galleries
gift shops	barber shops
department stores	shoe stores
cold drink stands	banks
snack bars	bakeries
book and record shops	telephones
underground parking	children's rides
above ground ramp parking	income tax service
movie theaters	automotive service
special holiday programs	sporting goods stores
fountains	drug stores
art shows	flower gardens
benches to sit on	sculptures
hobby shops	celebrity visits (sports figures, etc.)
hobby shows	politician's visits
toy stores	Santa Claus
specialty shops	Easter displays (flower shows)
specialty food shops	television in rest areas
specialty restaurants	choir and band performances
rest rooms	art shows
furniture stores	hobby displays

STEP 4   **Classifying the Proof Details.**   When you look over your list, you can see that the proof details fall into four main categories: (1) stores for every purpose, (2) service facilities, (3) parking areas, (4) rest and recreation facilities. With these categories, the analysis chart for the

limited subject of planned malls would look like this:

PLANNED SHOPPING MALLS

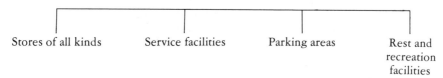

Stores of all kinds   Service facilities   Parking areas   Rest and recreation facilities

STEP 5   **Writing the Tentative Thesis Statement.**   After you have limited your subject by analysis, you can write a tentative thesis statement. The first part of a thesis is a general statement called the **major inference.** The major inference asserts your opinion, judgment, conclusion, or generalization about your subject. The major inference for a theme about shopping malls might be:

> *The mall concept of planned shopping centers offers the buyer everything under one roof.*

Your reader, however, needs more of an idea about where your exposition will take him. If you examine the bottom of your analysis chart, you can add to your general statement the main categories or classes of your discussion. These categories are called the **minor inferences.** Your complete thesis statement will then look like this:

> *The mall concept of planned shopping centers offers the shopper everything under one roof by providing stores for every purpose, varied service facilities, unlimited parking, and unusual rest and recreation facilities.*

The thesis statement, then, consists of three parts:

1. The limited subject:
   mall concept for planned shopping centers

2. The major inference:
   offers the buyer everything under one roof

3. The minor inferences:
   provides stores for every purpose
   provides varied service facilities
   provides unlimited parking
   provides unusual rest and recreation facilities

The categories of the discussion are called minor inferences because each of them is a generalization which must be further supported with proof details in the form of facts and examples.

STEP 6   Writing the Introductory Paragraph.   The thesis statement controls your paper; it gives the major and minor inferences which will be developed in the body of your paper. While the thesis begins the paper, it is only one part of the introductory paragraph. The introductory paragraph consists of two parts: the lead-in statement or statements, and the thesis statement.

THE LEAD-IN

The thesis statement contains the limited subject. The lead-in introduces the general subject and narrows it to the specific subject. The purpose of the lead-in is to arouse the reader's interest in the subject and to focus his attention on the thesis. The lead-in, in other words, is the attention-getter for your theme, while the thesis is the control center for your theme.

You saw the analysis of the subject of shopping malls presented graphically in chart form. It is often helpful to see how an introductory paragraph looks in graphic form; it is much like an inverted triangle because it begins with the general subject and narrows to the specific thesis.

General subject:
   commercial areas
Narrowed subject:
   shopping centers
Specific subject:
   malls
Thesis:
   major inference
   minor inferences

American cities are often notable for the inefficiency and ugliness of their *commercial areas.* Most *shopping centers* have developed without adequate planning for function or attractiveness. *The mall concept of planned shopping centers offers the shopper everything under one roof by providing stores for every purpose, varied service facilities, unlimited parking areas, and unusual rest and recreation facilities.*

STEP 7   Setting up the Tentative Framework.   Now that you have written the introductory paragraph, you are ready to set up the framework of the theme:

General subject: commercial areas of cities
Narrowed subject: shopping centers
Limited subject: the mall concept
Title: THE SUPERSHOP

Thesis: The mall concept of planned shopping centers offers the buyer everything under one roof by providing stores for every purpose, varied service facilities, unlimited parking areas, and unusual rest and recreation facilities.

    I. Stores for every purpose
   II. Varied service facilities
  III. Unlimited parking areas
  IV. Unusual rest and recreation facilities

Notice that the lead-in statement, while it will appear in the theme, is not part of the framework, which begins with the thesis. The minor inferences, pulled down from the thesis in order as they are written, indicate the major categories of the discussion that will form the body of the paper. Each minor inference from the thesis will function as the controlling inference in the topic sentence of each developmental paragraph.

STEP 8   **Limiting the Subject Further.**   Now that you have set up a framework by presenting the thesis and listing the minor inferences, you are ready to study your list of proof details and to place them under the appropriate minor inferences. However, given the number of details you already have listed, together with additional information you will want to add to support the minor inferences, you realize that you will have far too much to handle in a five hundred to eight hundred word theme, which is only about two to four typewritten pages of double-spaced text.

Once again you must limit your subject and rewrite the thesis according to the new limitation. Which of the four categories should you choose for discussion? You may decide that one of the mall ideas — the rest and recreation facilities — is a distinct innovation. This innovation is absent from the older, random growth type of shopping center, so you select this for your new limited subject. It is time to review your list again and to sift out only those details which pertain to the rest and recreation facilities of a mall. You might select these proof details:

children's rides
snack bars
juice bars
benches
fountains
flower gardens
sculptures
special holiday programs
art shows
hobby exhibits

visits by sports figures
garden shows
visits by TV and movie stars
visits by politicians
Santa Claus
television viewing areas
choral groups
telephones
rest rooms
speciality restaurants

Once again the problem is to bring order out of this random assortment of details. Again you use the logical operation of classification by grouping these details according to some basis of similarity. The rest and recreation facilities of a mall can be classified into six main categories:

1. Landscaped areas for relaxation   4. Play facilities for children

2. Restrooms   5. Displays for special interests

3. A variety of eating experiences   6. Shows for special events

As you look over these six categories, you realize that there is still too much information to handle in a five hundred to eight hundred word theme. The next question is, which of the categories can be eliminated by the writer and still let him get across the idea that a mall is an innovation in shopping centers? Upon reflection you realize that shopping areas other than malls offer conveniences and some recreation facilities for children. It is the other four categories that really make a mall distinctive.

THE FINAL ANALYSIS CHART

Your final analysis chart will look like this:

REST AND RECREATION IN A MALL

Lanscaped areas   Eating facilities   Special interest   Special event
for relaxation   displays   shows

REVISING THE THESIS

The thesis statement revised in accordance with your further limiting of the subject will look like the following:

A special attraction in the new shopping malls are the rest and recreation facilities, which provide landscaped areas for relaxation, a variety of eating experiences, displays for special interest groups, and shows for special events.

Here is an analysis of the new thesis:

1. Limited subject:
   the rest and recreation facilities of malls

2. Major inference:
   they are a special attraction for shoppers

3. Minor inferences:
   provide landscaped areas for relaxation
   provide a variety of eating experiences
   provide displays for special interest groups
   provide shows for special events

REVIEWING THE LEAD-IN

Now that you finally have limited your subject so that you know you can handle it in a short paper, you will want to look over the lead-in you wrote in order to make sure that it is still appropriate for the newly revised thesis statement and to make sure that it leads directly into the thesis. The first two sentences are still suitable:

1. American towns are often characterized by the inefficiency and ugliness of their commercial areas.

2. Most shopping centers have developed without adequate planning for function or attractiveness.

But now you really need another narrowing sentence to lead into the new thesis. You could add:

3. The new mall concept for planned shopping centers offers the shopper everything under one roof.

You are retaining your old major inference and using it now as another narrowing sentence in the lead-in. The inverted triangle for your revised introductory paragraph will look like the following:

General subject

Narrowed subject

Specific subject

Thesis

American cities are often notable for the ineffi-ciency and ugliness of their *commercial areas.* Most *shopping centers* have developed without adequate planning for function or attractive-ness. However, the new *mall concept* for planned shopping centers offers the shopper everything under one roof. *One of the special attractions in any mall is the rest and rec-reation facilities, which provide landscaped areas for relaxa-tion, a variety of eating experiences, displays for special interest groups, and shows for spe-cial events.*

STEP 9   Setting up the Framework for the Analysis Theme.   The framework for your revised theme sets up like this:

General subject: Commercial areas of cities
Limited subject: The rest and recreation facilities of a mall
Title: THE PAMPERED SHOPPER

Thesis: One of the special attractions in any mall is the rest and recrea-tion facilities which provide landscaped areas for relaxation, a variety of eating experiences, displays for special interest groups, and shows for special events.

    I. Landscaped areas for relaxation
   II. Variety of eating experiences
  III. Displays for special interest groups
  IV. Shows for special events

STEP 10   Understanding How Classification and Division Work Together.   You have seen from the analysis of the shopping mall topic that classification and division operate together. Notice that the writer, in order to make a logical analysis, had to classify and divide his subject on only one basis at a time. First he classified the areas of his home town on the basis of **function.** When he decided to write about the commercial area, he then classified this subject on the basis of **type of activity.** When he selected shopping centers as a further limitation, he then subclassified this subject on the basis of **type of planning.** Finally, when he decided that planned shopping malls would be the subject for his paper, he subclassified malls on the basis of **types of service** provided for the shopper. In order to further analyze his subject, he then divided each type of service into its **component parts.** On each level of analysis, then, he classified, subclassified, and divided on only one basis at a time.

A look at analyses of some other subjects will demonstrate the necessity for classifying and dividing on only one basis at a time. An analysis of the subject of *cars,* for example, might begin in one of several ways:

Subject: cars
Basis of analysis: foreign and domestic
               major American manufacturers
               size
               cost

If the topic were *bridges,* it might be analyzed in the following manner:

Subject: bridges
Basis of analysis: types
               movable
               fixed

               construction principle
               pier
               truss
               arch

               building material
               wood
               concrete
               steel

When you subclassify a subject, you can shift the basis of analysis. The important thing to remember is that on each level of analysis the basis of analysis must be consistent. The subject of bridges can again serve as an example. Suppose that you chose as your subject *fixed bridges*. This subject was selected from the analysis of bridges on the basis of type. If you were to further analyze this subject, you would most likely shift your basis of analysis and subclassify on the basis of construction principle:

Subject: fixed bridges
Basis of analysis: construction principle
        single beam
        suspension
        arch
        truss
        cantilever
        Bailey

If you decided to write a detailed analysis of the subject of fixed bridges constructed according to the *arch principle,* for example, you would continue to subclassify — but probably next on the basis of construction materials:

Subject: fixed arch bridges
Basis of analysis: construction materials
        cement
        steel

DIVIDING A SINGULAR SUBJECT

Singular subjects require analysis by division. In order to make a logical division, you must divide on only one basis at a time. Once again the subject of bridges will serve as an example. Suppose you chose for your subject *moveable bridges.* There are five types of moveable bridges:

Subject: moveable bridges
Basis of analysis: types
        transporter
        pontoon
        vertical lift
        swinging drawbridge
        Bascule

A civil engineering student living in an area of waterways with many drawbridges might find it interesting to investigate the single subject of the Bascule bridge. He would analyze this subject by division on the basis of component parts:

Subject: the Bascule bridge
Basis of analysis: component parts
> bridge leaf
> pit
> trunion pin
> motor
> driving gear
> bridge drive rack
> counter weight

Division of a subject usually involves an analysis of the component parts, but it can also involve an analysis in time or an analysis of the steps or stages of a subject. An analysis of any one of the systems of a car is an example.

Subject: the fuel system of a car
Basis of division: stages in the combustion cycle
> intake
> compression
> power
> exhaust

A further division of each one of these stages would involve the parts of the car concerned with each of the stages.

STEP 11 **Recognizing Problems in Analysis.**   You should avoid three errors that will produce a confusing or illogical analysis.

CROSS RANKING

If you classify or divide on more than one basis at a time, you are actually shifting the basis of analysis. This problem is called **cross ranking.** Here are two examples:

Subject: cars

sports	Basis of analysis: *purpose*
compact	Basis of analysis: *size*
economy	Basis of analysis: *price*

Subject: sports

wrestling	Basis of analysis: *mat sport*
judo	Basis of analysis: *mat sport*
cross country	Basis of analysis: *track sport*
tumbling	Basis of analysis: *mat sport*

OVERLAPPING

Your classifications or divisions on any one level of analysis must be **mutually exclusive.** This means that one entry cannot be subclassified or subdivided under any one of the other entries. Two examples of overlapping follow:

Subject: college divisions
> allied health
> business administration
> communications
> radiologic technology
> social science

Overlapping occurs in this analysis because radiologic technology is a subdivision of allied health.

Subject: campus Greeks
> sororities
> fraternities
> Sigma Nu

Overlapping occurs in this analysis because Sigma Nu is an individual fraternity and is thus a subdivision of fraternities.

INCOMPLETENESS

Your analysis of a subject should be as complete as possible for the limited subject you select. The number of subclassifications and subdivisions you have depends upon the length of your paper and the number of details you wish to include. Suppose you were consulting a consumer's guide for a complete analysis of compact cars manufactured by American companies. The analysis would be incomplete if it looked like this:

Subject: American-made compact cars
> American Motors
> General Motors
> Chrysler Corporation

The Ford Motor Company is obviously missing. Similarly, you would not have a complete analysis of tire brands if the guide's analysis looked like the following:

Subject: American tires
          Goodyear
          Goodrich
          Firestone
          General

The analysis is incomplete because Uniroyal and many other manufacturers are not included.

Analysis in a college catalogue or a consumer's guide or an analysis of an organization or an idea or a problem or a process should be as complete as possible. These are **formal analyses.** However, informal analyses — the kind you do every day — do not demand such completeness. It is quite possible, for example, that for your own purposes you want only to analyze compact cars manufactured by American Motors and the Chrysler Corporation. Under these circumstances, you would not need to include the other companies.

Name _____

Date _____

Section _____

EXERCISE 6-1   IDENTIFYING THE BASIS OF ANALYSIS

In each of the following groups, underline the item that is inconsistent with the others. Then identify the basis of analysis that has been used for the other terms in the group.

Example:

baseball
hockey
polo
<u>tumbling</u>
tennis

Basis of analysis: sports that
require striking equipment

1. library
    hospitality center
    bookstore
    learning resource center

    Basis of analysis: _____

2. registrar
    librarian
    director of financial aid
    counselor

    Basis of analysis: _____

3. set construction
    history of the theater
    lighting
    set design

    Basis of analysis: _____

4. choir
    symphonic orchestra
    brass band
    jazz ensemble

    Basis of analysis: _____

5. wool
    cotton
    silk
    dacron

    Basis of analysis: _____

6. slobs
    bleeding hearts
    gossips
    paranoid schizophrenics
    spongers

Basis of analysis: _____

7. chamber choir
    opera workshop
    college glee club
    string quartet

Basis of analysis: _____

8. Ferrari
    Porsche
    Corvette
    Jaguar

Basis of analysis: _____

9. ranch
    colonial
    Cape Cod
    Spanish
    duplex

Basis of analysis: _____

10. generosity
    high IQ
    gentleness
    good humor

Basis of analysis: _____

Name _____

Date _____

Section _____

EXERCISE 6-2 IDENTIFYING ANALYSIS PROBLEMS

In each of the following groups, there is a major analysis problem.
Name the problem or problems, because some groups may have one,
two, or all of the problems *(cross ranking, overlapping, incomplete
analysis)*.

1. **Clubs**   Problem: _____
   honorary societies
   student government association
   Greek council

2. **Administration**   Problem: _____
   dean of academic affairs
   dean of student affairs
   chairman of communications division
   dean of business affairs

3. **Students**   Problem: _____
   women students
   engineering students
   honor students
   married students

4. **Academic Major**   Problem: _____
   engineering students
   business administration students
   construction technology students
   architecture students

5. **Degree Programs**   Problem: _____
   accounting
   electronics
   journalism
   police science
   nursing
   radiologic technology

Name —————————————————————————

Date —————————————————————————

Section —————————————————————————

EXERCISE 6-3   WORKING CLASSIFICATION AND DIVISION

Select one subject from the list below. Subclassify the subject into at least three classes. Then divide each of the classes into subclasses. Name the basis of analysis for each.

Example:

Subject: Pollution
          air   Basis of analysis: element polluted
          land
          water

Subject: Water Pollution
          garbage   Basis of analysis: types of pollutant
          sewage
          chemical
          thermal

Subject choices:

1. Music
2. Hobbies
3. Campus activities
4. Wars
5. Television commercials

Subject:
      Subclasses: Basis of analysis:

Subject:
      Subclasses: Basis of analysis:

THE BASIS OF ANALYSIS AND THE THESIS STATEMENT

You already know that the thesis statement must contain (1) the limited subject, (2) the major inference, and (3) the minor inferences. Your work on Exercises 6-1 and 6-2 should help you to see that the minor inferences should not be cross ranked or overlapped. Each minor inference should be important enough so that interesting and adequate proof details can be supplied to support it.

One point concerning the thesis statement that has not yet been discussed is the necessity for stating the minor inferences in terms that are grammatically parallel. Following is an example of a thesis statement that is awkward because it is not grammatically parallel:

A high school band entering state competition is judged on concert performance, how well they march, and dress inspection.

The minor inferences *concert performance* and *dress inspection* are parallel because they are both noun phrases (nouns modified by adjectives), but the minor inference *how well they march* is a clause. Cast in grammatically parallel terms, the thesis would read:

A high school band entering state competition is judged on concert performance, marching ability, and dress inspection.

Thus, when you construct your thesis, you should pair nouns with nouns, infinitive phrases with infinitive phrases, noun phrases with noun phrases, dependent clauses with dependent clauses, independent clauses with independent clauses.

The last point you need to remember is that in a well-constructed thesis statement the basis of analysis is clear. If it is clear, it will indicate the pattern of development and will help the reader to follow your exposition.

The **bases of analysis** are:

types of any subject
characteristics of a subject
parts of a system, institution, mechanism, operation, or object
parts of a problem
parts of a solution
parts of an argument
divisions in time

EXERCISE 6-4 CRITICIZING THESIS STATEMENTS

Following are thesis statements written by freshman composition students in preparation for their first analysis theme. They chose subjects from personal experience. Criticize each of the thesis statements by identifying (1) the limited subject, (2) the major inference, (3) the minor inferences, (4) the basis of analysis. If the thesis is faulty, indicate the problem you find in it. If the thesis is satisfactory, write S in the space following **Thesis problem.** Thesis problems are listed below.

Thesis problems:

A. Limited subject not readily apparent
B. Subject not limited enough
C. Cross ranking of minor inferences
D. Overlapping of minor inferences
E. Dead-end minor inferences (too little or no factual information needed)
F. Minor inferences not grammatically parallel
G. No minor inferences
H. Illogical thesis

Example:

Thesis: Cepheids, though relatively rare, have, because of their special nature, an importance to people examining the universe. Polaris is one of these rare stars.

Limited subject: _____

Major inference: _____

Minor inferences: _____

Thesis problem(s): _____

1. **Subject:** Pay Television
   Thesis: Pay television should be introduced because it offers a finer selection of programs than those produced by most commercial sponsors and also that the regular TV networks would be forced to show better programs because of the competition.

   Limited subject:

   Major inference:

   Minor inferences:

   Basis of analysis:

   Thesis problem(s):

2. **Subject:** The College Cafeteria
   Thesis: Students should give the college cafeteria a try because the food is well prepared, the portions are large, the cost is reasonable, but the service is slow.

   Limited subject:

   Major inference:

   Minor inferences:

   Basis of analysis:

   Thesis problem(s):

3. **Subject:** The Neglect of Gifted Students
   Thesis: A lack of funds, the shortage of trained personnel, and the pressure of more crisis-oriented priorities are the major reasons for the widespread neglect of gifted children in our public schools.

   Limited subject:

   Major inference:

   Minor inferences:

   Basis of analysis:

   Thesis problem(s):

4. **Subject:** Preparing Desserts

   Thesis: For baked desserts the basic equipment needed includes bowls of several sizes, tableware, spatulas, a mixer, and regulated measuring instruments such as cups, glasses, and spoons.

   Limited subject:

   Major inference:

   Minor inferences:

   Basis of analysis:

   Thesis problem(s):

5. **Subject:** Commercial Air Passengers

   Thesis: Commercial air passengers can be divided into three major groups: the tourist, the standby, and the businessman.

   Limited subject:

   Major inference:

   Minor inferences:

   Basis of analysis:

   Thesis problem(s):

6. **Subject:** Modelling

   Thesis: Agency modelling, the most profitable type of fashion modelling, is unique in that the models wear only certain styles, they are paid by the hour, and they have to be prepared for shows at a moment's notice.

   Limited subject:

   Major inference:

   Minor inferences:

   Basis of analysis:

   Thesis problem(s):

7. **Subject:** Little Leagues

   Thesis: Little Leagues should be abolished because they discriminate against the child who is not a natural athlete, they allow parental prejudice to interfere with the selection of players during a game, and they do not set examples of good sportsmanship.

   Limited subject:

   Major inference:

   Minor inferences:

   Basis of analysis:

   Thesis problem(s):

8. **Subject:** Highway Drivers

   Thesis: Various types of drivers can be seen on any highway today. The three main types are the "Sunday driver," the "impatient driver," and "the cautious, defensive driver."

   Limited subject:

   Major inference:

   Minor inferences:

   Basis of analysis:

   Thesis problem(s):

9. **Subject:** The Beatle Phenomenon

   Thesis: In order to see why the Beatles remained on top of the rock world for so long, it is necessary to examine their popularity in terms of the individual members of the group, the tour years, and the musical innovations in their work.

   Limited subject:

   Major inference:

   Minor inferences:

   Basis of analysis:

   Thesis problem(s):

EXERCISE 6-5   CRITICIZING LEAD-IN STATEMENTS

Underline the lead-in statement (it may be one or several sentences) in the following introductory paragraphs to analysis themes. If the lead-in is inappropriate or ineffective or if there is no lead-in, write one you think would be satisfactory.

1. **Subject:** A Telephone Operator's Job

   An operator for Southern Bell Telephone Company not only has the job of putting through long distance calls but also of handling the many aspects of local calls. Local calls consist of emergencies, information, dialing assistance, and complaints.

   Rewrite of lead-in, if necessary:

2. **Subject:** Chinese Characters in Writing

   Chinese characters, which appear so puzzling to the people of the Western Hemisphere, are written hieroglyphically. This is especially true of the simple words which form the basis of all Chinese characters. Chinese characters can roughly be divided into two major categories — simple, basic words derived from the shape of objects they stand for and complicated words formed by the combinations of the basic words.

   Rewrite of lead-in, if necessary:

3. **Subject:** *Good Housekeeping* Magazine

   Good Housekeeping magazine is a widely read women's publication because it contains so many ideas focusing on different points of fashion, particularly in clothing. A wide selection and variety of styles can be seen in the four major classes of clothing featured: home-sewn garments, hand-knitted garments, vogue fashions, and designer copies.

Rewrite of lead-in, if necessary:

4. **Subject:** Russian Historical Movies

   The historical film about Russia, *War and Peace,* is among the most interesting movies made by virtue of its scenic splendor, its character portrayal, and its background of war and subsequent upheavals.

Rewrite of lead-in, if necessary:

5. **Subject:** Playing the Clarinet

   Playing the B flat clarinet to a point of perfection takes many hours of practice. Most of the areas in which a clarinetist would be interested are solo work, ensemble setup, and orchestral work. But in order for the clarinetist to function in any of these areas, he must work hard on the basic exercises. Clarinet exercises which specifically improve playing involve embouchre, technique, tone, and mastery of scales and arpeggios.

Rewrite of lead-in, if necessary:

EXERCISE 6-6   WRITING THESIS STATEMENTS

Following are three subjects. The minor inferences are given. Write a thesis statement which contains the limited subject, the major inference, and the minor inferences.

1. **Subject:** Corneal contact lenses
   Thesis:

   Minor inferences:
   - I. Bring greater freedom of movement
   - II. Provide greater protection from injury
   - III. Allow increased self-confidence

2. **Subject:** Home aquariums
   Thesis:

   Minor inferences:
   - I. Selecting the type of tank
   - II. Determining the kinds of fish
   - III. Choosing the accessory materials

3. **Subject:** Television commercials
   Thesis:

   Minor inferences:
   - I. Report straight information
   - II. Enlist "testimonials"
   - III. Incorporate humor

EXERCISE 6-7 WRITING THE INTRODUCTORY PARAGRAPH

Write an introductory paragraph for one of the thesis statements you have just written. The lead-in sentences, followed by the thesis, will form the introduction to the subject. Go back to page 100, and examine the inverted triangle introductory paragraph for *shopping malls.* Before writing your introductory paragraph, complete the exercise below that corresponds to your subject.

INTRODUCTORY PARAGRAPH: CORNEAL CONTACT LENSES

General subject

Narrowed subject

Specific subject

Thesis statement

INTRODUCTORY PARAGRAPH: HOME AQUARIUMS

General subject

Narrowed subject

Specific subject

Thesis statement

INTRODUCTORY PARAGRAPH: TELEVISION COMMERCIALS

General subject

Narrowed subject

Specific subject

Thesis statement

Name _____

Date _____

Section _____

EXERCISE 6-8   EXAMINING ANALYSIS CHARTS AND INTRODUCTORY PARAGRAPHS

On the following pages you will see analysis charts made by freshman composition students. In each case the student elected to write on a subject he already knew a great deal about — his job, his hobby, or a special interest. Study these analysis charts to see to what extent the student had to classify and divide to get a subject that would be manageable in a theme of five hundred to eight hundred words.

Opposite each chart is a worksheet on which you can make a critique of the student's introductory paragraph. The critique sheet on *Comics* is filled in as an example of a completed critique. Notice that the sentences in each introductory paragraph are numbered for easy identification. You can answer the questions on the critique sheet by placing the number of the correct sentence(s) in the blank.

INTRODUCTORY PARAGRAPH

(1) Every Sunday millions of Americans wake up and sit down to read the comic section of their morning newspapers. (2) Although many people snicker and laugh at the comics, most ignore the simple juncture between the comics and the readers' lives. (3) *This parallel is often startling, and readers can better see the connections if the comics are first classified into four general categories — the hilarity of family life, the problems encountered while growing up, the amusing side of military life, and the more serious side of adventure comics.*

General subject:

Limited subject:

Interest statement:

   1. What does it consist of (which sentence numbers)?
   2. Why might you want to read the paper?

Thesis statement:

   1. Is the limited subject clearly evident?
   2. What is the major inference?
   3. How many minor inferences are there?
   4. List the minor inferences:

   5. Are the minor inferences stated in grammatically parallel terms?
   6. What is their grammatical construction?
   7. Does the basis of analysis for the thesis indicate classification or division?

Convert the introduction into the framework for the paper.

THESIS:

   I.
   II.
   III.
   IV.

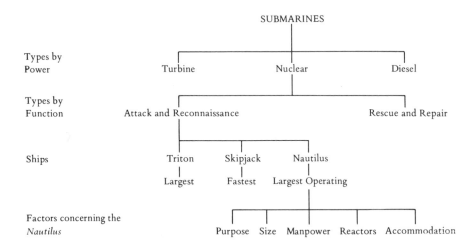

THESIS STATEMENT: Of the nuclear submarines, the *Nautilus* is probably the most advanced in the attack and reconnaissance class; five factors are involved in its function and operation: purpose, size, manpower, reactors, and accommodation.

INTRODUCTORY PARAGRAPH:

(1) Submarines are a very important weapon in our Navy. (2) Their power systems can be turbine, diesel, or nuclear. (3) In recent years it is the nuclear submarine which has generated the most interest for the general public. (4) Nuclear submarines are classified according to their function — Rescue and Repair or Attack and Reconnaissance. (5) The *Nautilus* is probably the most advanced submarine in the Attack and Reconnaissance class; five factors are involved in its function and operation: purpose, size, manpower, reactors, and accommodation.

General subject:

Limited subject:

Interest statement:

1. What does it consist of (what sentences?)
2. Why would you want to read the paper?

Thesis statement:

1. Is the limited subject clearly evident?
2. What is the major inference?
3. How many minor inferences are there?
4. List the minor inferences:

5. Are the minor inferences stated in grammatically parallel terms?
6. What is their grammatical construction?
7. Does the basis of analysis for the thesis indicate classification or division?

Convert the introduction into the framework for the paper.

THESIS:

   I.
   II.
   III.
   IV.

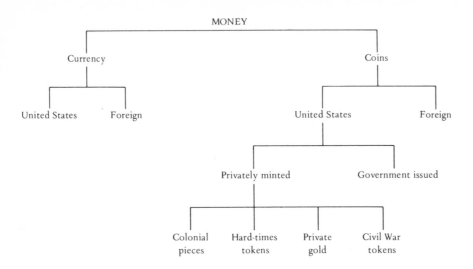

THESIS: Privately minted American coins, which are extremely valuable to a collector, are identified by four major types: Colonial pieces, Hard Times tokens, private gold, and Civil War tokens.

INTRODUCTORY PARAGRAPH

(1) Since 1652, when the first coin intended for use in America was struck, many types of money have circulated in this country. (2) The most familiar to Americans today are the government-issued coins. (3) The most interesting to collectors, however, are the privately minted coins which were struck out of necessity and circulated freely during several periods in our history. (4) Privately minted American coins, which are extremely valuable, can be divided into four major types: Colonial pieces, Hard Times tokens, private gold, and Civil War tokens.

General subject:

Limited subject:

Interest statement:

1. What does it consist of (what sentences)?
2. Why would you want to read the paper?

Thesis statement:

1. Is the limited subject clearly evident?
2. What is the major inference?
3. How many minor inferences are there?
4. List the minor inferences:

5. Are the minor inferences stated in grammatically parallel terms?
6. What is their grammatical construction?
7. Does the basis of analysis for the thesis indicate classification or division?

Convert the introduction into the framework for the paper.

THESIS:

  I.
 II.
III.
IV.

Name _____

Date _____

Section _____

EXERCISE 6-9   MAKING AN ANALYSIS CHART

Select one subject from the list below and make an analysis chart. Work the chart down by classifying and dividing until you get a limited subject with several categories that you think could be developed in a five hundred to eight hundred word theme.

Subjects:
1. Pets
2. Popular music
3. Camping
4. American magazines
5. Gardens
6. Snobs
7. Boats
8. Newspapers
9. Instructors
10. Aspects of a character
11. Movies
12. Motorcycles
13. Crime
14. Musical instruments
15. Campus activities
16. Religions
17. Day-care centers
18. Part-time jobs
19. Commercials
20. Hobbies
21. Condominiums

General subject:

ANALYSIS CHART

Thesis:

EXERCISE 6-10   WRITING A THESIS STATEMENT FROM THE ANALYSIS CHART

Taking your minor inferences from the bottom of your analysis chart, write a thesis statement in which the classifications or divisions are evident.

Thesis:

Limited subject:

Major inference:

Minor inferences:

Name _____

Date _____

Section _____

EXERCISE 6-11   MAKING A LIST OF PROOF DETAILS

Now make a list of proof details that support your minor inferences.

Name _____

Date _____

Section _____

EXERCISE 6-12   CLASSIFYING THE PROOF DETAILS

Examine your list and group the entries that have something in common. Then consider:
1. Do you have more classifications than appear in your thesis?
2. If so, would you like to add this class or category to the thesis in the form of another minor inference?
3. If you add another category to the thesis, can you still manage the paper in five hundred to eight hundred words?
4. If you think you have too many categories in your thesis to begin with, decide which one(s) you can omit and still write an interesting paper.

Reminder: When you estimate word count, assume that you are writing full sentences around your list of proof details. The average typewritten page of double-spaced text runs about 225 to 250 words.

Now cast the framework for your paper.

TITLE:

Thesis (revised if necessary):

   I.
  II.
 III.
 (etc.)

EXERCISE 6-13   CLASSIFYING PROOF DETAILS UNDER MINOR INFERENCES

Now you have a thesis and a framework for a theme. Place the proof details under the minor inferences they will support. Be sure that you have *at least* four substantial proof details for each minor inference.

Thesis:

Minor inference	I.
Proof details	A.
	B.
	C.
	D.
Minor inference	II.
Proof details	A.
	B.
	C.
	D.
Minor inference	III.
Proof details	A.
	B.
	C.
	D.

Reminder: This outline provides for the required three minor inferences. If you have additional minor inferences, include them as IV, V, and so on.

Name _____

Date _____

Section _____

EXERCISE 6-14 WRITING THE INTRODUCTORY PARAGRAPH WITH LEAD-IN AND THESIS

Write the introductory paragraph.

Name _____

Date _____

Section _____

EXERCISE 6-15   USING THE CRITIQUE SHEET TO ANALYZE THEME PREPARATION

Select a student from your class to criticize your proposed paper. Tear out Exercises 6-13 and 6-14 and attach to this sheet. You can also use this sheet to criticize your own proposed paper. When you get the papers back (or when you catch your own problems), you can then make any revisions necessary.

Author:

Critic:

Thesis:

   1. What is the limited subject?

   2. What is the major inference?

   3. What are the minor inferences?

   a. Are the minor inferences grammatically parallel?
   b. Can the writer support this thesis within the word limit of the assignment?
   c. If not, can you suggest further limitation?
   d. How many developmental paragraphs are there likely to be?
   e. Are there any thesis problems? (Check page 113 for the kinds of thesis problems and list any you find.)

Lead-in:

1. Is it appropriate for the subject?
2. Does it create enough interest to make you want to read the paper?
3. If not, can you suggest revision?

Proof details:

1. Are there at least four proof details to support each minor inference?
2. Does each proof detail specifically relate to the minor inference?
3. If not, list the proof details which are irrelevant. (Example: IID, IIIA, and so on.)

STAGE 7

THE OUTLINE

1. Recognizing Types of Outlines
2. Learning the Mechanics of Outlining

In working through Stage 6, you have seen that it is a long way from a random list of ideas on a subject to an orderly presentation of those ideas to your reader. But you have also seen that once you have put your inferences into a thesis statement and formed a brief outline by pulling down the minor inferences to form headings for the major categories of your paper, you have really roughed out the whole theme. In Stage 7 you will be working with the formal outline, which is a systematic arrangement of all your inferences and proof details showing the complete analysis of your subject.

Many freshmen consider outlines an artificial exercise which has little or no relation to the actual themes they write. But you know from your work with classification and division in Stage 6 that outlining is actually a natural process which comes about as a result of your attempt to show the relationships between your main ideas and your proof details. All you need to learn now are the technicalities of formal outline writing.

Consider the first stage in building construction, the architect's blueprint. The blueprint from which the builder will work shows the basic outline of the entire building; in addition, the blueprint illustrates the division of space, the location of doors and windows, and diagrams and locations of all the systems — heating, cooling, wiring, and plumbing. The blueprint can be changed up until the time of construction; after that, changes are cumbersome and costly. The outline for a piece of expository writing is similar to the blueprint for a building: the outline is the design for a structure of ideas; the blueprint, for a physical structure.

In addition to the fact that the outline is a necessity for effective organization, it will also save valuable time in the writing process itself. The outline will assist you in the following operations:

1. **The outline helps you to decide on the method of presentation.**
   Having decided upon your purpose, your major and minor inferences through analysis of your subject, you will have to decide which order of presentation is most suitable: order of importance, chronological order, spatial order, or causal order.
2. **The outline assists you in judging adequacy of content.**
   When you arrange your proof details under the category to which they belong, you can see at a glance whether you have sufficient support for each inference.
3. **The outline assists you in judging proportion in your paper.**
   While there is no standard rule about the number of proof details under each inference, the outline will tell you at a glance if any category is out of proportion. For instance, if you have only two proof details under one category, perhaps what you considered a major category was not one at all, or you have not considered other possible proof details for the inference.
4. **The outline assists you in judging the logic of your paper.**
   By looking at an outline, you can tell at a glance whether each supporting detail "adds up" to support the category under which it is classified. If there are any classification problems such as cross ranking or overlapping, the problem will be evident immediately.

STEP 1   **Recognizing Types of Outlines.**   There are two types of outlines: the **sentence outline** and the **topic outline.** The sentence outline is often used by the beginning writer because it helps to formulate and organize ideas in complete thought patterns. The topic outline, commonly used by the more experienced writer, consists of brief phrases or single words which note the key idea of each sentence. Both types of outlines use the same mechanics for showing the order and the relative importance of the major categories of discussion and their supporting details.

Here are two outlines written by a student in preparation for his analysis theme on his hobby of coin collecting.

SENTENCE OUTLINE

PRIVATELY MINTED TOKENS OF AMERICA

<u>Thesis statement:</u> To a collector, three of the most interesting types of privately minted coins are the Hard Times tokens, the Civil War tokens, and gold coins.

I. The first of these to be minted was the Hard Times tokens.
   A. There were three reasons for issuing these coins in the 1830s.
      1. A severe depression began to develop.
      2. The face value of existing coins fell below the value of the metal.
      3. Many people began to hoard large quantities of coins.
   B. There are two types of Hard Times tokens.
      1. One is the political token.
      2. The other is merchants' coins.
   C. The government ignored their production and distribution.

II. The second type to be minted was the Civil War token.
   A. There were two reasons for issuing these coins.
      1. Hoarding created a massive coin drain.
      2. Merchants needed coins.
   B. The tokens were struck in several metals and were the size of our present-day cent.
   C. The tokens are divided into three groups.
      1. Tradesmen's tokens were used to provide change and to advertise dealers' wares.
      2. Political tokens carried propaganda slogans.
      3. Patriotic or unpatriotic tokens carried slogans for or against the government's position on the Civil War.
   D. The government considered these coins illegal and confiscated them.

III. The third to be minted was gold coins.
 A. There were three reasons for their
    coinage.
    1. There was an aute shortage of regular
       coinage issued by the United States
       mint.
    2. It was difficult to transport coins
       from the East to the West.
    3. It was easier for gold mining
       companies to pay in gold.
 B. There are four kinds of gold coins.
    1. The first of these was the N.G.N.
       coin.
       a. It was made in the shape of an
          ingot.
       b. It carried the initials N.G.N.
    2. The second was the Templeton Reid
       issues.
    3. The third kind was those produced by
       the mining companies.
    4. The fourth was the Mormon gold
       pieces.
       a. They were issued for public
          convenience because of difficulty
          of paying in gold dust.
       b. The imprints on these coins were
          unusual.
          (1) The five dollar gold piece
              carried a religious theme.
          (2) Other gold pieces showed an
              animal or bird.
 C. The government later set up assay
    offices to authorize the minting of gold
    coins.

Concluding statement: In the past, regularly
issued coins have sometimes become so scarce
that citizens were forced to produce temporary
substitutes to carry on business.

TOPIC OUTLINE

PRIVATELY MINTED TOKENS OF AMERICA

Thesis statement: To a collector, three of the
most interesting types of privately minted coins
are the Hard Times tokens, the Civil War tokens,
and gold coins.

I. Hard Times tokens
   A. Reasons for issue
      1. Severe depression
      2. Devalued coins
      3. Hoarded coins
   B. Types of tokens
      1. Political tokens
      2. Merchants' coins
   C. Government's position

II. Civil War tokens
   A. Reasons for issue
      1. Hoarding of coins
      2. Facilitation of trade
   B. Description of coins
      1. Metals used
      2. Size of coin
   C. Types of tokens
      1. Tradesmen's tokens
         a. Used to provide change
         b. Used to advertise wares
      2. Political tokens
      3. Patriotic or unpatriotic tokens
         a. For the Civil War
         b. Against the Civil War
   D. Government's position

III. Gold coins
   A. Reasons for coinage
      1. Acute shortage of U.S. minted coins
      2. Difficulty of transporting coins
      3. Ease for gold mining companies

    B. Types
        1. N.G.N. coin
            a. Shape
            b. Imprint
        2. Templeton Reid issues
            a. Origin
            b. Denomination
        3. Mining companies' coins
            a. Denomination
            b. Shape
        4. Mormon gold pieces
            a. Reasons for issue
            b. Description
                (1) Five dollar gold piece
                (2) Others
    C. Government's position

Concluding statement: In the past, regularly
issued coins sometimes became so scarce that
citizens were forced to produce temporary
substitutes to carry on business.

STEP 2   **Learning the Mechanics of Outlining.**   The outline is headed by the
title and opens with the thesis statement. Each minor inference or
classification category that appears in the thesis appears in the same
order in the body of the outline under a Roman numeral. For example,
in the paper on "Privately Minted Tokens of America," the writer
arranged the minor inferences "Hard Times tokens, the Civil War
tokens, and gold coins." The first one, "Hard Times tokens," then
appeared as Roman numeral I, "Civil War tokens" appeared as Roman
numeral II, and "gold coins" as Roman numeral III. If the proof details
(A,B,C,D, and so on) include other minor points of evidence, those
points are represented by Arabic numerals (1,2,3,4, and so on) and
arranged under the proof detail of which they are a part.

The examples you have seen for the paper "Privately Minted Tokens of America" represent five stages of classification and division.
Although a three stage outline is usually adequate for a five hundred to
eight hundred word theme, a writer could use a four, five, or six stage
outline for longer papers with a great deal of detailed information. The
form for a six stage outline would look like the following:

THE SIX STAGE OUTLINE

TITLE

Thesis statement:

I.
  A.
  B. 1.
      2.
          a.
          b.
          c.
              (1)
              (2)
                  (a)
                  (b)
II. continue . . .
Concluding statement:

Regardless of how many stages you have for your outline, there are certain basic rules to follow:

RULES FOR OUTLINING

1. Center the title above the outline in capital letters.

2. Then write the thesis statement. The thesis statement carries no numeral because it controls the entire paper and is not a subdivision in itself.

3. Be sure that the order of the minor inference or classification category for each Roman numeral follows the order presented in the thesis statement.

4. Be consistent in form. If you have a sentence outline, write all entries as full sentences. If you have a topic outline, write all entries in topic form. Do not mix forms.

5. Write the entries in parallel grammatical form. For example, in a topic outline, make all Roman numeral entries nouns, noun phrases, or gerund phrases. Similarly, keep the entries on the next level of classification parallel.

6. Make sure that there are two or more entries on every level of classification. That is, every A must have a B, every 1 must have a 2. The logical reason for this is that nothing can be broken into fewer than two parts.

7. Place a period after every numeral and every letter of the outline except those in parentheses.

8. Capitalize the first word of each entry.

9. Use no end punctuation in a topic outline.

10. Single space the entries within a Roman numeral category, and double space between Roman numerals.

11. Keep corresponding numerals and letters in vertical columns.

12. Place Capital A under the first letter of the first word entry in Roman numeral I. Similarly, all other numbers and letters follow this pattern. (Note model outlines.)

DISCUSSION

If you compare the sentence outline with the completed theme, you will see that the student has expanded each of his basic sentence entries, varying the sentence structure and elaborating on details.

THEME

PRIVATELY MINTED TOKENS OF AMERICA

Since 1652, when the first coin intended for use in the American colonies was struck, many types of money have been circulated in this country. The most familiar to most Americans today are the government—issued coins; however, the most interesting are probably the privately minted coins circulated in isolated areas of our country by private companies, private citizens, assayers, bankers, and special interest groups. To a collector, three of the most interesting types of privately minted coins are the Hard Times tokens, the Civil War tokens, and gold coins.

The first of these coins, the Hard Times tokens, were minted during the 1830s. The name derives from the fact that America was suffering a severe depression which reached its peak in 1837. Because the face value of our official coins fell below the value of the metal of which they were made, many people began to hoard large quantities of coins, creating a severe coin shortage. To combat this practice and to carry on business, merchants had coins made by private mints. The coins, struck in copper in the size

of a large United States cent, are of two
general groups, political tokens and merchants'
coins. The theme of the imprint on the
political tokens centered around President
Jackson's fight against the United States Bank
and supported the President's position with
slogans and symbolic devices. The merchants'
coins, also known as tradesmen's coins, carried
advertisements. Although the Hard Times tokens
were unauthorized, the government overlooked
their production and distribution because of
their great need.

But the Panic of 1837 was not the only period
in our country's history when temporary coins
had to be issued because the people hoarded
minor coins. During the Civil War the hoarding
of coins by the citizens created a massive coin
drain and forced merchants into having tokens
made to facilitate trade. These tokens, struck
in several metals including copper, brass, iron,
and nickel, are the size of our present-day
cent. The tokens are divided into three groups:
tradesmen's tokens and anonymously issued pieces
with either political, patriotic, or unpatriotic
themes. The tradesmen's tokens, issued by
various firms, were used to provide change and
to advertise dealers' wares. These coins bore
either an implied or explicit promise of
redemption in goods or money. The political
coins carried themes such as the one with the
bust of General McClellan, bearing the
inscription "Millions for contractors, not one
cent for widows." Tokens carrying slogans
supporting the United States were known as
patriotic coins. For example, one token shows
General Dix's words, "The American Flag -- If
anyone attempts to tear it down, shoot him on
the spot," encircling the flag. In contrast,
tokens carrying slogans calling for an end to
the war, such as "Peace at any cost," are known
as unpatriotic tokens. Like the Hard Times
tokens, the Civil War tokens were illegal and
were circulated for only a short time. However,
the government, unlike that of the 1837
depression, stepped in and confiscated the Civil
War tokens. Still, a rush to hoard coins was
not the only reason coins were privately minted.

The Gold Rush and the great distance between
the West Coast and the United States Mint in
Philadelphia provided other reasons for the
private minting of coins. First, there was an
acute shortage of regular coinage issued by the
United States Mint because it was difficult to
transport coins to the new settlers in the
West. Then, because the various mining
companies dealt in gold, it was easy to produce
a gold coin with which to pay the mining
employees. One of the first of the gold coins
was the five dollar gold coin in the shape of an
ingot and struck with the imprint of San
Francisco. It also carried the initials N.G.N.,
not identified until 1902 as Norris, Gregg, and
Norris. Another series is the Templeton Reid
issues, made in California in 1849 and issued in
denominations of ten and twenty-five dollars.
In addition to those coins, mining companies
produced other tokens: gold coins in
denominations of fifty dollars, called slugs;
twenty dollars, called double eagles; five
dollars, one dollar, fifty cents, and
twenty-five cents. The small denominational
coins and the dollar were struck in shapes both
octagonal and round. Like the coins of the
mining companies, the Mormon gold pieces were
inaugurated as a public convenience. As in
other gold mining sections, in Salt Lake City
there was much trouble in payment of small sums
in the form of gold dust. For this reason the
five dollar gold piece was issued in 1860. This
coin showed a beehive on one side and clasped
hands with a legend "Holiness to the Lord"
around the border on the other side. Other
Mormon gold pieces showed a lion or an eagle
holding a laurel branch and arrows in its
talons. Later, however, the United States
government stepped in and set up assay offices
in the West to authorize the minting of gold
coins.

Although today most of us take the change in
our pockets for granted, in past eras of our
history, regularly issued coins became so scarce
that citizens of the time were forced to produce
temporary substitutes in order to carry on
business.

EXERCISE 7-1 IDENTIFYING OUTLINE PROBLEMS

Following are two outlines. The first was written by a student as a topic outline, the second as a sentence outline. Using the principles you have learned about subject limitation and classification and division in Stage 6, and rules of outlining in Stage 7, criticize these two outlines. Then rewrite them, eliminating, relocating, or adding entries as the need arises.

OUTLINE A: Topic

```
     BRITAIN'S NATIONAL HEALTH SERVICE -- SOME
                       DRAWBACKS

Thesis statement: Although Great Britain has
free medical care available to everyone, their
nationalized health plan has some drawbacks:
shortage of government funds, inadequate
opportunity for physician specialization, lack
of incentive, and hospital admission delays.

    I. Shortage of government funds
       A. The financing is overwhelmingly
          governmental
          1. Must compete with education funds
          2. With transport funds
          3. With defense funds
       B. Britain devotes a smaller portion of its
          GNP to health care

   II. Inadequate opportunity for physician
       specialization
```

A. Large scale exodus of medical men out of
   Britain
   1. Net outflow of 400 per year
   2. One out of three medical school
      graduates leave
B. British hospitals are staffed by
   immigrant doctors
   1. Immigrant doctors from India,
      Pakistan and other nonwhite
      Commonwealth countries
   2. Account for more than 40 percent of
      medical staffs in British hospitals
   3. Trained only temporarily in Great
      Britain

III. Lack of incentive
   A. System encourages general practitioners
      to provide the minimum service
   B. System encourages general practitioners
      to refer any serious or complicated
      cases to specialists

IV. Hospital admission delays
   A. More than 500,000 seek hospital
      admission at present
   B. Average delay for tonsil removal is
      twenty-two weeks

Concluding statement: In reviewing some of the
drawbacks of the British system, the United
States should think twice before adopting a
medical system that is operated almost
exclusively by the central government and
financed almost entirely out of general tax
revenues.

OUTLINE B: Sentence

HOW TO SELECT A VACATION

Thesis statement: In planning a vacation, one
must consider the problems of choice, where to
go, how much to spend, and how to get there.

I. There are many spots to choose from in planning a vacation.
   A. There are resorts such as Miami Beach and Las Vegas and tranquil spots such as the Virgin Islands.
   B. There are many big cities which are often visited along with dude ranches.
   C. Instead of staying in one place, you can travel from spot to spot.
      1. From Miami Beach you can visit the Islands.
      2. From Mexico City you can travel to Acapulco.
      3. The resorts of Maine are only a short hop away from Canada.
   D. After you decide where you want to go, obtain a map of the nearby cities of interest.

II. The second problem is that of cost.
   A. The average vacation for two runs about $200 to $300 a week.
      1. A week's camping in a state or national park starts at about $25.
      2. You must also add round trip transportation and other extras.
   B. You can buy a package vacation before you go.
      1. It includes rooms and meals.
      2. You will know in advance how much you will have to spend.

III. Transportation is the third problem in planning a vacation.
   A. Besides driving you can travel by rail, plane, or ship.
   B. A cruise offers a carefree vacation.
      1. Everything is provided.
      2. The ship is your hotel.
   C. Cost varies with the cabin you choose.
      1. The tips are not included in the ship's price.
      2. When paying the tips it is best to give a lump sum at the end.

IV. Consequently it is essential that you plan
    in advance.
    A. Plan your trip from three to six months
       in advance.
    B. Package deals are only available certain
       times of the year.

EXERCISE 7-2   FILLING IN THE OUTLINE

In the outline form below, you are given the thesis statement and the minor inferences. Using the list of proof details on the following page, fill in the outline. At the bottom of the outline, list the detractors by number.

AN INSTRUCTOR'S MANUAL OF STUDENTS

Thesis statement: Any teacher can identify the unprepared students in a class by the techniques they use to conceal their lack of preparation. These students can be classified as the excuse experts, the class bluffers, and the students who organize group efforts to harass the instructor.

I. The excuse expert comes in two types, the no-show and the textbook terror.
   A.
      1.
      2.
      3.
      4.
   B. 1.
      2.
      3.
      4.

II. The class bluffers also come in two varieties, the verbal and the nonverbal.
   A.
      1.
         a.
         b.
         c.
      2.
         a.
         b.
         c.

B.
1.
2.
3.
4.

III. Perhaps most inventive are the students who participate in group efforts to harrass the instructor.
A.
B.
1.
2.
3.
C.
D.

Concluding statement: Therefore, it is easy for any instructor to spot the unprepared students.

Detractors:
A. _____
B. _____
C. _____

List of Details

1. The nonverbal bluffer is very inventive with gestures.
2. He rustles the pages of his spiral notebook audibly and shakes it to "locate" the homework he was up till 2:00 A.M. doing.
3. The no-show relies on at least four basic excuses.
4. "I had to be in court."
5. "I have a (tournament), (game), (job interview), (cross country training flight), (bronchitis)."
6. The textbook terror who is determined never to purchase a book or, if he has bought one, never to bring it to class, has his own set of excuses.
7. "I left the book in my boyfriend's car and the car was stolen."
8. "I can't possibly afford a textbook this month."
9. My wife just had a baby and the visiting hours are only during this class hour.
10. This bluffer takes superfluous notes to convince the teacher that what is being said is really important to him as well as to the instructor.

11. He seldom looks up while taking notes; the teacher will assume he is legitimately busy and call on another.
12. "I had to take my mother to the hospital and my father to the airport."
13. "I never read textbooks anyway."
14. Another kind of bluffer looks excessively bright-eyed and attentive so that the instructor will call on someone who is obviously withdrawn, sleeping, or hostile.
15. "My pet raccoon chewed the book up last night."
16. The verbal bluffers can be identified as the volunteer and the distractor.
17. He always asks a question about a current event or about a subject on which he knows that the teacher is hooked, thus inducing the class into a prolonged discussion.
18. The distractor will do anything to get the teacher off the subject and thereby avoid the issue of being questioned on the material for the day.
19. He always volunteers quickly for the questions he does know the answers to.
20. He volunteers basic information early in the class so the instructor thinks he is prepared and will look for others to call on.
21. He always asks extraneous questions which makes him look eager for extra information on the subject.
22. The volunteer is chiefly concerned to hide the fact that he isn't prepared.
23. A dedicated nonconformist, he challenges the teacher on every point, thus intimidating the instructor so he won't be called on.
24. In language classes he volunteers to translate the first three lines of the assignment — the only ones he has completed.
25. Some students are antagonistic and defensive at all times, forcing the teacher to handle them with kid gloves.
26. These students organize late teams and operate them in relays so that each day several come in tardy at staggered moments, thus creating problems for the instructor.
27. In the technique known as brainwashing, the students collectively try to convince the teacher that he never gave the assignment.
28. The tardy types upset the lecture.
29. The leaders organize mass resistance to handing in homework in order to bring forth lectures on responsibility and the meaning of education.
30. The late teams also cause attendance-taking problems.

31. The evader makes the answer to a question so general that in questioning him more closely, the teacher supplies the answer.

32. The latecomers make it possible for students to insist they didn't get papers handed back at one time or another.

33. The hesitator waits until a bright or enthusiastic student answers the question, then quickly adds, "that's just what I was going to say."

34. The harassment experts organize coughing and yawning extravaganzas which will bring about time-consuming lectures on maturity, thereby delaying the lesson for the day.

Name _____

Date _____

Section _____

EXERCISE 7-3 WRITING THE OUTLINE

On the page following the statements about President Kennedy is an incomplete outline. Complete the outline by arranging the sentences in a major inference (thesis), three minor inferences, and the supporting details. Since only the letter *A* is given under each Roman numeral, you will have to supply the other letters according to the number of proof details that relate to each minor inference. At the bottom of the outline, list the detractors (irrelevant statements) by number.

1. He was the youngest man ever elected President.
2. He won the presidency with his "New Frontier" program.
3. In June 1963 he federalized the Alabama National Guard to enforce integration of the University of Alabama.
4. He helped further civil rights legislation.
5. He was elected to the United States House of Representatives in 1946.
6. John F. Kennedy will be remembered for his effectiveness in furthering civil rights legislation, in strengthening foreign relations, and in establishing innovative domestic programs.
7. He organized the Peace Corps.
8. He recognized the importance of the nation's defense policies by increasing conventional weapons rather than nuclear weapons.
9. He asked Congress to pass legislation requiring hotels, motels, and restaurants to admit customers regardless of race.
10. He was inaugurated President on January 20, 1961.
11. In July of 1963 he signed a treaty with Russia banning atomic testing in the atmosphere, outer space, and under water.

12. One of his accomplishments was the strengthening of foreign relations.
13. He was the youngest man ever to die while serving as President.
14. He encouraged physical fitness tests, which were started in all United States schools.
15. The fifty mile hike became a fad.
16. In 1952 he was elected to the Senate.
17. Mrs. Kennedy won praise for her redecoration of the White House.
18. The Cuban crisis brought the United States and Russia to the brink of war.
19. He aided business by increasing tax benefits for companies investing in new equipment.
20. He asked Congress to grant the attorney general authority to begin court suits to desegregate schools on behalf of private citizens.
22. He brought youth and informality to the White House.
23. He established innovative special domestic programs.
24. The "hot line" direct communication system between Washington, D.C. and Moscow was set up.
25. He appointed two Supreme Court Justices.
26. In 1961 he helped establish the Alliance for Progress, a ten-year program of aid for Latin American countries to begin democratic reform.
27. He gave recognition to the creative arts by appointing a special advisor on the arts.
28. His farm program suffered defeat.
29. He encouraged space exploration; and, as a result, the first American in space, Alan B. Shepard, Jr., made a fifteen minute suborbital flight.
30. The hourly wage was increased from $1.00 to $1.25 as sponsored by the President.
31. The President's Trade Expansion Act cut tariffs so that the United States could trade freely with the European Common Market.
32. He federalized the National Guard in September of 1963 to ensure the integration of public schools in three Alabama cities.
33. He asked Congress to join the judicial and executive branches in "making it clear to all that race has no place in American life or law."
34. Because of these accomplishments, John F. Kennedy left his mark on the United States even though his term of office was brief.

PRESIDENT KENNEDY'S ACCOMPLISHMENTS

Thesis statement:

Major inference

    I. Topic sentence (Minor inference #1)

        A.

   II. Topic sentence (Minor inference #2)

        A.

  III. Topic sentence (Minor inference #3)

        A.

Concluding statement:

Detractors (list only the numbers):

WRITING SUGGESTION: THE ANALYSIS THEME

A. Choose a subject from the following list of suggestions. Limit the subject to a level that gives you a topic that can be handled in a theme of about five hundred to eight hundred words.

Construct a formal outline with at least three levels of classification.

B. Write your analysis theme from the outline, including transitional devices.

Suggested subjects: mass protest, customers at a check out (or complaint) counter, types of advertising campaigns, comedians, television commercials, current music, hobbies, sports, your job, types of magazines at a newsstand, college slang, comic strips, television cartoon characters, vacations, dates.

Or: From the picture below, select a subject that is suggested by one of the persons in the picture or by several persons. For example, you might classify types of fortune telling, types of people on a city street, etc.

PHOTOGRAPH 6.   (Photo by Steven Mays.)

OUTLINE RATING SHEET

	YES	NO
TITLE		
Appears above the thesis statement		
Indicates contents of paper		
THESIS STATEMENT		
Is the limited subject apparent?		
Is the major inference clear?		
Are the minor inferences clear?		
Are the minor inferences mutually exclusive (do they justify a separate category)?		
Is the basis of analysis clear?		
BODY		
Do the minor inferences appear as entries following the Roman numerals?		
Does each supporting proof detail (A, B, C) directly relate to the inference under which it is classified?		
Are there adequate proof details to support each minor inference?		
Is each minor inference developed in proportion to the others?		
CONCLUDING STATEMENT		
Does the statement summarize the paper without introducing additional material?		
MECHANICS		
Is the outline form consistent (all topic entries or all sentence entries)?		
Are the entries on each level of classification grammatically parallel?		
Does every A have a B? Does every 1 have a 2?		
Have you followed capitalization, punctuation, and spacing rules for the outline?		

OUTLINE RATING SHEET

YES   NO

TITLE

Appears above the thesis statement

Indicates contents of paper

THESIS STATEMENT

Is the limited subject apparent?

Is the major inference clear?

Are the minor inferences clear?

Are the minor inferences mutually exclusive (do they justify a separate category)?

Is the basis of analysis clear?

BODY

Do the minor inferences appear as entries following the Roman numerals?

Does each supporting proof detail (A, B, C) directly relate to the inference under which it is classified?

Are there adequate proof details to support each minor inference?

Is each minor inference developed in proportion to the others?

CONCLUDING STATEMENT

Does the statement summarize the paper without introducing additional material?

MECHANICS

Is the outline form consistent (all topic entries or all sentence entries)?

Are the entries on each level of classification grammatically parallel?

Does every A have a B? Does every 1 have a 2?

Have you followed capitalization, punctuation, and spacing rules for the outline?

ANALYSIS RATING SHEET

	Poor	Average	Good	Excellent

OUTLINE

____ Correct form
____ Complete

TITLE

____ Indicates contents of paper

INTRODUCTION

Lead-in statement
    ____ Interests the reader
    ____ Shows relevance to subject
Thesis statement
    ____ Limited subject apparent
    ____ Major inference clear
    ____ Minor inferences clear
    ____ Minor inferences mutually
        exclusive

BODY

Content
    ____ Topic sentence with controlling in-
        ference introduces each paragraph
    ____ Number of proof details
    ____ Quality of proof details
    ____ Relevance of proof details
Organization
    ____ Pattern of organization evident
    ____ Effectiveness of transition

Style   Poor   Average   Good   Excellent
_____ Appropriate language level
_____ Specific word choice
_____ Clear phrasing
_____ Sentence variety
_____ Individuality of expression

CONCLUDING STATEMENT

_____ Summarizes main points of paper
_____ Uses appropriate transition

MECHANICS

Manuscript form
_____ Title in capitals
_____ Pagination
_____ Margins
_____ Legibility and neatness
_____ Spelling
_____ Sentence structure
_____ Grammar
_____ Punctuation
_____ Capitalization
_____ Expression of numbers

Name _____

Date _____

Section _____

ANALYSIS RATING SHEET

	Poor	Average	Good	Excellent

OUTLINE

____ Correct form
____ Complete

TITLE

____ Indicates contents of paper

INTRODUCTION

Lead-in statement
    ____ Interests the reader
    ____ Shows relevance to subject
Thesis statement
    ____ Limited subject apparent
    ____ Major inference clear
    ____ Minor inferences clear
    ____ Minor inferences mutually
        exclusive

BODY

Content
    ____ Topic sentence with controlling in-
        ference introduces each paragraph
    ____ Number of proof details
    ____ Quality of proof details
    ____ Relevance of proof details
Organization
    ____ Pattern of organization evident
    ____ Effectiveness of transition

Style   Poor   Average   Good   Excellent
  _____ Appropriate language level
  _____ Specific word choice
  _____ Clear phrasing
  _____ Sentence variety
  _____ Individuality of expression

CONCLUDING STATEMENT

  _____ Summarizes main points of paper
  _____ Uses appropriate transition

MECHANICS

Manuscript form
  _____ Title in capitals
  _____ Pagination
  _____ Margins
  _____ Legibility and neatness
  _____ Spelling
  _____ Sentence structure
  _____ Grammar
  _____ Punctuation
  _____ Capitalization
  _____ Expression of numbers

Name _____

Date _____

Section _____

ANALYSIS RATING SHEET

	Poor	Average	Good	Excellent

OUTLINE

____ Correct form
____ Complete

TITLE

____ Indicates contents of paper

INTRODUCTION

Lead-in statement
    ____ Interests the reader
    ____ Shows relevance to subject
Thesis statement
    ____ Limited subject apparent
    ____ Major inference clear
    ____ Minor inferences clear
    ____ Minor inferences mutually
        exclusive

BODY

Content
    ____ Topic sentence with controlling in-
        ference introduces each paragraph
    ____ Number of proof details
    ____ Quality of proof details
    ____ Relevance of proof details
Organization
    ____ Pattern of organization evident
    ____ Effectiveness of transition

Style   Poor   Average   Good   Excellent

_____ Appropriate language level

_____ Specific word choice

_____ Clear phrasing

_____ Sentence variety

_____ Individuality of expression

CONCLUDING STATEMENT

_____ Summarizes main points of paper

_____ Uses appropriate transition

MECHANICS

Manuscript form

_____ Title in capitals

_____ Pagination

_____ Margins

_____ Legibility and neatness

_____ Spelling

_____ Sentence structure

_____ Grammar

_____ Punctuation

_____ Capitalization

_____ Expression of numbers

STAGE 8

DEFINITION

1. Learning to Write the Formal Definition
2. Recognizing Errors in Formal Definition
3. Writing the Extended Definition
4. Recognizing Errors in the Extended Definition
5. Writing the Extended Definition Theme

Your entire purpose in working from Stages 1 through 7 has been to communicate as specifically and as logically as possible. You accomplished your first purpose, to write specifically, by making your proof details concrete. You made your presentation logical by carefully analyzing and classifying your inferences and proof details. You know how to answer the question, "What do you mean by . . .?" because you know how to supply proof details for your inferences.

Now you will find that you often need another method of precise communication that answers the question, "What do you mean by . . .?" This method is called **formal definition**. Assume that you are in a group that is having a discussion of equal rights. You might hear any number of terms, such as *radical, conservative, affirmative action plan, sexism, male chauvinism, grey power,* etc. Any number of times during such a discussion, one or another of the speakers may be called upon to explain what he means. He would be asked to "define his terms."

Suppose you were having a discussion about the occult with some people who were fascinated with the subject and with others who were skeptical about it. You might hear such terms as *ESP, aura, séance, levitation, regression, graphology,* and *astrology.* Suppose now that you are a person who is interested in astrology but not very well informed about it. Someone in the group asks you just what astrology is all about.

In an attempt to explain, you might reply: "Well, astrology is when you tell things about a person's life by reading the stars."

Examine this statement. Would the other people in the discussion group understand now what astrology really is? Does your definition give an exact explanation? Does it tell them whether astrology is an animal, a vegetable, a mineral, a science, or a parlor game? Does it tell what kinds of things can be told about a person's life or how they can be told? Look at your definition again: "Astrology is when you tell things about a person's life by reading the stars."

The first problem with your definition is that the word *when* does not indicate the **class** of objects or ideas or processes to which astrology belongs. *When* indicates time. You wouldn't be any better off if you said, "Astrology is where you tell things about a person's life by reading the stars," because *where* indicates location, not a class of things.

The second problem with your definition is the word *things*. **What kinds of things** does astrology tell about a person's life?

The third problem with the definition lies in the phrase *by reading the stars*. **How** does an astrologer read the stars? Someone in the group might recall having seen a picture of a storybook astrologer wearing a pointed hat encircled with figures of the sun, the moon, and the stars; that person might ask you if "reading the stars" is the only way an astrologer works.

Now you need some expertise. You need to know how to write the most exact and useful kind of definition, the **formal definition.**

STEP 1   **Learning to Write the Formal Definition.**   Writing the formal definition involves two operations. First, you must place the **term** in the **class** to which it belongs. Because you are using classification, the formal definition is also sometimes referred to as a **logical definition.** Second, you must show how the term differs from all other members of the particular class into which you have placed it. This is called the **differentia** because you are differentiating your term from other members of its class. A formal or logical definition, then, has three parts: the term, the class, and the differentia.

Think for a moment about what class astrology belongs to. You will find that it is not an exact science and that it therefore must be classified as a *pseudoscience*. A pseudoscience is a practice or an art for which there is conjecture but no scientific proof. Other pseudosciences would be palm reading, séances, and tarot card reading. Now you can see why you need the third part of a logical definition — the differentia. You must explain how astrology differs from the other pseudosciences.

You may now want to consult several dictionaries and perhaps an encyclopedia or two. Drawing from several general reference sources, you can explain the differentia in the way that would be most clear for your reader. Here is the way your one-sentence formal definition for astrology will look:

TERM	CLASS	DIFFERENTIA
Astrology (is)	a pseudoscience	which claims to foretell the future of human affairs and earthly events by the study of the relative positions and hence the influences of the sun, the moon, and the stars.

If you wanted to define palmistry, the class would remain the same, but the differentia would have to change:

Palmistry (is)	a pseudoscience	in which the palmist reads a person's character or aptitudes, his past and possible future, from the general shape of his hand and fingers and the lines, mounts, and marks of the palm.

Now look at the formal definitions for some other words which many people use without much precision:

A neurotic (is)	an emotionally disturbed person	characterized by excessive use of energy for unproductive purposes to control anxiety, compulsions, or phobias.
Soul (is)	a slang expression native to the Black culture	which indicates that a person is in harmony with himself and that he expresses in an uninhibited way such intensities of life as joy, sorrow, hardship, and brotherhood.
A hot rod (is)	an automobile	rebuilt or remodeled with a highly improved engine and body design for increased speed and acceleration.

STEP 2   **Recognizing Errors in Formal Definition.**   Before you can write a good formal definition, you will need to be able to recognize certain common definition errors:

CIRCULAR DEFINITION

Do not repeat the term or a derivative of the term in the differentia.

Example: A *radical* is a person having *radical* views.

Correction: A radical is a person who favors fundamental or extreme change, specifically of the social structure.

NONPARALLEL GRAMMATICAL FORM

The grammatical structure must be maintained in the sentence pattern of a formal definition. The sentence pattern is:

Subject (noun) + linking verb + subject complement (noun)

Incorrect: Cramming is when a student attempts to learn most of the contents of a course in a day or two.

Discussion: This definition is incorrect because there is no subject complement. The *when* clause functions as an adverb; it is not the noun or noun phrase needed to indicate the class to which cramming belongs.

Correction: Cramming (noun) is a method of study (noun phrase) in which a student prepares for an examination in a hurried, intensive way for the purpose of learning the contents of a course in a short time.

IMPROPER CLASSIFICATION

A. The class is overinclusive (too broad).

TERM	CLASS	DIFFERENTIA
Incorrect:		
A pig is	an animal	characterized by a long, broad snout; a thick, fat body; cloven hoofs; sexual immaturity; and a weight under 120 pounds.

Discussion: The class *animal* is overinclusive because there are many classifications of types of animals.

TERM	CLASS	DIFFERENTIA

Correction:

A pig is	a young swine	characterized by a long, broad snout; a thick, fat body; cloven hoofs; sexual immaturity; and a weight under 120 pounds.

Incorrect:

A draftsman's compass is	an instrument	consisting of two pointed legs connected at one end by a pivot used for drawing arcs or circles and taking measurements.

Discussion: The class *instrument* is overinclusive because an infinite number of mechanisms are instruments.

Correction: A draftsman's compass is a mechanical drawing instrument consisting of . . .

B. The class is overrestrictive (too narrow).

TERM	CLASS	DIFFERENTIA

Incorrect:

A pig is	a domesticated swine	etc.

Discussion: The class *domesticated swine* is overrestricted because it excludes wild pigs.

IMPROPER DIFFERENTIA

A. The differentia is overinclusive (too broad).

TERM	CLASS	DIFFERENTIA

Incorrect:

A poet is	a creative writer	who has great imaginative and expressive gifts and who possesses a great sensitivity to language.

Discussion: This differentia includes every kind of creative writer.

B. The differentia is overrestrictive (too narrow).

TERM	CLASS	DIFFERENTIA

Incorrect:

A poet is	a creative writer	who writes rhymed, rhythmical lines.

Discussion: The differentia is overrestrictive because it excludes poets who write in blank verse, which is not rhymed, or in free verse, which is neither rhymed nor necessarily rhythmical.

Correction:

A poet is	a creative writer	who composes verse.

HIGHLY TECHNICAL LANGUAGE

TERM	CLASS	DIFFERENTIA

Incorrect:

Dysgraphia is	a transduction disorder	resulting from a disturbance in the visual motor integration of a child.

Discussion: The instructor of children with learning disabilities would be able to understand this definition, but a general audience learning about particular disorders in the learning process probably would not.

Correction:

Dysgraphia is	a learning disorder	in which the child sees or knows what he wants to write but cannot make his motor system carry out his idea; hence, he cannot write correctly.

EXERCISE 8-1   WRITING A FORMAL DEFINITION

Select three of the following words and write a formal definition for each. Check your definitions against Step 2 to make sure that you have not committed any of the errors in formal definition. Try first to write the definition from your own understanding of the word. Then, check your definitions against those in two different dictionaries.

TERM	CLASS	DIFFERENTIA
1. Underground		
2. Maturity		
3. Personality		
4. Pornography		
5. Hypocrite		

Name _____

Date _____

Section _____

FORMAL DEFINITION RATING SHEET

	Poor	Average	Good	Excellent

Term: _____

Completeness (term, class, differentia) ☐ ☐ ☐ ☐

Faults:
____ Circular
____ Class too broad
____ Class too narrow
____ Class not grammatically parallel
____ Differentia too broad
____ Differentia too narrow
____ Language too technical

Term: _____

Completeness (term, class, differentia) ☐ ☐ ☐ ☐

Faults:
____ Circular
____ Class too broad
____ Class too narrow
____ Class not grammatically parallel
____ Differentia too broad
____ Differentia too narrow
____ Language too technical

Term: _____

Completeness (term, class, differentia) ☐ ☐ ☐ ☐

Faults:
____ Circular
____ Class too broad
____ Class too narrow
____ Class not grammatically parallel
____ Differentia too broad
____ Differentia too narrow
____ Language too technical

STEP 3   Writing the Extended Definition.   In many cases you will find that the formal sentence definition is adequate for the purpose. In other cases you may decide that your readers will want or need further explanation of a particular term. When a definition goes beyond the formal sentence definition it is called an **extended definition.** The length of an extended definition depends on the writer's purpose and the reader's needs. A single paragraph may be adequate; on the other hand, the writer may need an entire chapter to explain a particular term. Sometimes an entire book is actually an extended definition or a series of extended definitions.

When you write an extended definition you have many options. As a brief example of options, ask your classmates what they know about the apparently simple subject of *asphalt* — since people ride on it every day, they ought to be familiar with it. One student may try to describe it in terms of color, texture, or consistency. Another may know where it comes from; still another may tell you where it is used and under what circumstances. One student might try to give a synonym for asphalt, and another might explain how it differs from other surfacing materials. If you were to assemble all the comments and do a bit of research yourself in some dictionaries or in an encyclopedia, you would find that there are ten methods by which you could extend a formal definition that would give a basic understanding of the simple subject of *asphalt.* Following are examples of the ten basic methods of extending a formal definition.

Formal definition: Asphalt is a bituminous surfacing material used in paving, roofing, and waterproofing.

1. *Etymology:* The word comes from the Middle English *asphaltoun,* which comes from the Late Latin *asphaltus;* these words came originally from the Greek word *asphaltos,* meaning "binding agent used by stone masons."

2. *Synonym:* It is sometimes called *mineral pitch.*

3. *Description:* Asphalt is a brownish-black solid or semi-solid mixture; it is composed of bitumens, and it has a strong odor before it solidifies.

4. *Origin:* It is obtained naturally from native deposits.

5. *Process or growth:* Asphalt can also be obtained as a petroleum byproduct.

6. *Negation* (what it is not): Asphalt is not tar, although people sometimes call it that. Neither is it cement.

7. *Comparison:* It is like tar in its appearance, in that it is a dark, oily, viscous substance.

8. *Contrast:* But asphalt, composed of bitumens, is obtained from native deposits or as a petroluem byproduct; in contrast, tar, which is composed of hydrocarbons, is produced by the destructive distillation of organic substances such as wood, coal, or peat. Cement differs from asphalt in that it is an adhesive consisting of powdered, calcined rock and clay materials.

9. *Example:* Asphalt, commonly referred to as "blacktop," is used for highways and driveways in areas which are subject to the stress of abrupt changes in weather or extremes of weather of one type or another because it "gives" and is less likely to buckle or crack than cement. Combined with gravel, asphalt is also used as a roofing and waterproofing material because of its weathering qualities.

10. *Quotation:* According to the County Highway Commission, "asphalt is a prime surfacing material because it is relatively stable, it is not greatly affected by extremes of heat and cold, and it is easily obtainable."

THE ORDER OF EXTENDED DEFINITION

The order in which you use the types of sentences as proof details to extend your formal definition depends upon their appropriateness to your subject and your own preference. If there is an etymology for a word, it is often helpful to use that first because it reveals the history of the word and the changes that it has undergone. It is sometimes useful to give a synonym next because a reader may be more familiar with the synonym than he is with the term itself. If, however, the synonym is more obscure than the original term, it is best not to use it. Description as a method of extending a definition can include size, weight, color, special details, and composition. Origin is a good method to include, for it explains the actual source, cause, or circumstances connected with the beginning of a word. Students sometimes confuse etymology and origin. Etymology refers strictly to the derivation of the word; origin explains where the object or idea comes from. Process or growth explains the stages from origin to present object, material, or idea. Negation is used when it would be useful to explain what the word is not in order to avoid confusion among several terms. Comparison and contrast often follow negation naturally in an extended definition, for the reader can see the term compared to something it is like and then see how it differs from something with which it has been compared. Finally, examples are always helpful because they show specifically how the object, idea, or substance being described is actually used and where it appears. These, then, are the ways that you can extend your formal sentence definition in order to give your reader more information about a term.

STEP 4   **Recognizing Errors in the Extended Definition.** While the ten methods of extending a formal definition are helpful, they present certain problems if they stand alone as the only definition or if they are used in place of the formal definition. Here are examples of what would happen if you were to use the following types of definition alone:

1. **Example:** An example of a stream of consciousness novel is James Joyce's *Ulysses*.

Discussion: While examples are excellent ways of illustrating a term, they don't help much if you don't know what the term means in the first place and if you aren't familiar with the example given — in this case, the book. Thus, *stream of consciousness novel* would have to be defined first.

2. **Description:** A discotheque has psychedelic lighting and decorations, and very loud music.

Discussion: The term *discotheque* must be placed in a class of dancing establishments before it can be described in further detail.

3. **Comparison:** A hypocrite is like a pretender.

Discussion: If you don't have a precise formal definition of *hypocrite,* your reader is not ready to see in what ways he is like a pretender.

4. **Synonym:** A hypochondriac is a malingerer.

Discussion: No two words in the English language mean exactly the same thing. For instance, a hypochondriac and a malingerer are alike in that both sometimes use illness to escape work or unpleasant duties. But the difference is that the hypochondriac truly believes he is ill, whereas the malingerer only pretends to be ill. Therefore, unless you were to give a formal definition of *hypochondriac* first, the comparison would be incomplete and inexact.

THE PARAGRAPH OF EXTENDED DEFINITION

Here is how the extended definition of *asphalt* looks in paragraph form. Notice that the writer has added a lead-in statement and a topic sentence which is a generalization about asphalt. His extended definition begins with the formal sentence definition. Notice also that he has used his quotation as an appropriate summary sentence.

ASPHALT

During the Depression era of the 1930s the
Works Progress Administration (WPA) authorized a
project for covering the brick paving in
American towns and cities with asphalt. Through
this project many thousands of people were given
work, and millions were introduced to a new and
smoother kind of motoring. Today virtually
everyone travels on asphalt roads; but most
people do not know much about this common
substance. What is it? Asphalt is a bituminous
surfacing material used in paving, roofing, and
waterproofing. The word comes originally from
the Greek asphaltos, meaning "binding agent used
by stone masons." It is sometimes also called
mineral pitch. Asphalt is a brownish—black,
semi—solid mixture, and it has a strong odor
before it solidifies. It is obtained from
native deposits, but it can also be obtained as
a petroleum byproduct. Asphalt is not tar,
although people often call it that. Neither is
it cement. It is like tar in its appearance, in
that it is a dark, oily, viscous substance. But
asphalt, which is composed of bitumens, is
obtained from native deposits or as a petroleum
byproduct, whereas tar, which is composed of
hydrocarbons, is produced by the destructive
distillation of organic substances such as wood,
coal, or peat. Cement differs from asphalt in
that it is an adhesive consisting of powdered,
calcined rock and clay materials. Asphalt is
used in areas which are subject to the stress of
abrupt changes in weather or extremes of weather
of one type or another because it "gives" and is
less likely to buckle or crack than cement.
Combined with gravel, it is also used as a
roofing material because of its weathering
qualities. According to the County Highway
Commission, "asphalt is a prime material for
surfacing roads because it is relatively stable,
it is not greatly affected by extremes of heat
and cold, and it is easily obtainable."

STEP 5   **Writing the Extended Definition Theme.**   You have seen how the formal definition can be extended to a full paragraph by using some or all of the ten methods of extended definition as proof details. Some subjects, however, lend themselves to a multiparagraph composition. The paragraphs divide naturally into the kinds of information to be given — perhaps origin, process, and growth, then description, and then examples. The student paper which follows, written on the subject of *charisma,* is a good example of how a particular term lends itself to extended definition in multiparagraph form. Notice how the student's introductory paragraph consists of the lead-in statement and the thesis, an inference about the subject. Notice also that the body of the paper begins with the formal definition. Except for those in the introductory paragraph, the sentences are numbered so that you can complete Exercise 8-2.

CHARISMA

In the late 1950s the media began to use the term <u>charisma</u> with increasing frequency, particularly in connection with John F. Kennedy. Soon the word was applied to people in the social world and in the entertainment and sports fields. Charisma is a difficult word to define precisely, but it can be better understood by examining its history and application.

(1) Charisma is the ultimate quality of a person that inspires enthusiastic popular support or admiration through sheer personality or physical appearance. (2) Also called <u>charism</u>, it is in some ways like charm, presence, and captivating authority. (3) One who possesses it can direct human affairs with much greater ease than one who does not, for the people whose affairs are being directed willingly follow the path set by one with charisma.

(4) The history of the word helps to explain the elusive qualities the word connotes. (5) The word comes from the Greek <u>charis</u>, a noun meaning "favor," and <u>charismata</u>, another noun meaning "gifts"; <u>chariszesthai</u> is a Greek verb

meaning "to favor."   (6) <u>Charisma</u> passed intact
from the Greek to the Latin and was used by
early Christians to denote God-given gifts to
special people for the good of others.   (7) In
the New Testament, I Corinthians (12: 8-10), the
missionary Paul lists eight <u>charismata</u>:

> For to one is given by the Spirit the word of
> wisdom; to another the word of knowledge by
> the same Spirit; to another faith by the
> same Spirit; to another the gifts of healing
> by the same Spirit; to another the working
> of miracles; to another prophecy; to another
> divers kinds of tongues; to another the
> interpretation of tongues.

(8) Thomas Aquinas redefined charismata
simply as the fullness of knowledge of divine
things, the power of expounding divine truth,
and the power of miracles.   (9) The word
<u>charisma</u> has been transposed over the centuries
from the theological sphere to the social and
political spheres.   (10) Charisma has come to
refer to those with a gift for enchanting and
influencing people without necessarily
appealing to their intellects.   (11) Like wit,
sensitivity, and artistic talent, charisma is
not dependent upon a single virtue but is a
combination of numerous personality traits which
mix together to create boundless charm.
(12) Charm, however, is a working between
individuals, whereas charisma is a working
between an individual and the public.   (13) One
of the most illustrative examples of the
application of the word <u>charisma</u> to a public
person is the late President John F. Kennedy.
(14) The results of the television debates
held during the 1960 presidential campaign
demonstrated the power of charisma.   (15)
Richard Nixon argued issues in the standard
debating style while John Kennedy reiterated his
prepared campaign statements, relaxed and

smiling into the cameras. (16) Public support
went to Kennedy after the debates, and the death
blow went to Nixon, who lacked Kennedy's
charisma. (17) Since his death, Kennedy's
charisma, together with that of his family, has
increased. (18) He is no longer able to charm
the public by his presence, but his memory and
his family continue to enthrall them.

   (19) Although the professional image-makers
attempt to bottle and sell charisma, this
quality is not something which is transferable,
like a share of stock, nor is it teachable like
a foreign language or a dance step. (20)
Charisma is more like an eleventh finger or a
third eye; it is an innate ability. (21) This
somewhat magical talent for bewitching masses
of people has grown in importance with the
growth of the mass media which has widened
the charismatic's audience to worldwide
proportions. (22) This gift "given by the
Spirit" is the ultimate asset to every public
figure in our electronic age.

EXERCISE 8-2   IDENTIFYING METHODS OF EXTENDED DEFINITION

Each sentence in the body of the theme on charisma is numbered. Fill in the blanks below by identifying the method of extended definition which each sentence represents. Keep in mind that each sentence may illustrate more than one method of extending the definition.

METHODS

Formal definition

1. Etymology
2. Synonym
3. Description
4. Origin
5. Process or growth

6. Negation
7. Comparison
8. Contrast
9. Example
10. Quotation

SENTENCES

1. _____
2. _____
3. _____
4. _____
5. _____
6. _____
7. _____
8. _____
9. _____
10. _____
11. _____

12. _____
13. _____
14. _____
15. _____
16. _____
17. _____
18. _____
19. _____
20. _____
21. _____
22. _____

WRITING SUGGESTION: THE EXTENDED DEFINITION

1. Write a paragraph or a short multiparagraph theme of extended definition. Define any word you choose, but if you have no special word in mind, you might try one of the following: mod, radical, conservative, reactionary, muckraker, communist, freedom, censorship, classic car, philatelist, bigot, goldbricker.

Or: Examine the photograph below. Many images may come to you. Choose a term that comes to mind and use it for your extended definition.

PHOTOGRAPH 7.   (Photo by Dave Patrick.)

2. Consult at least three dictionaries before writing your extended definition. One should be the *Oxford English Dictionary.* Another should be an unabridged dictionary such as Webster's *Third New International Dictionary.* This would also be a good opportunity to consult a specialized dictionary — there are many of these on a variety of subjects. They are listed in the card catalog of the library under "Dictionaries" by subject. For example, if you choose to define a slang term, you could consult *The Dictionary of American Slang,* ed. Harold Wentworth and Stuart Berg Flexner; *A Dictionary of Slang and Unconventional English,* ed. Eric Partridge; *Dictionary of American Underworld Slang,* ed. Hyman E. Golding; or the *Dictionary of Contemporary Usage,* ed. Bergan Evans and Cornelia Evans.

3. Begin your paper with a lead-in statement. If you write only a paragraph, the formal definition will follow the topic sentence; if you write a theme, the formal definition will follow the thesis.

4. Extend your formal definition by using at least seven of the ten methods listed below. You may use each method more than once, but count it only as one method. You may also try all of the methods if you like. The order in which you use the methods is up to you and will be determined by appropriateness to the term you are defining.

METHODS

Formal definition

1. Etymology	6. Negation
2. Synonym	7. Comparison
3. Description	8. Contrast
4. Origin	9. Example
5. Process or growth	10. Quotation

5. Beginning with the formal definition, number each of your sentences. After each sentence place in parentheses the method of extension you have used.

Example: (12) Charm, however, is a working between individuals, whereas charisma is a working between an individual and the public. (contrast)

If you are criticizing another student's paper or if your instructor is grading yours, the blanks provide a place to check each method used to extend the definition. If a method is misused or if a method is missing and you think its inclusion would make a better definition, then you or the instructor can comment in the space provided.

EXTENDED DEFINITION RATING SHEET

FORMAL SENTENCE DEFINITION

Poor Average Good Excellent

Completeness (term, class, differentia)			

Faults:

_____ Circularity
_____ Class too broad
_____ Class too narrow
_____ Class not grammatically parallel
_____ Differentia too broad
_____ Differentia too narrow
_____ Language too technical

EXTENDED DEFINITION

| | | |
---|---|---|---

1. _____ Etymology
   Comment:

2. _____ Synonym
   Comment:

3. _____ Description
   Comment:

4. _____ Origin
   Comment:

5. _____ Process or growth
   Comment:

6. _____ Negation
   Comment:

7. _____ Comparison
   Comment:

8. _____ Contrast
   Comment:

9. _____ Example
   Comment:

10. _____ Quotation
    Comment:

STAGE 9

PROCESS ANALYSIS

1. Directional Process Analysis
2. Informational Process Analysis
3. Learning the Organization for the Process Theme
4. Examining Student Models of Process Themes

Process analysis is a method of explaining how something is made, how it is used, how it is operated, how it is organized, or how it developed. There are two kinds of process analyses, **directional** and **informational.**

STEP 1 **Directional Process Analysis.** A directional process analysis is the "how to do it" kind of process analysis. Everywhere you look, you see this kind of analysis, which is actually a set of directions written in the imperative mood. Consider directions in a phone booth, for example:

> Remove receiver.
> Deposit ten cents.
> Listen for dial tone.
> Dial number.

Other examples of directional process analysis are recipes, instructions for assembling toys and furniture, developing film, remodeling a kitchen, or starting your own business. Directional analyses can be only a few lines long, or they can be a complete essay or even a book.

STEP 2 **Informational Process Analysis.** While directions instruct a person in the actual performance of a process, the informational description informs the reader about a particular process for the purpose of increasing his general knowledge. There are three basic types of informational process. The first is the historical, which describes how an idea, an event, or an institution came about. In this category you might see such subjects as "The Evolution of Equal Rights for Women," "How the Senate Investigated the Watergate Scandal," and "How the United Farm Workers Became a Union."

The second type of informational process describes a scientific, mechanical, or natural process. In this category you might learn about such subjects as "How Hurricanes Are Seeded," "How a Battery Ignition System Works," and "How Detergent Discharges Affect Natural Waterways."

The third type of informational process is that which describes a logical or organizational process. In this category you would see such subjects as "How a Crime Is Investigated," "How a Sales Campaign Is Planned," and "How a Bill Becomes a Law."

Explaining a process clearly and concisely is one of the most difficult forms of analysis. You may recall the times that you have had to follow directions or to assemble a product only to find that certain steps were omitted or obscurely described, causing you untold frustration, loss of time, or even making it impossible for you to complete the process at all. Perhaps you have asked directions to a particular place and have found people so inept at giving directions that you had to stop several times for instructions. You would be equally frustrated in reading an informational process if the writer failed to include all the relevant steps in explaining the sequence of events that led to an historical event; a scientific, mechanical or natural process; or a logical or organizational process.

STEP 3   **Learning the Organization for the Process Theme.**

TITLE

Write a precise, descriptive title that indicates whether the process will be directional or informational.

| *Example:* | Directional: | HOW TO PITH A FROG |
| | Informational: | PITHING A FROG |

OUTLINE

Write an outline. The information given below under BODY will show you the kinds of entries which must appear in the process analysis outline in addition to the thesis statement.

INTRODUCTORY PARAGRAPH

1. **The Lead-in Statement.** As with other types of themes, the introductory paragraph begins with a lead-in statement, which consists of two parts:

   a. It should contain one or several sentences that explain why you are writing this particular analysis.

   b. It should contain a formal definition which includes, if possible, *who* performs the process, *where* it is performed, *when* it is performed, and *why* it is performed. An example of the lead-in statement for the process analysis "Pithing a Frog" follows:

(explanation) {
```
    Many college students find biology one of
their most difficult subjects, some because of
the terminology and others because of the
laboratory experiments.  One of the experiments
which actually defeats some students is the
dissection of a frog.  There are two reasons for
this: first, the student is afraid that he will
not be able to control the frog, and, second, he
fears that the frog will suffer in the pithing
process which precedes the dissection.  Both of
```
}

(definition) {
```
these fears may be overcome if the pithing
process is understood and done correctly.
Pithing a frog is a laboratory process in which
the biology student plunges a dissecting needle
into the back of a frog's skull and backbone in
order to deaden the central nervous system so
that the frog can be used for dissection.
```
}

2. **The Thesis Statement.** In most types of writing, the thesis statement contains the major inference and the minor inferences that indicate the categories of discussion. In the process analysis, however, the thesis statement lists the main steps of the process. There are two considerations for writing the thesis for a process analysis.

   a. If the process has no more than five main steps, the thesis is written as follows:

General example: _____(process)_____ includes _____
(Informational process)   main steps:
            first, _____ing the _____;
            second, _____ing the _____;
            third, _____ing the _____;
            and, finally, _____ing the _____.

Specific example: Pithing a frog involves three main steps: first, holding the frog; second, pithing the brain; and third, pithing the spinal cord.

b. If the process cannot be reduced to five main steps or fewer, do not list all of the steps. Instead, state the total number of steps, mentioning only the first and final step.

General example: _____(process)_____ involves _____ main steps, beginning with _____ and ending with _____.

Specific example: In the process of preparing a balance sheet, an accountant follows nine steps, beginning with obtaining balances from the general ledger of the asset liability and capital accounts and ending with determining if the total assets equal the total liabilities and proprietorship.

BODY

1. **If the process is one which requires specific equipment and materials, then Roman numeral I will be headed "Equipment and materials."** Provide a precise list of all tools, equipment, supplies, and apparatus.

Vague example: The student needs three items.

Precise example: The student experimenter needs a live frog, a dissection needle, and a pair of plastic gloves.

2. **Discuss the individual steps in the order they are listed in the thesis statement.** Define the first step in a formal definition or state the purpose of the step if understanding the purpose is necessary to the reader.

Example of stated purpose not necessary: The student holds the frog securely in his left hand with the frog's hind legs extended downward toward the floor.

Example of stated purpose necessary: He then pushes the dissecting needle down through the spine, stopping only when he reaches the hump in the frog's back. This is done to sever the spinal cord so that no natural reflexes will occur while dissecting.

3. **Define or explain any term which might possibly confuse or puzzle the reader.**

Example: The process of making a blister package consists of placing an object in a blister (plastic bubble), covering it with a card, and sealing both cards together by applying heat and pressure.

4. **Define an abbreviation the first time it is used.**

Example: The pilot then determines the TC (true course) of the line; and using the proper procedure, he finds the MH (magnetic heading) of the line.

5. **Indicate any special conditions, requirements, preparations, and precautions.**

Example of special precaution: If the student takes longer than five minutes to pith his frog, he is causing the animal pain.

Example of special condition: The medical assistant must also consider the importance of selecting the proper site for injection; the site should be as far as possible from major nerves and vessels and capable of holding a large volume of the injected fluid.

6. **Indicate directional process by using imperative mood.** Imperative mood gives a command with the subject *you* implied. This means that you will not write "you should" or "you must" for directional process.

Incorrect example: In planning a cross country flight, first you need to locate the course line and draw it on the chart.

Correct example using imperative mood: In planning a cross country flight, locate the course line and draw it on the chart.

7. **Indicate informational process by using indicative mood.** The subject *you* is not used.

Incorrect example: In planning a cross country flight, first you need to locate the course line and draw it on the chart.

Correct example using indicative mood: In planning a cross country flight, the pilot must first locate the course line and draw it on the chart.

The following guide explains the voices and moods to be used in process analysis.

Imperative Mood
Imperative mood, with the subject *you* implied, is used for giving directions.

Example: The first step in blister packaging is to start the sealer. *Take* the cord in hand, *plug* it into a 110 volt outlet, and *wait* approximately fifteen to twenty minutes for the unit to warm up. While waiting for the unit to warm up, *load* the blisters with the objects. Then *clear* off an area around the sealer and *place* a product in each blister.

Indicative Mood

Indicative mood, active or passive voice, is used for giving information. However, use active voice whenever possible because it makes your writing more direct.

Example of active voice: The first step in blister packaging is to start the sealer. The *operator takes* the cord in his hand and *plugs* it into a 110 volt outlet. *He waits* approximately fifteen to twenty minutes for the unit to warm up. During this time the *operator loads* the blisters with the objects. *He* then *clears* off an area around the sealer and *places* a product in each blister.

Example of passive voice: The first step in blister packaging is to start the sealer. The cord *is taken* in the operator's hand and *is plugged* into a 110 volt outlet. Fifteen to twenty minutes *is needed* for the unit to warm up. During this time, the blisters *are loaded* with the objects. An area around the sealer *is* then *cleared* off and a product *is placed* in each blister.

CONCLUSION

One or more of the following can be covered in the conclusion. Some of the points may already have been covered in the introduction.

1. **Discuss the advantages of the process.**

   Example: Data processing during registration saves both time and money for the college and the students.

2. **Discuss the disadvantages of the process (if any).**

   Example: The only disadvantage to administering an intramuscular injection is that all muscular sites available are very close to major nerves and vessels.

3. **Discuss the effectiveness of the process.**

   Example: Blister packaging best protects the products from the elements, provides an eye-catching display, and protects the merchant from the high incidence of pilferage today.

4. **Evaluate the results of the process.**

   Example: Candles made by rubber molds can be given as personalized gifts, or they can be sold to friends and specialty shops at a profit.

5. **Discuss the importance of the process.**

   Example: Preparing a balance sheet is important because it will accurately reflect the financial condition of a business on a specified date.

6. **Discuss how the process is related to other processes or to other work that is being done or reported on.**

   Example: Blister packaging is related to many other modern packaging processes such as skin packaging and shrink packaging.

STEP 4   Examining Student Models of Process Themes.   Following are two themes with their outlines. The first, "How to Pith a Frog," is written to give **directions.** The second, "Sorting the Mail," is written to provide **information.** Both themes were written from personal experience.

DIRECTIONAL PROCESS ANALYSIS: OUTLINE

```
               HOW TO PITH A FROG


    Thesis statement: To succeed in this process,
    follow these four main steps: first, assemble
    the materials; second, hold the frog correctly;
    third, pith the brain; fourth, pith the spinal
    cord.

       I. Assemble the materials.
          A. Get the dissection needle.
          B. Get a pair of plastic gloves.

      II. Hold the frog correctly.
          A. Hold it in the left hand.
          B. Press its snout between the index and
             middle finger.
          C. Search for a shallow groove in back of
             the frog's skull.

     III. Pith the brain.
          A. Feel the shallow groove.
          B. Push the needle into the skull.
             1. Twist and turn the needle.
             2. Withdraw the needle.
```

IV. Pith the spinal column.
   A. Point the needle toward the hind legs.
   B. Push the needle through the spine.
   C. Sever the spine.
   D. Withdraw the needle.

Concluding statement: Biology students find that
following this process is not as disagreeable as
they had imagined because, performed properly,
it prevents the frog from feeling any pain.

DIRECTIONAL PROCESS ANALYSIS: THEME

HOW TO PITH A FROG

Many college students find biology one of
their most difficult subjects, some because of
the terminology and others because of the
laboratory experiments. One of the experiments
which actually defeats some students is the
dissection of a frog. There are two reasons for
this: first, the student is afraid that he will
not be able to control the frog, and, second, he
fears that the frog will suffer in the pithing
process which precedes the dissection. Both of
these fears may be overcome if the pithing
process is understood and done correctly.
Pithing a frog is a laboratory process in which
the biology student plunges a dissecting needle
into the back of a frog's skull and backbone in
order to deaden the central nervous system so
that the frog can be used for dissection. To
succeed in this process, follow these four main
steps: first, assemble the materials; second,
hold the frog correctly; third, pith the brain;
and fourth, pith the spinal cord.
   First, assemble the materials needed to pith
the frog. The equipment needed in this process
is a live frog, a dissecting needle, and a pair
of laboratory gloves. The dissecting needle is
similar to a sewing needle in appearance, but
the dissecting needle is approximately four
times longer and five times wider than the
standard one-and-a-half inch sewing needle. The
dissecting needle, unlike the standard needle,

has a cylindrical wooden handle at its base.
The plastic gloves can be of the disposable
variety. Once the materials are ready, proceed
to the next step.

In the second step hold the frog securely
in the left hand with the frog's hind legs
extended downward toward the floor. Place the
frog's snout between the index and middle
finger, pressing the thumb on the frog's back.
Using the fingernail from the index finger on
the right hand, search for a shallow groove in
the back of the frog's skull. When you have
located this groove, proceed to the third step,
the pithing of the brain.

To pith the brain, keep the dissecting needle
parallel with the top of the frog's head and
push the needle into the skull. Twist and turn
the needle from side to side and continue this
movement as the needle is withdrawn.
Technically the frog remains alive: his heart
still beats, but he feels no pain because his
nervous system is destroyed. Killing the frog
in this manner will not damage internal organs
which are observed during dissection.

The final step is to sever the spinal cord.
This must be done because natural reflexes may
occur during the dissecting process. With the
dissecting needle, make a 180 degree turn and
point the dissecting needle toward the frog's
hind legs and parallel with its backbone. Then
push the dissecting needle down through the
spine, stopping only when it reaches the hump in
the frog's back. This action severs the spinal
cord. Withdraw the needle. The frog is now
ready to be dissected.

In conclusion, the advantages of pithing a
frog for dissection outweigh the disadvantages.
First, killing the frog in this manner is humane
because the frog feels no pain once the nervous
system is destroyed. Then too, pithing also
preserves the frog's internal organs for
dissection. There is, however, a single
disadvantage to the process. If the pithing
process lasts longer than five minutes, the frog
will suffer pain. Therefore, the process

requires dexterity and precision on the part of the experimenter. However, biology students find that following this process for accurate pithing is not as disagreeable as they had imagined because performed properly, it prevents the frog from feeling any pain.

INFORMATIONAL PROCESS ANALYSIS: OUTLINE

SORTING THE MAIL

Thesis statement: First, letters are sorted, separated, and postmarked; second, they are distributed by state, city, and country; third, they are sorted into primary and secondary cases; and, finally, mail is sorted by individual carriers.

    I. Letters are sorted, separated, and postmarked.
       A. Mail is grouped by size.
       B. Mail is sent to separate sections.
       C. Mail is cancelled.
          1. Letters are prepared by clerks for cancelling.
          2. Letters are prepared and cancelled by automatic machines.

   II. Letters are sorted according to their destination.
       A. Out-of-town mail is sorted first.
       B. Mail to a city within a state is sent in "directs."
          1. Only large cities have "directs."
          2. "Directs" save time.
       C. Letters are sent to sectional centers labeled "foreign."
          1. Letters are sorted by foreign country.
          2. Letters are placed in pouches.

  III. Letters are sorted into primary and secondary cases.
       A. The mail is sorted into primary cases.
          1. It is sorted by zip code.
          2. It is sorted by special postal box numbers.

      B. The mail is then sorted into secondary
         cases.
         1. Here it is sorted by section.
         2. It is also sorted by carrier number.

  IV. The final letter sorting stage is done by
      the carrier.
      A. The mail is separated by streets and
         house numbers.
      B. The letters are pulled.
      C. The mail is bundled and sent to relay
         boxes.
      D. The mail is sorted into individual mail
         boxes.

<u>Concluding</u> <u>statement</u>: Mail that is improperly
sorted during any stage of delivery can easily
be lost or delayed for days, weeks, or even
years.

INFORMATIONAL PROCESS ANALYSIS: THEME

SORTING THE MAIL

    The postal system is one of our most
important means of sending letters and
information to distant places. Millions of
letters and parcels are mailed directly to all
parts of the world. These letters and parcels
could easily become lost and be sent to the wrong
people were it not for the system of sorting
used by the post office. First, letters are
sorted, separated, and postmarked; second, they
are distributed by state, city, and country;
third, they are sorted into primary and
secondary cases; and finally, mail is sorted by
individual carriers.
    Postal clerks must separate or group the
mail, a process known as "culling." After the
mail is brought in from collection boxes
throughout the city, it is sorted, separated,
and postmarked. The mail is a mixture of large
envelopes, letters, small parcels, catalogs,
newspapers, and other items. Letters, large
envelopes and flats, small parcels, and air
mails are grouped individually and sent to

separate places in the post office to be
postmarked. In small post offices, other clerks
stack the letters face up with the stamps in the
same position and feed the letters into a
machine that cancels (marks) the stamps so that
they cannot be used again. In large post
offices, however, automatic machines prepare
letters for cancellation and cancel the stamps.
The postmark prints on the envelope the date and
time of mailing -- A.M. or P.M. After each
piece of mail has been postmarked, it is ready
for the second stage of sorting.

In the second stage clerks group the letters
or parcels according to their destination.
Out-of-town mail is sorted according to states.
Some states, such as Illinois, California, and
New York, have large cities within them that
receive a large amount of mail. As a result,
the mail for these cities is separated and sent
in mail pouches called "directs" because the
mail is sent directly to the city instead of
being sent to a sectional center within the
state where mail is received for all parts of
that state. "Directs" are valuable because they
eliminate some of the handling involved in
shipping the mail. In addition to the sorting
of the mail by states and cities, sorting must
also be done for foreign countries. Most of the
sorting to foreign countries is done at
sectional centers. At these "foreign" sectional
centers, the mail is sorted by country and
placed into appropriate pouches. Once the mail
has been through the second stage of sorting, it
is sent to the individual states, cities, and
countries to which it belongs. Upon its arrival
at one of these destinations, it is ready for
the third stage of sorting.

When the mail reaches its destination, the
third stage of sorting begins. In this stage,
the mail is sorted into primary and secondary
cases. In the primary cases, the mail is sorted
with other mail according to zip code and
according to the specific mail route. Each zone
has a zip code for that area, and the last two
numbers of the code represent a section of the

city. Therefore, the mail is sorted at the
primary cases by these zones. However, the mail
may also be sorted by special postal box
numbers, and primary cases often have spaces for
banks, public utility companies, or various
professional buildings which receive a large
volume of mail. After the mail is sorted at the
primary cases, it is then taken to the secondary
cases, where it is sorted by carrier number to
identify with an individual carrier. Each zone
within the city is divided into sections and
numbers to identify with an individual carrier,
and the secondary cases are marked so that the
mail is sorted to individual letter carriers.
Once the clerks sort the mail so that every
carrier or postman will get all the mail for the
people living along his route, the mail is ready
for the final stage.

In the final stage, individual mailmen, known
as carriers, are given their own bundle of mail
to be sorted. Now the mail is separated
according to the house numbers on the streets
the carrier serves. Each carrier has a case
with each street listed separately. The letters
are filed by street numbers and then pulled and
bundled for delivery. The mail is then
carefully tied and taken by trucks to relay
boxes along the carriers' routes because letter
carriers cannot possibly carry at one time all
the letters, magazines, and catalogs that they
must deliver each day. Carriers who deliver
mail by walking a route must return to the relay
boxes because postal rules say that they cannot
carry more than thirty-five pounds at one time.
The carriers who deliver mail from vehicles, on
the other hand, carry the whole day's delivery
in the truck. Once the postman takes the mail
from the relay box and drops a letter into a
person's mailbox, he will have completed the
final stage of sorting the mail.

Sorting the mail is the most important
process in the proper handling of mail.
Consequently, mail that is improperly sorted
during any stage of delivery can easily be lost
or delayed for days, weeks, or even years.

WRITING SUGGESTION: THE PROCESS ANALYSIS THEME

A. Select one of the topics listed below. Following the guidelines in Step 3, write first the outline and then the process theme.

General topics

Planning a hiking trip, trip to a foreign country, cross country flight, debate, political campaign, etc.

Selecting a used car, a camper, an apartment, diving equipment, etc.

Judging a contest, debate, parade, etc.

For the business person

Balancing a checkbook
Preparing a balance sheet
Laying out an advertisement
Preparing an advertising campaign
Programming a computer
Obtaining a patent

For the do-it-yourself type

Soldering an electrical connection
Tuning a motor
Making a Japanese tomato ring
Refinishing furniture
Painting a house
Restoring an antique
Building a _____

For the hobbyist

Making a terrarium
Making candles, glasses from old bottles, a table from industrial spools, batik fabrics, etc.
Making a home aquarium
Making a rock, herb, vegetable, annual, or perennial garden
Developing black and white film

For the medical assistant

Giving a hypodermic injection
Preparing a porcelain filling
Taking a venus blood sample
Taking X-rays
Administering artificial respiration
Performing _____ chemical process
Assisting the doctor in the _____ procedure

For the occultist

> Reading a horoscope
> Reading a palm
> Reading tarot cards

For the pet lover

> Grooming a dog, horse, etc.
> Raising a hamster, monkey, etc.
> Training an animal
> Showing an animal

For the political scientist

> Campaigning for a political candidate
> Taking a poll
> Organizing a precinct
> Publicizing a candidate

For the sleuth

> Apprehending a suspect
> Making an arrest
> Applying handcuffs
> Identifying fingerprints
> Tracing a bullet

For the outdoorsman

> Pitching a tent
> Selecting a campsite
> Hunting with a bow and arrow
> Fishing for _____
> Scuba diving

B. The photograph on page 202 illustrates one process in pottery making — shaping. Write a process analysis about any one of the stages in pottery making.

PHOTOGRAPH 8. (Photo by Dave Patrick.)

PROCESS ANALYSIS RATING SHEET Poor Average Good Excellent

OUTLINE

—— Correct form
—— Complete

TITLE

—— Indicates directional or
informational process analysis

INTRODUCTION

—— Interest statement
   —— Explains why process being
     described
   —— Gives formal definition of
     process
—— Thesis statement
   —— If no more than five main steps,
     lists steps.
   —— If more than five main steps,
     mentions number of steps and
     lists only first and last.

BODY

—— Lists materials and equipment needed
—— Discusses main steps in order as listed
in thesis
—— Defines or explains unfamiliar terms
—— Defines abbreviations first time used
—— Uses indicative mood

CONCLUSION

—— Discusses advantages of process
—— Discusses disadvantages (if any)
—— Discusses effectiveness of process
—— Evaluates results of process
—— Discusses importance of process
—— Mentions how process is related to
other similar processes

PROCESS ANALYSIS RATING SHEET   Poor   Average   Good   Excellent

OUTLINE | | | |
____ Correct form
____ Complete

TITLE | | | |
____ Indicates directional or
informational process analysis

INTRODUCTION | | | |
____ Interest statement
    ____ Explains why process being
    described
    ____ Gives formal definition of
    process
____ Thesis statement
    ____ If no more than five main steps,
    lists steps.
    ____ If more than five main steps,
    mentions number of steps and
    lists only first and last.

BODY | | | |
____ Lists materials and equipment needed
____ Discusses main steps in order as listed
in thesis
____ Defines or explains unfamiliar terms
____ Defines abbreviations first time used
____ Uses indicative mood

CONCLUSION | | | |
____ Discusses advantages of process
____ Discusses disadvantages (if any)
____ Discusses effectiveness of process
____ Evaluates results of process
____ Discusses importance of process
____ Mentions how process is related to
other similar processes

STAGE 10

COMPARISON AND CONTRAST

1. Using Comparison and Contrast for Evaluation
2. Comparing and Contrasting for General Knowledge
3. Using Analogy as Loose Comparison
4. Writing the Thesis for the Comparison/Contrast Theme
5. Structuring the Outline for the Comparison/Contrast Theme
6. Examining Student Models of Comparison/Contrast Themes

When you discover the **similarities** between two or more objects, ideas, institutions, or people, you are analyzing by **comparison**. When you discover the **differences,** you are analyzing by **contrast.** As with any kind of analysis, when you compare and contrast a set of subjects, you are increasing your store of knowledge.

STEP 1 **Using Comparison and Contrast for Evaluation.** Comparison and contrast is most commonly used for practical purposes of evaluation. Analysis by comparison and contrast helps you to make decisions about what products to buy, what decisions to make, and what actions to take. Suppose, for example, that you are planning to buy a van camper for a summer tour of the states. One of the first things you need to know about making a logical analysis by comparison and contrast is that all of the items or subjects under consideration must be in a comparable class. If you were on a limited budget, you certainly would not start comparison shopping by considering a Winnebago and a Volkswagen Campmobile. Instead, you would probably investigate the VW Campmobile, the Ford Econoline, and perhaps also the Chevrolet Campco since all are in a comparable size and weight class. Once you have established the likenesses, your main concern in selecting a camper would involve the contrasts. Thus, you would be likely to select as points of difference such items as initial price, type of warranty, gas consumption, use of space, basic equipment, and ease of obtaining repairs while on the road. A comparison and contrast analysis, then, involves a **set of subjects** (two or more) and a number of **points of comparison or contrast.** Most people, no matter what their interests or their occupations, often find it necessary to make comparison/contrast analyses.

STEP 2   **Comparing and Contrasting for General Knowledge.**   In addition to evaluation as a very practical reason for comparison and contrast analysis, you will find that comparison and contrast can greatly increase your store of knowledge and that this can be done in two ways:

1. You may compare and contrast two subjects, both of which you know something about and both of which are of interest to you. Analyzing the two subjects on selected points of comparison or contrast, or both, reveals basic principles or ideas which can broaden your knowledge and inform your reader. Many people, for instance, think of communes as a recent development in America; they do not realize that communes are very much a part of America's history. A writer interested in the development of communes in the United States could profitably compare and contrast the nineteenth century Brook Farm community of Massachusetts with the twentieth century Twin Oaks community of rural Virginia, based on B. F. Skinner's *Walden II.* The points of comparison/contrast that would give a revealing picture would be basic ideology, initial money pledged, method of work distribution, cultural activities, marriage and child rearing practices, and relationship to the community at large.

2. You may compare and contrast two subjects, one of which is known and one of which is relatively unknown, in order to make the unknown subject more understandable. Suppose, for example, that while reading an article about England, you learned that Scotland Yard was a branch of England's Criminal Investigation Department (CID). Your government professor mentioned that the CID is parallel in many ways to our FBI, but that in fact the CID is the most well-known and highly respected investigation department in the world. Here is a case where you could learn a great deal about an unknown in terms of the known. An extremely informative paper would result from a comparison/contrast analysis of the FBI and the CID on the following points: established purpose, services offered to other agencies, departments within each organization, types of investigations conducted, personnel structure, and personnel selection methods.

Regardless of the set of subjects you use in comparison and contrast analysis, the **class** in which you place those subjects is determined by your particular interest. Suppose that within a city limit there were two or three five acre tracts of undeveloped land for sale. If you were the city planner in charge of recreation and preservation, your special interest would lead you to classify these parcels of land as park and recreation areas. In this case your points of comparison and contrast in recommending a purchase to the city commissioners would be the cost to the city, the location in relation to public transportation and density areas, the natural resources already present, the cost of developing the land, and the tax rates. On the other hand, if you were a housing developer, your interest would lead you to classify these parcels of land as high density profit parcels. In selecting one parcel of land to recommend for purchase by your corporation, your points of comparison and contrast would be zoning possibilities; initial cost; proximity to schools, churches, and stores; and the cost of developing the land.

EXERCISE 10-1 CLASSIFYING SETS OF SUBJECTS

Put two of the following sets of subjects into a particular class, and then give a few points of comparison or contrast for each set.

Example:
  Set: Acrylic paints and oil paints
  Class: Artist's materials
Points of comparison: A. Both are effective media
                         B. Both have wide color range possible

Points of contrast: C. Drying time differs
                         D. Texture achieved differs

Sets of subjects

1. Set: England and United States
   Class:
   Points of comparison:
   Points of contrast:

2. Set: Community Colleges vs. Four-Year Universities
   Class:
   Points of comparison:
   Points of contrast:

3. Set: Living at home; living on your own
   Class:
   Points of comparison:
   Points of contrast:

4. Set: Male and female teachers
   Class:
   Points of comparison:
   Points of contrast:

EXERCISE 10-2   CHOOSING SETS FOR COMPARISON/ CONTRAST ACCORDING TO INTEREST

A. Choose two sets of subjects of interest to you. Be sure each set of subjects is in the same class. (Whales and sharks won't work because one is a mammal and one is not.)

B. Then state at least three points on which you would compare or contrast your subjects. You may wish to use only comparison or only contrast here.

Example:

Set: Panasonic Ranger and Sony 8

Class: Car tape players

Points of comparison: A. Sound

Points of contrast: B. Ability to withstand vibration

C. Advertised wattage vs. actual wattage

D. Cost

1. Set:

   Class:

   Points of comparison:

   Points of contrast:

2. Set:

   Class:

   Points of comparison:

   Points of contrast:

STEP 3   **Using Analogy as Loose Comparison.**   Up to this point you have seen that subjects suitable for comparison/contrast analysis were in the same general class and were of equal importance. However, another kind of comparison involves subjects that are not of the same general class or importance. This is a loose comparison known as **analogy.** Analogies are not strict or exact comparisons; but in using them, the writer attempts to make his reader see the similarities between two subjects in a striking, thought-provoking, or unusual way.

One of the most common analogies currently used is the comparison of a computer to a human brain. Obviously, one is a natural object and one a man-made object; they are, however, loosely comparable in that both are capable of planning, computing, and producing results. A general science teacher might resort to analogy in order to enlighten his class about the structure of the human eye by comparing it to a camera. He would explain that the similarities lie in their reactions to light, their methods of receiving images, their methods of focusing light image, and their methods of limiting light reception.

This kind of analogy is often used for teaching purposes. Another form of analogy, the **figure of speech,** is often used for illustrative and artistic purposes. In these figures of speech, called similes and metaphors, a person or an object or even an abstraction is likened to something outside of its own class. The writer thus attempts to sharpen the reader's understanding of a complex idea, to increase his sensory perception, or to make him see a new image.

A **simile** indicates comparison by use of the words *like* or *as.* For example, the poet Langston Hughes would say, "A dream dries up like a raisin in the sun." The user of cliché similes would say, "He shot out of there like a bullet."

In a **metaphor** the comparison is implied. The expression "The ship plowed the sea" implies that the ocean is a vast field and that the ship will cut through it as the tractor does the earth. Adjectives can also form metaphors; for example, one hears such expressions as "a blue outlook," "a bittersweet experience," "a ringing declaration," and "the camera's eye."

Sophisticated writers often extend analogies to a paragraph or more; poets, obviously, use the device extensively. However, because analogy is primarily imaginatively illustrative rather than strictly logical, you will be concerned in your next paper with strict comparison and contrast. In other words, you will be choosing a set of two subjects and three or more points of comparison, contrast, or comparison/contrast for the purpose of making an evaluation or increasing your general knowledge.

STEP 4   **Writing the Thesis for the Comparison/Contrast Theme.**   Subjects can be treated either by comparison or by contrast alone, or by a combination of both comparison and contrast. Your choice depends upon the point you are trying to make and the scope of your paper. The thesis must clearly indicate which method you are using. You will recall that the thesis for the analysis paper states the limited subject, the major inference, and the minor inferences which indicate the categories of development. The thesis statement for the definition paper is a generalization about the word to be defined. The thesis statement for the process paper introduces the process and mentions the major steps to indicate the categories of development.

Comparison and contrast is a complex type of analysis because it involves not just one, but a set of two or more subjects which are then compared, contrasted, or compared and contrasted on at least two, and usually more, points. The thesis statement, then, must be carefully set up so that the reader knows exactly what to expect. Here are some examples of thesis statements for comparison/contrast analysis:

1. METHOD: **Comparison**
   TITLE: Two Revolutions
   THESIS STATEMENT: The American Revolution and the Russian Revolution are similar in respect to the methods used in gaining the support of the majority, the tactics used in the revolutions, the use of outside help, and the outcome.
   (This student used four points of comparison.)

2. METHOD: **Contrast**
   TITLE: Ocean Racers and Cruising Boats
   THESIS STATEMENT: Ocean racers and cruising boats differ with respect to hull construction, engine performance, and safety equipment.
   (This student chose three points of contrast.)

3. METHOD: **Comparison/Contrast**
   TITLE: Formica vs. Wood Furniture
   THESIS STATEMENT: Although formica and wood furniture differ in durability, workmanship, and ease of cleaning, they are similar in strength and in types of pieces manufactured.
   (This student chose three points of contrast and then two points of comparison.)

4. Suppose you choose a subject which, for your particular purposes, you want to treat exclusively by comparison, and yet you want to anticipate your readers' awareness that there is, after all, a basic difference between your set of subjects. You can then handle the thesis statement like this:

METHOD: Basically **comparison**
TITLE: Two Dictators: Perplexing Patterns
THESIS STATEMENT: Although Mussolini and Stalin were of different nationalities, their early backgrounds are strangely similar in that they both had dominant fathers who influenced their lives greatly, they both abandoned their proposed professions, they both took a great interest in journalism, and both early grew accustomed to prison walls.
(The student mentions the difference immediately, then moves to the similarities.)

5. Similarly, if you have a subject which you want to treat exclusively by contrast yet there are obvious similarities between the sets involved, then you can handle the thesis like this:

METHOD: Basically **contrast**
TITLE: Marble for Elegance
THESIS STATEMENT: While cultured marble and quarried marble are both in demand in the luxury building trade, many people do not realize that these two materials differ with respect to origin, ease of installation, and sanitation.
(The student discusses likeness in the initial statement and proceeds to the points of difference.)

6. In the combination comparison/contrast theme, the thesis is, of course, completely self-explanatory because you clearly delineate exactly what points of likeness and what points of difference you plan to discuss, as in Thesis Example 3, "Wood vs. Formica Furniture."

STEP 5   **Structuring the Outline for the Comparison/Contrast Theme.**   In the kinds of themes you have written up to this point, you have seen that there is really only one way to write an outline and that the major points of your discussion, indicated by Roman numerals, are dictated by the order of points made in your thesis statement. However, because in the comparison/contrast theme you are dealing with a set of two or more subjects and any number of points of comparison and contrast, you have two options for organizing the outline.

THE BLOCK METHOD OF OUTLINING

The first method is called the **block method** because you present your first subject and then discuss in order each point of comparison and/or contrast you plan to make. Next, you present your second subject and discuss in turn the corresponding points of comparison and/or contrast. This is a simple method of organization; and it is effective if you have a readily understood set of subjects, and the points of comparison and contrast are relatively few and uncomplicated. This method would not be too effective, however, if you had many points of comparison and contrast that contained statistics, complicated details, or technical information. By the time your reader reached the second "block" of your paper, which discussed your second subject in the set, he would be inclined to forget much of the information that had been presented about your first subject in the first block.

Here is an example of an outline for a comparison/contrast analysis developed in block form:

METHOD: **Comparison and contrast**
TYPE OF OUTLINE: **Block**
TITLE: Vacations: By Air or Sea?
THESIS STATEMENT: Air travel and sea travel are similar in that they achieve the ultimate objective of the tourist; but they vary with respect to cost, duration, itineraries, and special features.

    I. Air travel
        A. Costs
        B. Duration
        C. Itineraries
        D. Special features
    II. Sea travel
        A. Costs
        B. Duration
        C. Itineraries
        D. Special features

THE ALTERNATING BLOCK METHOD OF OUTLINING

The **alternating block method** of outlining involves setting up the major categories by points of comparison and/or contrast rather than by the subjects to be compared and contrasted. This method is usually preferred when there are a number of points to be compared and contrasted or when detailed information is included under the points to be compared and contrasted.

Here is an example of an alternating block outline form:

METHOD: **Contrast**

TYPE OF OUTLINE: **Alternating Block**

TITLE: Air Cooled and Water Cooled Engines

THESIS STATEMENT: When purchasing a car, people should be aware of the differences between air cooled and water cooled engines before they make a decision. Although these two types of engines are both four cycle internal combustion motors, they differ with respect to parts, maintenance, and performance.

    I. Parts
        A. Air cooled engines
        B. Water cooled engines
   II. Maintenance
        A. Air cooled engines
        B. Water cooled engines
  III. Performance
        A. Air cooled engines
        B. Water cooled engines

BLOCK AND ALTERNATING BLOCK OUTLINES: SAME SUBJECT

Now you can look at a block outline and an alternating block outline on the same subject. Notice that in the block form the subjects are the entries for the Roman numerals; the points of comparison and contrast are the capital letters.

On the other hand, in the alternating block outline, the points of comparison are the entries for the Roman numerals, and the two subjects of the set are then entered alternately as capital letters A and B.

In the following block outline about the Seminoles and Cherokees, there are only two major paragraphs, one which discusses the Seminoles and then one which discusses the Cherokees.

In the alternating block outline, there are four major paragraphs in the paper; each paragraph discusses in detail the differences between the two tribes one point at a time.

Notice that whether the block or the alternating block form of outline is used, the thesis and the concluding statements remain the same.

SEMINOLE AND CHEROKEE INDIANS

Thesis statement: Although the Seminole and Cherokee Indians live on reservations, their life styles differ with respect to tribal customs, financial earnings, living quarters, and feelings toward white men.

BLOCK

I. SEMINOLE
  A. Tribal customs
  B. Financial earnings
  C. Living quarters
  D. Feelings toward white men
II. CHEROKEE
  A. Tribal customs
  B. Financial earnings
  C. Living quarters
  D. Feelings toward white men

ALTERNATING BLOCK

I. Tribal customs
  A. SEMINOLE
  B. CHEROKEE
II. Financial earnings
  A. SEMINOLE
  B. CHEROKEE
III. Living quarters
  A. SEMINOLE
  B. CHEROKEE
IV. Feelings toward white men
  A. SEMINOLE
  B. CHEROKEE

Concluding statement: Although the Seminoles and the Cherokees are considered the same by most Americans, they do differ in many respects.

EXERCISE 10-3 CONVERTING FROM BLOCK TO ALTERNATING BLOCK OUTLINE

Convert the block outline to alternating block form.

SITE-BUILT HOMES VS. MOBILE HOMES

Thesis statement: People who are moving to a new area or who are preparing to retire must often make a decision whether to buy a site-built home or to purchase a mobile home. The prospective buyer should consider carefully the differences in initial building costs, grounds maintenance, building upkeep, and safety factors.

BLOCK	ALTERNATING BLOCK
I. Site-built homes	
A. Initial building cost	
B. Grounds maintenance	
C. Building upkeep	
D. Safety factors	
II. Mobile homes	
A. Initial building cost	
B. Grounds maintenance	
C. Building upkeep	
D. Safety factors	

Concluding statement: Unless the buyer weighs these factors, he may make a hasty decision that he will regret in the future.

STEP 6   **Examining Student Models of Comparison/Contrast Themes.**   Following is an outline in alternating block form written by a student who selected as her subject the differences in the writings of two novelists.

METHOD: **Contrast**

TYPE OF OUTLINE: **Alternating Block**

THE WORKS OF RAY BRADBURY AND J. R. R. TOLKIEN

Thesis statement: Both Ray Bradbury and J. R. R. Tolkien, whose books are widely read, are authors of escape literature. Their works differ, however, in the types of characters they use, the bases for the stories, and the presentation of the stories.

  I. Types of characters
     A. Ray Bradbury
        1. Actual people
           a. In full-length novels
           b. In collection of stories
        2. Variety of characters
           a. In full-length novels to provide minor plots
           b. In collection of stories to present separate happenings
     B. J. R. R. Tolkien
        1. Fictitious characters
           a. Hobbits
           b. Dwarves and elves
           c. Fairies
           d. Gollums and other animals that talk
        2. Variety of characters
           a. Each with separate history
           b. Each with separate place in society
           c. Each with something to do with author's protagonist

 II. Bases for the stories
     A. Ray Bradbury
        1. Uses present time
           a. Dandelion Wine
           b. Something Wicked This Way Comes

        2. Uses time in the future
          a. The Martian Chronicles
          b. The Golden Apples of the Sun
    B. J. R. R. Tolkien
        1. Uses imaginative history of the past
          a. Farmer Giles of Ham
          b. "The Homecoming of Beorhtnoth
            Beorhthelm's Son"
        2. Uses elements of Celtic, Nordic, and
          English folklore
          a. The Lord of the Rings
          b. The Hobbit

III. Methods of presentation
    A. Ray Bradbury
        1. In futuristic stories
          a. Little or no explanation of
            progress
          b. Ordinary situations transformed
            into fantasy
        2. In present times
          a. Presentation of characters
          b. Ordinary situations transformed
            into fantasy
    B. J. R. R. Tolkien
        1. Detailed explanations
          a. Of histories
          b. Of characters
          c. Of physical surroundings
          d. Of situations
        2. Fantasy transformed into ordinary
          situations

Concluding statement: The differences between
these two authors are endless, yet their works
are among the most popular books read today. In
spite of the differences, the basic purpose of
their writing is to entertain a reading public
which has an ever-growing taste for escape
through fiction.

Following is an outline, also in alternating block form, written by a
student who selected as his subject the similarities in the American and
Russian revolutions.

METHOD: Comparison

TYPE OF OUTLINE: Alternating block

TWO REVOLUTIONS

Thesis statement: The similarities in the
American and Russian revolutions involve the
methods used in gaining the support of the
majority, the tactics used, the kinds of outside
help obtained, and the final outcome of the
revolutions.

I. Methods used in gaining support of majority
   A. Americans
      1. Emphasized dislike of rule by foreign
         monarch
      2. Protested taxation without
         representation
      3. Offered Continental Congress
         solution
   B. Bolsheviks
      1. Organized against oppressive rule by
         Czar Nicholas II
      2. Rallied against starvation among the
         peasants
      3. Proposed solution of soviets

II. Tactics used in war
   A. Americans
      1. Planned underground
      2. Demoralized enemy
      3. Used surprise attack (Battle of
         Trenton)
   B. Bolsheviks
      1. Planned underground
      2. Demoralized enemy
      3. Used surprise attack (St. Petersburg
         uprising)

III. Outside help obtained
    A. Americans
        1. Used French arms
        2. Used French military aides
        3. Used French navy
        4. Took advantage of France's war with
           England
    B. Bolsheviks
        1. Used German revolutionary literature
        2. Used German arms
        3. Used German funds
        4. Took advantage of Germany's
           hostility with Czarist Russia

IV. Final outcome
    A. Americans
        1. Political changes
            a. Defined central government's
               powers
            b. Gave states powers
        2. Economic and social changes
            a. Encouraged industry at home
            b. Created interstate commerce
            c. Extended territory by Northwest
               Ordinance
    B. Bolsheviks
        1. Political changes
            a. Overthrow of Czar
            b. Government by Lenin
        2. Economic and social changes
            a. Peasants gained farmland
            b. Workers gained control of
               factories
            c. Workers controlled local soviets

Concluding statement: Though Americans look at
the Communist movement as an evil of today's
world, they must remember that the ultimate
purpose of the American and the Russian
revolutionaries was the same -- to obtain a
better standard of living and a better way of
life for the people of their respective nations.

COMPARISON THEME

TWO REVOLUTIONS

Although the ideological differences between America and Russia are constantly stressed, a study of the revolutions of both nations reveals some remarkable similarities. The likenesses in these two revolutions involve the methods used in gaining the support of the majority, the tactics used, the kinds of outside help obtained, and the final outcome of the revolutions.

In gaining the support of the people, both the American and the Bolshevik revolutionaries took advantage of the people's hatred toward their rulers. The American colonists disliked being ruled by a monarch in another land. Their major complaint was that they were being taxed but had no voice in local affairs. As a result, the Continental Congress offered the angry colonists a solution -- a republic in which every citizen had a voice in national affairs. Similarly, in Russia the working classes were discontent with the oppressive rule of Czar Nicholas II. The peasants were starving while the Czar and his family dined extravagantly and indulged in countless luxuries. Consequently, the Bolsheviks also offered a solution -- a classless society in which all men would be treated as equals.

Once the two revolutionary groups accepted the ideological solutions, they employed similar tactics in their revolutions. Both American and Russian leaders went underground to plan the war against the oppressors. Both revolutionary groups used methods to demoralize the enemy in attempts to slow him down. The Americans constantly harassed the already weary British troops with war cries and stealthy night raids on British camps. The Bolsheviks used propaganda to demoralize the enemy. Such slogans as "Peace, bread, and land" made the weary Czarist soldiers more anxious to leave their posts. Both revolutionary groups used the element of tactical surprise to defeat the foe. This is exemplified by the Americans in the Battle of Trenton and by the Russians in the uprising in St. Petersburg.

In addition to using similar tactics, both revolutionary groups sought the help of foreign countries. The American Revolution was supported by French arms, French military aides, and the French navy. Because the French were at war with England at the time, they felt that any loss for the English was a French gain. In a similar manner, German funds, arms, and revolutionary literature helped the Bolshevik cause. Germany was fighting a war with Russia, and any collapse of the Russian political structure would very possibly end this war.

In the outcome both the American and the Russian revolutionaries won important political and social changes. In America the people for the first time had a voice in the nation's affairs. In the summer of 1787, a new government was framed when representatives met in Independence Hall. At this convention, the powers of the central government were clearly defined and the states were given specific powers and control over their own government. During this period the Constitution of the United States was formed. In addition to political gains, economic changes led to international trading for the United States. Rather than import goods from Europe, Americans were urged to buy products manufactured at home. In addition, the Northwest Ordinance of 1787 created a new territory for expansion. In Russia the peasants began to have control of their country. Once the Czar was overthrown and the new Russian government headed by Lenin was formed, the peasants were given control of the farmland for a short period of time. Meanwhile, economic and social changes brought about the control of the factories by the workers. In addition to controlling the factories, the workers played an important role in the local soviets.

Many Americans tend to look at the Communist movement as an evil of today's world. They should remember, however, that the ultimate purpose of both the American and the Bolshevik revolutionaries was the same -- to obtain a better standard of living and a better way of life for the people of their respective nations.

WRITING SUGGESTION: THE COMPARISON/CONTRAST THEME

1. Following is a list of suggested subjects for a comparison, contrast, or comparison/contrast theme. If you prefer, choose a subject from your own area of interest.

   Two types of fishing
   AM radio/FM radio
   Two cars in the same class
   Two card games
   Two teaching styles
   One sport: professional and amateur
   Television shows (select only one type — for example, two situation comedies, two talk shows, two variety shows, etc.)
   Two lifestyles
   Artists (select only one type — for example, painters, vocalists, rock groups, dancers, etc.)

   Or: Study the photograph on page 225. Select a set of subjects suggested by the photograph and write a comparison/contrast paper.

2. After you have selected your set of subjects, decide upon at least three points of comparison, contrast, or comparison and contrast.

3. Develop your thesis according to the guidelines in Step 5. Make sure that the thesis clearly indicates whether you are using comparison, contrast or both.

4. Construct your outline and indicate type of outline — block or alternating block.

5. If your outline indicates that your theme might exceed the word limitation suggested by your instructor, then consider eliminating one or more of the points of comparison and/or contrast.

6. Use appropriate transitional devices in your theme: *similarly, likewise, similar to, just as, in a like manner,* for comparison; and *in contrast, however, but, nevertheless, on the other hand, still, unlike, different from, opposed to, on the contrary,* to indicate contrast.

PHOTOGRAPH 9. (Photo by Dave Patrick.)

COMPARISON/CONTRAST RATING SHEET

	Poor	Average	Good	Excellent

OUTLINE
____ Indicates block or alternating block
____ Indicates comparison, contrast or C/C
____ Complete
____ Correct form

INTRODUCTORY PARAGRAPH

Lead-in
____ Interests reader
____ Shows relevance to subject
Thesis statement
____ Subject sets apparent
____ Points of comparison/contrast clear

BODY

Content
____ Topic sentence with points of
comparison/contrast introduces
each sentence
____ Number of proof details
____ Quality of proof details
____ Relevance of proof details
Organization
____ Pattern of organization evident
____ Effectiveness of transition
Style
____ Appropriate language level
____ Specific word choice
____ Clear phrasing
____ Sentence variety
____ Individuality of expression

CONCLUDING PARAGRAPH

Poor	Average	Good	Excellent

_____ Summarizes main points of paper
_____ Uses appropriate transition

MECHANICS

Manuscript form
_____ Title in capitals
_____ Text double-spaced
_____ Pagination
_____ Margins
_____ Legibility and neatness
_____ Spelling
_____ Sentence structure
_____ Grammar
_____ Punctuation
_____ Capitalization
_____ Expression of numbers

Name _____

Date _____

Section _____

COMPARISON/CONTRAST RATING SHEET

	Poor	Average	Good	Excellent

OUTLINE

_____ Indicates block or alternating block
_____ Indicates comparison, contrast or C/C
_____ Complete
_____ Correct form

INTRODUCTORY PARAGRAPH

Lead-in
_____ Interests reader
_____ Shows relevance to subject
Thesis statement
_____ Subject sets apparent
_____ Points of comparison/contrast clear

BODY

Content
_____ Topic sentence with points of
       comparison/contrast introduces
       each sentence
_____ Number of proof details
_____ Quality of proof details
_____ Relevance of proof details
Organization
_____ Pattern of organization evident
_____ Effectiveness of transition
Style
_____ Appropriate language level
_____ Specific word choice
_____ Clear phrasing
_____ Sentence variety
_____ Individuality of expression

CONCLUDING PARAGRAPH

	Poor	Average	Good	Excellent
____ Summarizes main points of paper				
____ Uses appropriate transition				

MECHANICS

	Poor	Average	Good	Excellent

Manuscript form
____ Title in capitals
____ Text double-spaced
____ Pagination
____ Margins
____ Legibility and neatness
____ Spelling
____ Sentence structure
____ Grammar
____ Punctuation
____ Capitalization
____ Expression of numbers

Name _____

Date _____

Section _____

COMPARISON/CONTRAST RATING SHEET

	Poor	Average	Good	Excellent

OUTLINE

____ Indicates block or alternating block
____ Indicates comparison, contrast or C/C
____ Complete
____ Correct form

INTRODUCTORY PARAGRAPH

Lead-in
____ Interests reader
____ Shows relevance to subject
Thesis statement
____ Subject sets apparent
____ Points of comparison/contrast clear

BODY

Content
____ Topic sentence with points of
comparison/contrast introduces
each sentence
____ Number of proof details
____ Quality of proof details
____ Relevance of proof details
Organization
____ Pattern of organization evident
____ Effectiveness of transition
Style
____ Appropriate language level
____ Specific word choice
____ Clear phrasing
____ Sentence variety
____ Individuality of expression

CONCLUDING PARAGRAPH

	Poor	Average	Good	Excellent

____ Summarizes main points of paper

____ Uses appropriate transition

MECHANICS

Manuscript form

____ Title in capitals

____ Text double-spaced

____ Pagination

____ Margins

____ Legibility and neatness

____ Spelling

____ Sentence structure

____ Grammar

____ Punctuation

____ Capitalization

____ Expression of numbers

STAGE 11

CAUSE AND EFFECT

1. Reasoning from Causes to Effects
2. Reasoning from Effects to Causes
3. Writing the Thesis Statement for Analysis by Cause and Effect
4. Recognizing Pitfalls in Causal Analysis
5. Recognizing Cause and Effect Analysis in Research

"Why can't I save any money?" "Why do I always get my papers in late and lose a letter grade?" "Why can't I ever tell a person that something he does bothers me?" "Why does every car I buy cost me so much money in repairs?" "Why do the kids get sick just when we are about to leave on vacation?" Don't you hear yourself and other people ask at least some of these kinds of questions from time to time?

While these are questions, they are also statements of effects; and they are important questions because the results affect the quality of your life. If you could analyze the causes that bring about these effects, you could eliminate some of the problems which make your life confusing, uncomfortable, or otherwise not as satisfactory as you would like it to be.

In the realm of public experience, as well as personal experience, there are hundreds of questions that concern causes and effects. These questions, too, directly and indirectly affect people's lives. "Why are high school dropouts on the increase?" "Why are urban renewal housing units so ugly and so unserviceable?" "What is the effect of busing on the nation's schools and school children?" "Why is the rate of repeated offenses so high among discharged convicts?" "How did it happen that a sizeable part of a Colorado city was built on land known to be contaminated by radioactivity?" "Why are there so few programs for the exceptionally bright child in our nation's public schools?"

In order to answer any of these questions, you need a systematic and logical method to investigate the causes that produce these effects. This method is analysis by cause and effect. Your starting place, of course, is with the subject itself, but there are two reasoning approaches to analysis by cause and effect.

STEP 1   Reasoning from Causes to Effects.

A. You can start with a set of observable circumstances, and with sufficient data you can arrive at a conclusion which is stated in the form of a possible or predictable effect. The subject of child abuse is a case in point. A great deal of research has been conducted recently on the types of child abuse, the kinds of adults who do the abusing, and the kinds of children who are abused. The reason for this research, of course, is that the problem of child abuse is becoming an increasingly serious one in the United States. Here is a given set of circumstances:

Johnny is three years old.
He is a middle child.
The boy is highly active.
His parents are under thirty years of age.
His mother suffers from feelings of rejection.
Johnny's father was overdisciplined and was severely
    beaten by his own parents when he was a child.
Johnny's mother has difficulty coping with her everyday
    household duties and with the management of three
    children who are under four years of age.

A possible effect of this set of circumstances is that Johnny might be an abused child. Researchers on the subject would predict that Johnny is a possible candidate for child abuse because there are so many factors in his life that correlate with those of abused children.

B. You can start with a set of circumstances (causes) and draw a verifiable conclusion (effect). A set of circumstances about an elementary school child who stutters illustrates this approach to analysis by cause and effect. Since it is estimated that over 1.5 million of our elementary school children stutter, much research is concerned with this problem. Here is the given set of circumstances concerning David, age eight:

David has certain physiological problems.
He has abnormal movements of two muscles in the middle ear.
He also has badly misaligned teeth.
He has an unusually high and narrow hard palate.

David has some psychological problems.

He has been upset since the birth of his baby brother.

His other brothers and sisters speak for him.

His parents place great emphasis on David's speech patterns and constantly correct him.

His parents are involved with many projects and do not demonstrate a great deal of affection for David.

A verifiable effect is that David is a stutterer.

STEP 2   Reasoning from Effects to Causes.   "Why" questions begin with the effect. The natural question when discussing effects is, "What caused this?" In this kind of causal analysis, you can begin with an observable conclusion (effect) and work back to the cause or the causes.

Assume that an elementary school counselor received the following report from David's teacher:

David, age eight, has become a behavior problem in his second grade classroom. He is uncooperative in most activities, he disrupts the class, he has occasional temper tantrums, he displays convulsive physical movements, and he refuses to communicate verbally.

If the counselor is to help David, she must first find all of the causes that might be contributing to his behavior problem; hopefully, she may find the basic or primary cause that leads to these observable effects. The counselor must ask questions of those persons who are in a position to observe David. Thus, she asks questions of David's teacher, his doctor, the school psychologist who has already seen him, and his parents. Here is the list the counselor compiles which helps to lead her to the cause of David's problems:

From David's teacher:

David is uncooperative in class activities.

He has never mastered basic phonetic skills.

He wants constant attention while others are speaking.

During reading sessions, he must be isolated from class so that the other children will not be disturbed by his disruptive behavior.

He refuses to communicate orally; when he does try to do so, he stutters.

The other children laugh at him.

In place of speaking, he uses convulsive movements such as blinking his eyes, contorting his face, and jerking his hands and legs.

However, he will partake in singing or enacting a role in a playlet; when he does so, he does not stutter.

From the school psychologist:

   Game playing with David indicates that he is an anxious child.
   David displays some hostilities that are inappropriate to the situation.
   David will enact little "roles" with a normal speech pattern.
   David stutters in normal conversation.

From David's doctor:

   David has teeth that are misaligned and badly spaced.
   He has a hard palate that is unusually high and narrow.
   He has an abnormal movement of two muscles in the middle ear.

From David's parents:

   The birth of his baby brother made him jealous.
   His mother says that his father often severely reprimands him.
   His mother says that other children supply words for him when he stutters.
   Both his parents correct his speech when he talks.
   His father says that David's mother dominates the boy.

   The school counselor, after consultation with David's teacher, school psychologist, family doctor, and parents, comes to the conclusion that this child's stuttering originates from a combination of physiological and emotional circumstances and that the stuttering consequently causes a chain of behavioral effects. Having determined why David is a stutterer and what the effects of the problem are, the counselor can now recommend action to be taken by David's classroom teacher, by his parents, and by the school speech therapist to whom she will refer the child.

   In summation, then, there are two methods of reasoning using causes and effects:

Induction: When you begin with a set of observable data which lead into a predictable or verifiable conclusion (effect), you are using **inductive** reasoning.

Deduction: When you begin with an observable conclusion (effect) and lead away from that conclusion by supplying a set of pertinent contributory proof details, you are using **deductive** reasoning.

Deduction and Induction Working Together: Notice that David's teacher sent the counselor a report which was stated in the form of a series of conclusions about David's behavior in class. The counselor then began to collect from other sources facts and observations about David. Working inductively from this set of facts, the counselor drew the deduction that David's problems grew primarily from the fact that he is a stutterer.

STEP 3 **Writing the Thesis Statement for Analysis by Cause and Effect.**   Suppose that David's counselor was presenting her findings in a formal case study of David. The opening of her report would consist of a thesis statement as follows:

> Consultation with David S.'s teacher, school psychologist, family doctor, and parents reveals that his stuttering is caused by a combination of physiological and emotional circumstances and that the stuttering is primarily responsible for his behavioral problems in the classroom.

The thesis statement for analysis by cause and effect is similar to the thesis statement for analysis by classification and division because it has a major inference and minor inferences.

Major inference: Stuttering is primarily responsible for David's behavioral problems in the classroom.
Minor inferences: The stuttering is caused by physiological and emotional circumstances.

Name _____

Date _____

Section _____

EXERCISE 11-1 WORKING FROM CAUSES TO EFFECTS

From your own experience or observation, give a list of circumstances (causes) that lead up to a verifiable conclusion (effect).

Name _____

Date _____

Section _____

EXERCISE 11-2 WORKING FROM EFFECT TO CAUSE

From your own experience or observation, state an effect and list the possible circumstances (causes) that could be responsible for that effect.

STEP 4   **Recognizing Pitfalls in Causal Analysis.**   You have studied analysis by classification and division, by process, by definition, and by comparison and contrast. But analysis by cause and effect is perhaps the most difficult because of the several pitfalls to a logical and thorough analysis. You will need to familiarize yourself with these problems in cause and effect reasoning.

1. **Hasty generalization:** There are few males in the nursing profession today because females are better at tedious, repetitious tasks and are more sympathetic than are men.

Discussion: History, mistaken assumptions, stereotyping, prejudice, pay scales, and many other causes enter into this situation.

2. **Either/Or fallacy:** America: Love it or leave it.

Discussion: Somewhat akin to hasty generalization in that such reasoning fails to take account of more than one cause; this kind of reasoning assumes only two alternatives for coping with a country's ills. Worse yet, it fails to take account of any causes of the ills.

3. **After this, therefore because of this:** Permissive child raising is common in affluent communities. Senseless vandalism is sharply rising in these affluent communities. Therefore, permissiveness causes vandalism in children.

Discussion: Formally called the *post hoc ergo propter hoc* fallacy, or *post hoc* for short, this kind of reasoning involves being misled by time sequence in establishing the cause of an effect.

4. **Insufficient cause:** Jean-Paul does not express himself well verbally at kindergarten because he comes from a bilingual family.

Discussion: Some research does indicate that children raised in a bilingual home have expression problems in the early grades. But there may be other reasons for Jean-Paul's problem. He could have a hearing impediment, he might be uninterested, he might have a low maturity level, or he might be anxious in a new school situation. This problem of reasoning from insufficient cause is also akin to hasty generalization.

5. **Mistaking the nature of a cause:** Herman falls asleep every day in his English class; it is obvious that he is bored.

Discussion: Herman's teacher attributes his sleeping to boredom; actually Herman is recovering from mononucleosis.

EXERCISE 11-3   RECOGNIZING PITFALLS IN CAUSAL ANALYSIS

From your own experience or observation, supply an example for each of the problems in cause and effect reasoning.

1. **Hasty generalization**

2. **Either/Or fallacy**

3. **Post hoc fallacy** (after this, therefore because of this)

4. **Insufficient cause**

5. **Mistaking the nature of a cause**

STEP 5   **Recognizing Cause and Effect Analysis in Research.**   You are probably aware by now that most causal analysis involves moving out of the area of personal experience and moving into the area of research. Right now you can give yourself a little practice in causal analysis (and possibly gain some insight into yourself as well) by working up a cause and effect paragraph on one of the questions presented in the opening of this chapter. For instance, you might find out once and for all why you can never get your papers in on time, if that's your particular problem.

However, as you work through Part 2 of this book you will be writing a limited research paper that will be concerned with one aspect of a social, economic, or political problem in America. Subject matter of this nature cannot be investigated without careful attention to causes and effects, and such investigation cannot be undertaken without careful training in the basics of library research. You will receive this training in Part 2, and the writing suggestion dealing with cause and effect analysis will be delayed until after you have had this training. By examining the model on page 328 of Part 2, you can see how one student used cause and effect analysis in his paper on "Migrant Housing."

In working through the various stages of this book, you have been working with expository methods one at a time. In working with an extended definition, you saw how mixed expository methods work together to communicate information to a reader. The experienced writer who is dealing with extensive exposition of a subject uses a combination of all the expository methods.

Depending on the subject you choose, your research paper will include most of the expository methods you have studied — analysis by classification and division, definition, possibly process analysis, comparison and contrast, and, of course, analysis by cause and effect. But what makes the research paper different from a simple theme? In addition to the fact that you use mixed expository methods, you will present not only the problem, but also the possible solutions to the problem.

The outline below was written by a student who chose for the subject of her research paper the problem of "Stutterers in Our Elementary Schools." You can see from her outline that causal analysis is an essential part of her research paper.

STUTTERERS IN OUR ELEMENTARY SCHOOLS

Thesis statement: Stuttering, an increasing problem in elementary school children, if not corrected early, can result in severe frustration, withdrawal from society, and abnormal psychological development.

I. Causes of stuttering
   A. Physiological abnormalities
      1. Abnormal movements of two muscles in the middle ear
         a. Simultaneous contraction of muscles
         b. Reduced intensity of sound
         c. Cutout of auditory feedback signal
      2. Oral abnormalities
         a. Teeth
            (1) Condition: badly spaced or misaligned
            (2) Result: poor articulation
         b. Hard palate
            (1) Condition: unusually high or very narrow
            (2) Result: distortion of sounds
   B. Psychological abnormalities
      1. Early childhood disturbances
         a. Birth of baby brother or sister
         b. Absence of a parent for extended time
      2. Parent—child relationship disturbance
         a. Lack of affection
         b. Severe reprimanding
         c. Overdomination by parents
            (1) Continually correct child's speech
            (2) Continually speak for him
            (3) Permit siblings to speak for him

II. Result: Severe frustrations
   A. Rejection by peers
      1. Child laughed at
      2. Child isolated from class during play with peers
   B. Rejection by teacher
      1. Child isolated during reading sessions
      2. Child isolated during speech sessions
   C. Inability to express clearly personal views
      1. Stutters 10 percent of words spoken
      2. Stutters on first word of sentence
      3. Uses fragmented sentence
      4. Substitutes convulsive movements
         a. Shutting or blinking of eyes
         b. Sudden jerking of hands and/or legs
         c. Contorting of facial expressions

III. Result: Withdrawal from society
    A. Avoids oral communication
    B. Develops inferiority complex
       1. By continual suppression
       2. By continual correction
       3. By continual persecution

IV. Result: Abnormal psychological development
in school
    A. Becomes behavior problem in school
       1. Disrupts class for attention
       2. Refuses to cooperate during
          activities
    B. Maintains low maturity level
       1. Will not practice articulation
       2. Will not master phonetic skills
    C. Displays buried hostility

V. Solutions for stuttering children
    A. Home therapy
       1. Manage own affairs
       2. Speak for self
       3. Blow off steam
       4. Encourage warm parental relationship
    B. Classroom therapy
       1. Teacher consults with speech
          therapist
       2. Teacher improves child/peer
          relationships
       3. Teacher encourages child's oral
          expression
    C. Clinical therapy
       1. Vocal therapy
          a. Articulation principles
          b. Articulation reorganization
       2. Listening skills
       3. Mechanical devices
          a. Pacemaster
             (1) Times speech by metronome
             (2) Controls pace of speech
          b. Klein Speech Rectifier
             (1) Produces sounds through
                microphone over larnyx
             (2) Allows speaker to hear himself
                better

      c. Computer
        (1) Compares reference from
           memory banks
        (2) Allows speaker to make
           consistent decisions
        (3) Prevents distraction by others
     d. "Dial-a-Therapy"
        (1) Corrects speech patterns by
           phone
        (2) Diagnoses problem and
           treatment

Concluding statement: Each of the over 1,500,000
elementary school children who stutter can be
helped by parental guidance, classroom
cooperation, speech therapy, and mechanical
devices. Such attention given early will save
them from abnormal personal and academic
development.

Part 2

Finding and Using Information: the Basics of the Research Paper

STAGE 1

BEGINNING THE RESEARCH PAPER

1. **Choosing a Subject**
2. **Limiting the Subject**
3. **Understanding the Purpose of the Research Paper**

So far you have been relying primarily on personal experience for source material for your papers. Your subject matter has been drawn from jobs, hobbies, sports, school, travel, family, friends, cultural activities, organizations, and social life. In drawing on this source material, you were involved in observation, participation, conversation, and perhaps interviews.

PHOTOGRAPH 10. (Photo by Dave Patrick.)

The next step is to move beyond reporting personal experience into the area of research. Look at the photograph (p. 251) of the polluted river. As you look at this picture, a number of questions probably come to mind: "What caused this desolation?" "Who is responsible for the pollution?" "What are the pollutants?" "How many other rivers and bodies of water in America are polluted and to what extent?" "What happens to the plant and fish life?" "What happens to the water supply and the recreation potential when these bodies of water become polluted?" "Is it possible to keep progressing technologically and still preserve our natural resources?" "What is being done currently to correct this destruction?" "Ultimately, what are the solutions to prevent such problems?"

The more you find out about one problem, the more alert your natural sense of inquiry will become to other social, political, economic, and ecological events, discoveries, and changes that are going on all around you. But awareness is not enough. If you are to *participate* in discoveries, changes, and problem-solving, you will need to gather information. Information, the basis of all understanding, must first be collected, then sorted, and finally arranged carefully before it can be *used*.

The research paper is a project designed to help you master basic investigation skills and apply these skills to basic methods of exposition. A subject for a research paper can be almost any aspect of life in the past or present. Your subject for this first research paper, however, will be one aspect of a social, economic, political, or ecological problem in the United States. Because you will be using basic research sources and developing a very limited topic, your final product will be a **modified research paper.**

In thinking, reading, and writing about your subject, you will be drawing heavily on the composition skills you have already developed: subject limitation, thesis development, inference/fact distinction, classification and division, process analysis, cause and effect analysis, definition, and comparison and contrast analysis. In addition, you will be applying your newly acquired investigation skills and demonstrating your understanding of standard documentation procedures.

OBJECTIVES OF THE MODIFIED RESEARCH PAPER

There are four primary objectives of the modified research paper:

1. The first objective is to select a worthwhile subject to investigate and to limit that subject to a specific topic.

2. The second objective is for you to develop a working knowledge of some basic research sources (see p. 261).

3. The third objective is for you to learn note taking procedure so that you can make full use of your sources in a limited amount of time. You can do this by assembling your own sourcebook, a collection of articles on a particular subject. Your own sourcebook will contain articles which you find to be most useful and which you make copies of, articles from magazines, newspapers, and pamphlets or bulletins, and any other pertinent items such as photographs or records of interviews. Assembling your own sourcebook will help in several ways:

   a. You will be able to do more analytical reading of your sources because you can underline and annotate each source. This analytical reading will assist you because you will be able to take fewer and more precise notes and save yourself much time.
   b. You will be able to work at your own pace and wherever you wish because you will not have to do all of your note taking in the library.
   c. You will have your complete sources at hand to refer to should a question arise when you are writing the final paper.

4. The fourth objective is for you to write a documented paper which will make use of the composition skills you have already developed.

PROCEDURE FOR THE RESEARCH PAPER

In preparing this paper, you can follow a series of stages and steps which will help organize your time and the research material:

1. Assembling a preliminary bibliography
2. Reading for an overview of your subject
3. Selecting the most helpful sources for your specific topic and assembling them in a sourcebook
4. Assembling a working set of note cards
5. Writing an extended definition of your topic
6. Writing a paragraph of fact enumeration ("hard data") on your topic
7. Writing a cause and effect paragraph about the topic you have selected
8. Writing an extended introduction and formulating a thesis
9. Preparing a formal outline
10. Writing a rough draft
11. Preparing the final documented paper with title page, text, footnotes, and bibliography
12. Preparing a five minute oral presentation of your findings and recommendations

An illustration and a photograph of a packet containing a student's sourcebook, preliminary papers, and modified research paper appear here.

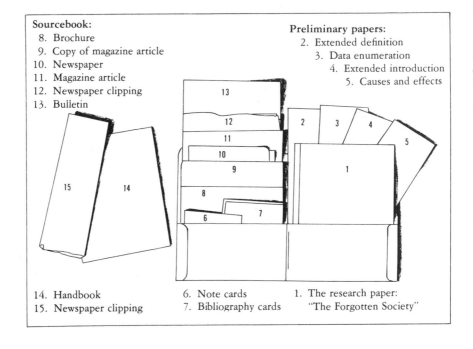

Sourcebook:
8. Brochure
9. Copy of magazine article
10. Newspaper
11. Magazine article
12. Newspaper clipping
13. Bulletin

Preliminary papers:
2. Extended definition
3. Data enumeration
4. Extended introduction
5. Causes and effects

14. Handbook
15. Newspaper clipping

6. Note cards
7. Bibliography cards

1. The research paper: "The Forgotten Society"

STEP 1   **Choosing a Subject.**   The first step in any research project is to select a general subject and limit it as soon as possible to a specific topic. Personal interest may lead you to a topic. A police science major, for example, may wish to explore the problem of teenage vandalism, or a sociology major may wish to investigate the problems of the aging in our society. If you are considering special education as a major field, you might choose to investigate the problems of the gifted child, the child with learning disabilities, or the mentally retarded child. If you have a favorite academic subject — political science, for example — you might want to investigate the problems involved in the legitimate operation of political campaigns. If you are interested in economics, you could investigate the area of consumer fraud and consumer protection. If you still don't have an idea for a topic, skim several recent news magazines and several issues of the newspaper to find a general subject.

STEP 2   **Limiting the Subject.**   The earlier in this project that you limit your subject to a specific topic, the more efficient your research will be. The following subjects are far too broad: aging, consumer fraud, crime, drugs, education, employment, environmental ills, justice, minorities, nutrition, politics, population control, prisons, transportation.

Assume that you are interested in environmental ills as a broad subject. Some limitations of this subject are pollution, endangered species, and endangered resources. Should you choose the subject of pollution, you would need to limit it further, perhaps selecting as your topic water pollution. For a limited research paper, you would limit this topic to a specific type of water pollution, narrowing it even more, perhaps, to a type of water pollution in your particular area of the country. A student in Maine, for example, chose the topic of water pollution by paper mills; a student in Florida chose the topic of industrial pollution in the Miami River.

In selecting and limiting your subject, you will want to take care to avoid certain pitfalls:

Prejudging the Subject   You may be interested in a subject and have already formed an opinion about it. For instance, one student who selected as his subject "safety devices for cars" had already decided that the federal government should make airbags mandatory equipment on all new automobiles. However, when he began to research the subject, he found that there were still too many problems with the airbag to warrant a conclusive decision about it. Had this student continued to maintain his position in his paper, reporting only the favorable aspects of the airbag, he would have committed a research blunder known as "bending the thesis." He would have defeated the whole purpose of research, which is to investigate a subject, to report objectively all information about it, and to propose solutions.

Choosing an Inconclusive Subject You will want to avoid choosing a subject about which there is too little information and about which you cannot draw a conclusion. For instance, coeducational housing in colleges might seem like a good subject, but in fact it is a relatively new situation on the American scene; you cannot have any conclusive information about how it will affect today's students in terms of marriage and role adjustment and how it will affect society in general until several decades have passed. Another subject that you might select because it is very timely is sex education in the public schools. However, if you think about it you will realize that in this case, too, there will be little *objective* evidence available either pro or con until several generations can be followed and nationwide data gathered. Still another example of an inconclusive subject would be that of letter grades vs. the pass/fail system of grading.

STEP 3 **Understanding the Purpose of the Research Paper.** Stage 2 will guide you in your search for information. First, however, you need to understand what a research paper is *not.* It is not a general summary of one book or a single periodical article on a subject. It is not a string of quotes from several sources joined together with a few of your own conjunctions and transitional devices. It is not personal opinion based only on personal observation. It is not just a report of the findings of others on a subject, nor is it merely a collection of facts.

What is it then? The research paper is the end result of a careful investigation of a subject which is important to you. Extended research papers, such as those you will be writing in upper division college work or in business or professional situations, cover previous knowledge on a subject as well as current information. In the case of this limited research paper, your investigation of a topic will be directed primarily toward gathering and presenting current information on the topic. Based on the information you gather, your paper will present a carefully formulated thesis. The paper will then demonstrate the thesis by presenting proof details in the form of facts gathered from reading about the subject, interviews, radio and television broadcasts, personal letters of inquiry, and visits to and observation of locations pertinent to the topic. Finally, the research paper draws a conclusion — one based not only on the judgment of experts, but on your own evaluation of the subject. However, this evaluation is always based on objective evidence. If the research paper involves a problem, then it will conclude with proposals for solutions. Again, these proposals are based not only on those suggested by the experts, but also on your own ideas which you have formulated through researching the subject.

STAGE 2

FINDING SOURCES

1. Distinguishing Between the Preliminary and the Final Bibliographies
2. Assembling the Preliminary Bibliography

Once you have selected a subject, your next step is to begin a systematic search for information. Information can be gathered from various sources which include general references (encyclopedias, dictionaries, yearbooks, and statistical abstracts), books, magazine and newspaper articles, bulletins and pamphlets, letters, radio and television broadcasts, and interviews. This list constitutes the **bibliography**.

STEP 1   Distinguishing Between the Preliminary and the Final Bibliography.

THE PRELIMINARY BIBLIOGRAPHY

There are two bibliographies for any research paper, the preliminary bibliography and the final bibliography. The preliminary bibliography is a complete list of all sources you have collected for the investigation of your subject. These sources are often written on index cards. As you actually examine the sources, you will find that some are helpful in researching your specific topic while others, which had promising titles, contain information you are not sure you can use. Those cards listing sources of doubtful value are set aside. The remaining cards constitute your **working bibliography**.

THE FINAL BIBLIOGRAPHY

The final bibliography consists of the sources actually used in your paper. These will be acknowledged at the end of the paper. This final bibliography is usually entitled **selected bibliography** or **works cited** because it lists only those sources from which you drew the specific information that appears in your paper and which you document with footnotes that give credit to these sources. The bibliography for a completed research paper appears on page 367.

STEP 2   Assembling the Preliminary Bibliography.   Your search must establish whether there is sufficient published information on your subject. One source, even if it is a complete book, does not constitute sufficient information for a research paper. Even for a very short paper you will need at least five different sources. One student found that a topic for which there was insufficient published material was "The Disadvantages of Food Stamps." This student found only one article, and that article mentioned only one disadvantage — too much red tape connected with the food stamp program. Since the student still wanted to investigate the subject of food stamps, he had to broaden the scope of his subject rather than limit it to "disadvantages." If you find that you have chosen a subject for which there are no periodical articles and you cannot enlarge the subject, then you have to change subjects.

Assuming, however, that you have in your early search determined that there is sufficient material from a variety of sources, it is now time to begin making a preliminary bibliography. Before you begin compiling the bibliography, you will need to familiarize yourself with the correct bibliography form for each type of source. You will need to know how to prepare the collection of note cards, which constitutes the preliminary bibliography and how to prepare the entries which appear on your bibliography sheet at the end of your paper. You will notice from your examination of the bibliography for the research paper on "Indian Education" that the sources are entered alphabetically. You will save time and effort if you take this listing of bibliography forms along with you to the library and prepare the cards properly at the outset. Then, when you are ready to assemble the final bibliography, you will need only to alphabetize your cards and copy them onto your bibliography sheet.

Varying styles for bibliography and footnote form exist. The most important point to remember in documenting a paper is to pick one style and use it consistently throughout the paper. The following pages illustrate one style for bibliography form. The first example shows the proper form for the bibliography card and the way the entry will look on the bibliography sheet.

BIBLIOGRAPHY FORMS

BOOKS

1. A book with one author

364.9 *C 594C*	Call number
Clark, Ramsey. *Crime in America.* *New York : Simon and* *Schuster, 1970.*	Author's name Title of book Facts of publication

The entry on the bibliography page will appear as follows:

> Clark, Ramsey. *Crime in America.* New York: Simon and Schuster,
>   1970.

The entry begins flush with the left margin.

The author's last name comes first because a bibliography is alphabetized.

The title of the book is underlined to indicate italics.

Publication information consists of the place of publication followed by a colon, the name of the publisher followed by a comma, and the date of publication.

If the entry runs beyond one line, subsequent lines are indented five spaces.

Bibliography lines are single spaced within each entry and double spaced between entries.

2. A book with two authors

> Chafetz, Morris E., M.D., and Harold Devone, Jr. *Alcoholism and
>   Society.* 4th ed. New York: Oxford University Press, Inc., 1962.

The form is the same as for a book with one author, except that the second author's first name comes first.

This entry is also an example of an edition other than the first.

If the book is a revised edition, then the abbreviation "Rev. ed." comes after the title.

3. **A book with three authors**

> Sutherland, Robert Lee, Julian Woodward, and Milton A. Maxwell. *Introductory Sociology.* 6th ed. Chicago: Lippincott, 1961.

In the case of cities that are well known, it is not necessary to give the state.

If a book has more than three authors, only the first author's name is given followed by a comma and "et al" or "and others." It is acceptable to use this form whenever there are more than two authors. The entry would appear as follows:

> Sutherland, Robert Lee, and others. *Introductory Sociology.* 6th ed. Chicago: Lippincott, 1961.

4. **An edited book**

> Hamalian, Leo, and Frederick R. Karl, eds. *The Radical Vision: Essays for the Seventies.* New York: Thomas Y. Crowell Company, 1970.

5. **A book with corporate authorship**

> National Institute on Amphetamine Abuse. *Amphetamine Abuse,* ed. J. Robert Russo. Springfield, Ill.: Thomas, 1968.

6. **An essay in an edited collection**

> White, Lynn, Jr., "The Historical Roots of Our Ecologic Crisis," in *The Radical Vision: Essays for the Seventies,* ed. Leo Hamalian and Frederick R. Karl. New York: Thomas Y. Crowell Company, 1970.

7. **A translated book**

> Revel, Jean Francois. *Without Marx or Jesus: The New American Revolution Has Begun,* trans. J. F. Bernard. Garden City, New York: Doubleday, 1971.

8. **A work of several volumes**

> Calhoun, Arthur Wallace. *A Social History of the American Family.* 3 vols. New York: Barnes and Noble, 1960.

9. **A book that is one of several volumes**

> Ferrell, Robert H. *George C. Marshall,* in *The American Secretaries of State and Their Diplomacy,* ed. Samuel Flagg Bemis. 18 vols., Vol. 11—, ed. Robert H. Ferrell. New York: Cooper Square Publishers, 1966.

The editorship of this series changed with volume 11.

10. **The Bible**

> Corinthians: ii. 14.

The King James version is assumed unless another version is specified.
Neither the Bible nor the books of the Bible are italicized.

ENCYCLOPEDIAS AND YEARBOOKS

11. **A signed encyclopedia article**

> Calderone, Mary S. "Sex Education," *Encyclopedia Americana,* 24 (1969), 629–629b.

The volume number of an encyclopedia is given in Arabic or Roman numerals according to the way it appears on the cover.

Inclusive page numbers are given for an encyclopedia article.

When a volume number is given, the "p." or "pp." for page or pages is dropped.

12. **An unsigned encyclopedia article**

> "Early Childhood Education: Overview," *The Encyclopedia of Education,* 3 (1971), 146.

In the absence of an author the entry begins with the title of the article in quotes.

13. **Statistical Abstract**

> "Marital Status by Sex and Age," *Statistical Abstract of the United States,* 92 (1971), 32.

Yearbooks are handled in the same way as encyclopedias. If no author is given, then the title of the article is given in quotes.

14. **Yearbooks**

> "The Energy Crisis: Gasoline Shortage," *Facts on File,* 1974, p. 122.

> American Hospital Association. "The Bill of Rights for Hospital Patients," *Reader's Digest Almanac and Yearbook,* 1974, p. 459.

PERIODICALS

15. **An unsigned magazine article**

> "Cities Suffocating in Trash: Crisis in Five Years," *Conservation News,* 38 (July 1973), 2–3.

When the volume number for a magazine is given, the date of publication is enclosed in parentheses followed by a comma.

Inclusive pages are given for a bibliography entry for a magazine.

The "p." for page or "pp." for pages is dropped when the volume number is given.

> "New Weapons Against Shoplifting," *U.S. News and World Report,* February 14, 1972, pp. 70–71.

The volume number is omitted for weekly periodicals.

16. **A signed magazine article**

> Daniel, Glenda. "Child Abusers: Parents Anonymous," *PTA Magazine,* 68 (September 1973), 32–35.

17. **An unsigned newspaper article**

> "Radioactive Waste Storage Is Nuclear Age Problem," *The Miami Herald,* December 3, 1973, sec. C, p. 1.

18. **A signed newspaper article**

> Blakeslee, Sandra. "Study Doubts That Smoking Causes Smaller Babies," *The New York Times,* January 15, 1972, sec. 7, p. 15.

MISCELLANEOUS SOURCES

19. **Public documents**

> U.S. Department of Transportation. *Transportation Noise and Its Control.* Washington, D.C.: U.S. Government Printing Office, June 1972.

The forms of public documents vary widely. Enough information should be given so that the reader can locate the reference.

20. **Bulletins**

> National Tuberculosis and Respiratory Association. "We Want Clean Air." New York, 1972 (NTRDA Bulletin).

Bulletins are very short; therefore, the title of a bulletin appears in quotes.

The forms of bulletins vary. Again, enough information should be given so that the reader can identify the type of source and its location.

21. **Pamphlets**

A pamphlet without an author

Alcohol and Alcoholism. Rev. ed Washington, D.C.: U.S. Government Printing Office, 1972. (Pamphlet of the National Institute on Alcohol Abuse and Alcoholism).

In bibliography form pamphlets are handled as much like books as possible.

Because the forms of pamphlets vary so widely, the entry is always identified in parentheses as a pamphlet.

A pamphlet with corporate authorship

Alcoholics Anonymous. *Profile of an AA Meeting.* New York, 1972 (Pamphlet of Alcoholics Anonymous).

A pamphlet with no date given

Committee on Aging: Council on Medical Service. *Health Aspects of Aging.* Chicago: The American Medical Association [n.d.] (Pamphlet of the American Medical Association).

No date is indicated by "n.d." in square brackets. The reader then knows that no date of publication or copyright is given and the omission is not yours.

22. **Interviews**

Davis, James, Chairman, Oriole County Housing Authority, Gaston, Georgia. Personal interview on Housing for the Aged, December 29, 1973.

or

Interview with James Davis, Chairman, Oriole County Housing Authority, Gaston, Georgia, December 29, 1973.

23. **Telecast or radio program**

"The Scene Tonight," ABC telecast on the problems of the aged, April 30, 1974: "Momma Lives on Miami Beach." Narrator, Clarence Jones.

In the preparation of your bibliography, you will develop a working knowledge of the basic kinds of sources necessary for any investigation:

the standard library card catalog
general and specialized encyclopedias
Readers' Guide to Periodical Literature
The New York Times Index
Essay and General Literature Index
yearbooks and statistical references

The following pages show you the actual steps taken by a student in his search for material on the general subject of "Drug Abuse." You will see the reasons for the order in which he consulted each type of source and the way he determined the usefulness of each source.

GENERAL ENCYCLOPEDIAS

The best way to begin research on a subject is to locate an article on it in an encyclopedia; in this way you can get an overview of the subject. This overview will point out important characteristics, background, and major subdivisions of the subject. Often the overview reading in an encyclopedia will help you in narrowing your subject to a specific topic. The *Encyclopedia Britannica,* the *Encyclopedia Americana,* and *Collier's Encyclopedia* are three encyclopedias that are useful for college-level research because the articles in them are written by experts or teams of experts on a given subject.

You will save yourself time if you first consult the Index volume of any encyclopedia. When you do so, be flexible in looking up your classification of the subject. You may already be too limited. For instance, the student who looked up "Education of the Mentally Retarded Child" did not find the subject listed this way; he had to look in the index under the larger classification of "Child Development." He then found his topic listed as a subclassification.

Reproduced on page 267 are entries from the index of the *Encylopedia Americana.*

Discussion: The student looks under "Drugs." He finds a "see" reference to "Drug Addiction and Abuse." When he looks under "Drug Addiction and Abuse," he notes that in boldface type there is a reference to Volume 9, page 414. He may assume that a general article on the subject appears there. At the same time further listings in the index suggest possibilities for the limitation of the subject "Drug Abuse."

Pages 268–70 are reproductions of the first and last pages of the article on "Drug Addiction and Abuse," from Volume 9 of the *Americana.* This is a very helpful article for overview reading on the subject.

414   DRUG ADDICTION AND ABUSE

DRUG ADDICTION AND ABUSE. It is
very likely that every society has had
mood-changing drugs and that there have
always been individuals who used them in
ways that were not socially approved. In
this sense, *drug abuse,* the socially non-
sanctioned use of a drug, is universal and
as old as history. Drug abuse varies from
culture to culture and from time to time
within the same culture. Since laws do not
always correspond to prevalent social attitudes, there may be times when users of
an illegal drug are not considered to be
drug abusers (for example, the people
who drank alcoholic beverages in the
United States during prohibition). From a
pharmacological viewpoint, attitudes toward drugs are often inconsistent or irra-
tional. Some drugs may be totally outlawed, while others with similar actions
are made generally available and may be
self-administered with full social approval.

The repeated use of some drugs can
cause a *psychological dependence,* in which
the effects of the drug or the conditions
associated with its use are felt by the user
to be necessary for his state of emotional
well-being. The intensity of the dependence may vary from a mild inclination to
use the drug to a strong craving or compulsion to use it. Severe psychological
dependence may result in a type of behavior characterized by a preoccupation
with the procurement and use of the drug.
This type of behavior is known as *compulsive drug use,* and since a great dependence
of any self-administered drug is generally
not socially approved, the term is usually
synonymous with *compulsive drug abuse.*
One obvious exception is the use of to-
bacco, where social acceptance is so complete that even heavy compulsive use,
which is damaging to the user's health, is
not currently considered to be drug abuse.

The term *drug addiction* has been defined in many ways, but in this article it is
used to mean a behavioral pattern of
compulsive drug use characterized by an
overwhelming involvement with the procurement and use of the drug and the high
tendency of the user to relapse to drug
use after a period of abstinence. Contrary
to popular belief, drug addiction is not the
same as physical dependance on a drug.
Physical dependence is a physical state pro-

duced by the administration of a drug
such that a characteristic pattern of signs
and symptoms appear when the drug is
withdrawn and disappear when the drug is
administered again. Physical dependence
can be produced by a wide variety of
drugs that are used in everyday medical
practice. Some drugs that produce physical dependence are not pleasant to take
and are neither abused nor used compul-
sively. Also, not all withdrawal symptoms
are associated with a craving for the drug
that produced the physical dependence.

Most of the drugs that are used for their
subjective effects can be divided into four
groups: narcotic analgesics, central nervous system general depressants, central
nervous system stimulants, and hallucinogens. The accompanying table illustrates
several generalizations that help to summarize the differences among these four
groups of drugs. (For additional information on specific drugs, see the individual
articles, such as AMPHETAMINE; BAR-
BITURATE; CODEINE; MARIHUANA; and
OPIUM. The hallucinogens are discussed
in the article HALLUCINOGENS and the
legal aspects of narcotics addiction are
covered in the article NARCOTICS, TRAF-
FIC AND CONTROL.)

MAJOR DRUGS USED FOR SUBJECTIVE EFFECTS

Narcotic Analgesics
  Codeine
  Heroin
  Meperidine
  Methadone
  Morphine

Central Nervous System
  General Depressants   Chronic
  Alcohol   use
  Anesthetic gases   produces
    and vapors   physical
  Barbiturates   depen-   Abuse
  Chloral hydrate   dence   reaches
  Chloridazepoxide   addictive
  Diazepam   propor-
  Ethchlorvynol   tions   Subject
  Glutethimide   to abuse
  Meprobamate
  Methyprylon
  Paraldehyde

Central Nervous System
  Stimulants
  Amphetamines
  Cocaine
  Methylphenidate
  Phenmetrazine

Hallucinogens
  Dimethoxy-methylamphetamine (DOM or STP)
  Dimethylated triptamine (DMT)
  Lysergic acid diethylamide (LSD)
  Marihuana
  Mescaline
  Psilocybin

Amphetamine and methamphetamine are now being manufactured by illegal laboratories, and these drugs are being used by affluent adolescents and middle class young adults as well as by economically deprived ethnic minorities. In 1965 the illegal manufacture or sale of stimulants was made a federal crime in the United States, and in 1968 even the possession of such drugs (when not medically prescribed) became a punishable offense.

Effects on the Mind and Body. The effects of general stimulants on the mind and body depend largely on who is taking them, whether they are taken orally or by injection, and the circumstances under which they are taken. In proper dosages, these drugs can be used to suppress appetite, improve one's mood, and restore to near normal levels the performance of one who is overcome with fatigue.

Given intravenously, amphetamines and cocaine produce similar effects. There is a very sudden pleasurable sensation that is often called a "flash" or "rush." By any route, both amphetamines and cocaine can induce a marked elevation of mood so that the user feels no need for sleep and is unrealistically optimistic and energetic. Some people, however, feel quite anxious and agitated when they take too much of such drugs.

When first used, amphetamines and other stimulants produce an increased heart rate and an elevated blood pressure. Eventually considerable tolerance develops to these effects on the heart and the blood vessels as well as to the effects on one's mood. To continue to experience the effect on mood, users often have to increase their dosage. In some cases, users have ingested more than 1,000 mg of amphetamines a day for months at a time. The average dose given for weight reduction is 30 mg per day.

Users of amphetamines may stay up continuously for several days, stop using the drug, and then fall into a deep exhausted sleep lasting one or more days. Even days after discontinuing the drug, some users find it extremely difficult to function normally without using am-

phetamines. Although it is not necessary to administer any medications to prevent a life-threatening or painful withdrawal syndrome, many users who abruptly discontinue using amphetamines experience profound psychological depression. Some continue using the drug to avoid this feeling.

Both the amphetamines and cocaine, when taken by any route, are potentially toxic. Some users become irritable and have a tendency to repeat certain behavior patterns. Some individuals develop a psychotic syndrome characterized by delusions of persecution (paranoid ideation) and auditory or visual hallucinations.

HALLUCINOGENS

The drugs classified as hallucinogens include some of the oldest and some of the newest drugs known to man. The use of cannabis (of which marihuana is one form) was first recorded more than 4,000 years ago, and psilocybin, which is found in certain mushrooms, was in use by Indians when the Spanish conquerors first came to Mexico. On the other hand, lysergic acid diethylamide (LSD) was synthesized in 1938, and some of the newer agents, such as 2.5-Dimethoxy-4-methylamphetamine (DOM, colloquially known as STP), were not discovered until the 1960's.

The patterns of hallucinogen self-administration in the United States are quite varied. There are many young people and mature adults who seem to accept the general values of society and yet experiment with marihuana, LSD, mescaline, and similar agents. The overwhelming majority of these people do not continue to use the drugs but return to the use of alcohol. Others, in spite of the legal penalties, continue to use marihuana one or more times per week in preference to alcohol.

The repeated self-administration of LSD and related hallucinogens by otherwise conventional citizens is becoming much less common, perhaps as a result of concern about possible serious consequences. There have been reports that LSD may increase the number of broken chromosomes in the white blood cells, but other drugs as well as ordinary viral infections also break chromosomes, and the significance of any drug-induced increase in breakage (if the reports are confirmed) is presently unknown. It also seems clear that the unsupervised use of LSD entails the risk of serious psychiatric difficulties. In addition, the laws against the manufacture and distribution of these drugs make it difficult for users to obtain uncontaminated drugs.

Effects on the Mind and Body. Although the term "hallucinogen" is used to refer to these drugs, their effects are more subtle and more difficult to describe than hallucinations. They cause dilated pupils and increases in blood pressure, temperature, and pulse rate. At low or moderate doses, such drugs alter both mood and perception. Familiar objects, situations, and relationships may seem novel, and the mood may vary from a sense of tranquillity to intense anxiety or panic. Higher doses usually produce visual or auditory hallucinations or both.

The hallucinogens as a class are not associated with certain kinds of behavior that are seen with other classes of self-administered drugs. Physical dependence does not develop, and except for marihuana, daily use of hallucinogens is virtually unknown. For many users, hallucinogens have much symbolic and social significance, but an overwhelming compulsion to take them does not occur. In this sense, addiction to hallucinogens does not occur. With daily use, however, tolerance does develop to the psychological effects of LSD, and this tolerance produces cross-tolerance to related drugs, such as mescaline, but not to marihuana. The long- and short-term effects of marihuana, LSD, and related drugs on the body and biochemistry of the brain are presently the subjects of intensive research efforts.

JEROME H. JAFFE, M.D.
University of Chicago

Bibliography

Chein, Isidor, and others, *The Road to H* (New York 1963).

DeRopp, Robert S., *Drugs and the Mind* (New York 1957).

Jaffe, Jerome H., "Drug Addiction and Drug Abuse," *Pharmacological Basis of Therapeutics,* ed. by Louis Goodman and Alfred Gilman, 3d ed. (New York 1965).

Knowlis, H., *Drugs on the College Campus* (Detroit 1967).

President's Commission on Law Enforcement and Administration of Justice, *Task Force Report: Narcotics and Drug Abuse,* Order No. Pr 36.8:L41/N16 (Washington 1967).

Wikler, Abraham, ed., *The Addictive States* (Baltimore 1968).

Wilner, Daniel, and Kassebaum, Gene G., *Narcotics* (New York 1965).

Discussion: In this article on "Drug Addiction and Abuse," you notice first of all the chart with the major drugs classified according to subjective effects. Then, as you skim the article, you observe that important terms that should be clearly defined and differentiated are italicized. Also notice on p. 268 that in the middle of the second column of this article there is the equivalent of a "see also" reference. It suggests that for additional information on specific drugs you should see the individual articles. It is at this point that the student investigating "drug abuse" decides that two categories of drug abuse interest him — hallucinogens and amphetamines — because these are two of the types of drugs commonly abused by college students. At the end of the article, there is a selected bibliography. The selected bibliographies that appear at the end of most encyclopedia articles can serve as a springboard to put you on to other sources. Notice here the book *Drugs on the College*

Campus. Since the student has already decided that he will investigate one aspect of college drug abuse, this book will certainly be one he will want to look at if he can locate it in his college or his city library.

Since the student decides that this *Americana* article is one that he will certainly draw from for his paper, he now makes a proper bibliography card.

Name of author Title of article in quotes	
Name of publication underlined to indicate italics	*Jaffe, Jerome H. M. D. "Drug Addiction and abuse," Encyclopedia Americana, 9 (1974), 414–418.*
Volume number in Arabic numerals as it appears on spine of the volume	
Publication date in parentheses because it follows a volume number	
Inclusive page numbers	
Annotation	*Gives drug classifications chart; defines many terms connected with drug abuse.*

Note that an annotation on a bibliography card is a short comment about the contents of a source. Annotating the bibliography card after examining the source is a good practice because the annotation will remind you about the contents and will indicate whether you think the source is definitely helpful, of possible use, or of no use.

THE CARD CATALOG

Having read an overview article on your subject in an encyclopedia, you will want to find out now whether any books on your subject are available. Thus, you will consult the card catalog, which indexes all the books in a library's circulating and reference collections. Each book owned by the library is described on a separate card, and these cards are filed alphabetically. A book will be found listed in the card catalog on four types of cards: author card, title card, subject card, and cross reference card.

At this point in your research, it is unlikely that you know the specific names of books on your subject; therefore, you will be looking for subject cards. The student researching "drug abuse" found the following three cards through subject headings.

```
613.83     Drug abuse.
N277a    National Institute on Amphetamine Abuse, 1st, Edwards-
            ville, Ill., 1966.
              Amphetamine abuse, edited by J. Robert Russo.
            Springfield, Ill., Thomas [ᶜ1968]
                 xii, 159 p.   illus.   24 cm.
                 Sponsored by the Delinquency Study and Youth Develop-
            ment Project. Southern Illinois University, Edwardsville, Ill.
                 Includes bibliographies.

                 1. Amphetamine. 2. Drug abuse.  I. Russo, J. Robert, ed.
            II. Southern Illinois University, Edwardsville. Delinquency
            Study and Youth Development Project. III. Title.

            HV5822.A5N3   1966       613.8′3      68-29687

            Library of Congress           [5]
```

Discussion: The title of this book is *Amphetamine Abuse.* It is edited by J. Robert Russo. It was published in Springfield, Illinois, by Thomas publishers in 1968. Notice that no single author is given; this is an instance of a book with corporate authorship — the National Institute on Amphetamine Abuse. The title, of course, indicates that the book will be useful, but further reading of the catalog card confirms this. The student sees that the book was sponsored by the Delinquency Study and Youth Development Project at Southern Illinois University in Edwardsville, Illinois. He also notices (after the entry "National Institute on Amphetamine Abuse") that this institute was the first and that it was held in 1966. Because the institute was sponsored by a university and the findings are therefore those of experts on the subject, the source appears to be a responsible one. The student immediately makes another bibliography card. When you make a bibliography card for a book, be sure to enter the call number so that when you are ready to examine the book, you need not return to the card catalog to find the location of the books in the stacks.

```
613.83
N277a


National Institute on Drug
abuse. Amphetamine Abuse,
ed. J. Robert Russo. Spring-
field, Ill.: Thomas, 1968.
```

The second card indexes a specialized dictionary.

```
                    ASK AT REFERENCE DESK
R            Drug abuse - Dictionaries.
615.1       Lingeman, Richard R
L755d          Drugs from A to Z, a dictionary [by] Richard R.
            Lingeman. New York, McGraw-Hill [°1969]
               xvi, 277 p.   21 cm.




            1. Drug abuse—Dictionaries.   2. Drugs—Dictionaries.   I. Title

            HV5804.L54                 613.8'3'03       68-30559

            Library of Congress              [15-2]
```

Discussion: The title of this specialized dictionary is *Drugs from A to Z.* Specialized dictionaries give more information than a regular dictionary, but in a shorter and more succinct form than you would find in an encyclopedia. They are often helpful for very specific information. Notice that the entry on the top of this card directs the student to the reference desk for this book. The letter R above the call number indicates that this particular book does not circulate; it is kept at all times for use in the reference room only. The additional instruction "Ask at reference desk" indicates that this book is one of the most frequently used of the general reference sources, and it is kept behind the librarian's desk rather than in the reference stacks so the student has quick access to it.

A third card with the subject heading "drug abuse" is especially useful to this student because it lists a book about the use of drugs by college and university students in his home state.

```
                    ASK AT REFERENCE DESK
613.83      Drug abuse - Florida.
D7942u      Drug Research Foundation, Inc.
               The usage of drugs by college and
            university students in the State of
            Florida. Submitted to Earl Faircloth,
            Attorney General of the State of
            Florida. Miami, Fla., 1970.
               73, 14p.   21cm.



               1. Drug abuse - Fla.   I. Florida.
            Attorney General.   II. Title.
```

Discussion: The student researching drug abuse notes that the Drug Research Foundation, Inc. is the collective authorship of this book, *The Usage of Drugs by College and University Students in the State of Florida.* Although no mention of amphetamines is made in the title, he may safely assume that a book with this title will contain information about amphetamine abuse, since it is a common form of drug abuse by college students. The student notes another entry at the top of the card directing him to the reference desk for this book. Although the call number does not carry the letter R, it is kept at the reference desk because it circulates so frequently that it often is lost.

Cross Reference Cards: The two types of cross reference cards are the "see" and the "see also" cards. A "see" card is the library's way of telling you that your subject will be found under a classification different from the one you are looking for.

```
Crime detection

    see

Criminal investigation
```

A "see also" card suggests other related subjects that can be investigated.

```
Presidents

    see also

    Executive Power

also names of Presidents
```

"See also" cards are filed after all other cards on the same subject. They are often a help in limiting your subject. Here is an example of a "see also" card found by the drug abuse researcher.

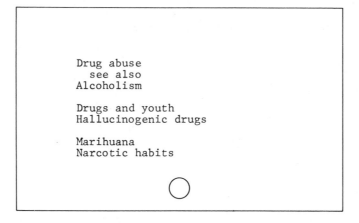

```
Drug abuse
     see also
Alcoholism

Drugs and youth
Hallucinogenic drugs

Marihuana
Narcotic habits
```

At this point the student researching this subject makes bibliography cards for the second and third books, making sure that the call number of each book is on the bibliography card. With these three sources obtained from the card catalog, the student can now get the books from the stacks and determine whether or not they will be helpful by looking at the table of contents. If the specific topic does not appear in the contents, the student can look in the index of the book, which gives more detailed listings, and also take a quick look at the preface, which will usually give the thesis, the scope, and sometimes a summary of the contents of a book. For example, look at the table of contents for the book *Amphetamine Abuse,* edited by J. Robert Russo. The fact that the book is edited indicates that it is probably a collection of essays on a single subject.

CONTENTS

I. Cultural Omen or Contemporary Problem?   3

II. Use, Misuse and Abuse of Amphetamine-Type Drugs   7
from the Medical Viewpoint
Maurice H. Seevers

III. Psychiatric Implication of Amphetamine Abuse   15
John D. Griffith

IV. The Drug Industry and Non-Narcotic Drug Abuse   32
M. C. Russell

Preceding the CONTENTS are pages containing:

1. Contributors (tells about the experts and their qualifications)

2. Preface (gives a summary of the book)

3. Acknowledgments (tells what people, foundations, organizations helped)

Discussion: Skimming the table of contents for the book *Amphetamine Abuse,* the researcher sees that there are nine separate articles on the subject of amphetamine abuse, each written from a different point of view. There is also a summary and a useful appendix. Furthermore, when this student examines the pages preceding the table of contents, he notices that not only is a preface included, but there is also a page of acknowledgements. The acknowledgement page of a book is helpful because it tells what persons, foundations, and organizations were involved in the publication of the book.

For a project as limited as this brief research paper, you will not have the time to do extensive reading; but you will want to look at as many sources as possible to know that you have found the ones most useful for your paper. Therefore, if you do locate a book on your topic and the table of contents indicates that a particular section is pertinent, you may want to use it.

READERS' GUIDE TO PERIODICAL LITERATURE

The Readers' Guide to Periodical Literature indexes by subject (and sometimes by author) the contents of over one hundred magazines. The yearly bound volumes of *Readers' Guide* index articles from March through February every year. If the bound volume for the recent year is not yet in your library, you can still locate very current articles on your topic because the *Readers' Guide* keeps indexing articles all year and publishes them in paperback supplements semimonthly between September and June and monthly between July and August. Once you learn to use the *Readers' Guide* you will be able to use other indexes for specialized fields because the formats of these indexes are the same as the format for *Readers' Guide.*

Reproduced here are excerpts from actual pages in the *Readers' Guide.* In his bibliography search on the subject of drug abuse, the student looks first under the entry "Drugs."

DRUGS
Clearing out old medicines: FDA's list of pro-
    scribed drugs. Time 96:94 D 7 '70
FDA publishes a list; ineffective drugs. Sci N
    98:431 D 5 '70
        See also
Doping in sports
Fertility drugs
Hallucinogenic drugs
Medicines. Patent, proprietary, etc.
Methadone

He notices a "see also" reference to specific categories. If this student had not already decided on the subject of drug abuse among college students, he could have gotten an idea for a topic from one of these references. For instance, "Doping in sports" might be an interesting topic to research. However, since this student is still undecided whether he will pursue amphetamine abuse or hallucinogenic abuse as a specific topic, he decides to look at the category of "Hallucinogenic drugs" to see what is indexed on that topic.

HALLUCINOGENIC drugs
Charlie Manson's home on the range. G.
Talese. il por Esquire 73:101-3+ Mr '70
Deceptions in the illicit drug market. F. E.
Cheek and others. il Science 167:1276 F 27
'70
Drug abuse and social alienation; address,
1970. A. I. Malcolm. il Todays Ed 59:28-31
S '70
Freaked-out spiders. il Newsweek 76:67 Ag
10 '70
Turned-on spiders spin weird webs. il Sci
Digest 67:80-2 Ja '70
See also
Amphetamines
LSD
Mescaline
THC

The articles listed here do not seem pertinent. The student notices, however, a "see also" reference to amphetamines. He notes that there was not a "see also" reference to amphetamines under the general heading of "Drugs." This is an example of why a student must be flexible in tracing subject headings. He now turns back to the As and locates the subject heading "Amphetamines." Under this subject heading he sees five citations for magazine articles. The last three listed appear to be very promising: "Slow Down for Pep Pills," " 'Speed' That Kills or Worse," and "Why Speed Kills." He then makes proper bibliography cards from these citations in *Readers' Guide.* In order to do so, he must understand what the various parts of the citation mean.

AMPHETAMINES
Amphetamine: differentiation by d and l
isomers of behavior involving brain nore-
pinephrine or dopamine. K. M. Taylor and
S. H. Snyder. bibliog il Science 168:1487-9
Je 19 '70
Pep pills for youngsters; treatment of hyper-
active children in Omaha. il U S News 69:
49 Jl 13 '70
Slowdown for pep pills; new restrictions.
Newsweek 76:77 Ag 17 '70
"Speed" that kills, or worse. J. Black. il
N Y Times Mag p 14-15+ Je 21 '70; Same
abr. with title Tempting siren called
"speed." Read Digest 97:153-7 O '70
Why speed kills. Newsweek 76:121 N 16 '70

What do these entries mean? Here is an explanation of the fourth article.

"Speed" that kills or worse is the title of the article.
J. Black is the author of the article.
il is the standard abbreviation which means the article is illustrated.
New York Times Magazine is the name of the periodical containing the article.
p 14–15+ indicates the pages on which the article appears (the + indicates that the article continues beyond page 15 on nonconsecutive pages).
Je 21 '70 is the date of the issue — June 21, 1970.
Same abr. with title Tempting siren called "speed" means that a condensed version of the original article appeared under this title in *Reader's Digest,* Volume 97, pages 153 to 157 in the October 1970 issue.

The student now consults the examples for bibliography forms (page 264) to see how to make a proper bibliography card for a magazine article with an author. The *Readers' Guide* citation converted to bibliography form would look like this:

Black, J. "'Speed' That Kills
or Worse," New York Times
Magazine, June 21, 1970,
pp. 14–28.

The bibliography card for the article "Why Speed Kills," which does not list the author, would look like this:

> *"Why Speed Kills*
> *Newsweek, November*
> *16, 1970, p. 121.*

The drug abuse researcher found these articles in the 1970–1971 volume of *Readers' Guide*. He needs, however, to get as much recent and current information on his topic as possible; therefore, he will consult both bound and paperback editions up through the most current editions in his library. Since he has now decided that the specific topic of "amphetamine abuse" appears most promising to research, he looks in the 1971–1972 volume of *Readers' Guide* and finds the following entry:

AMPHETAMINES

Adrenal release mechanisms. il Sci N 100:106 Ag 14 '71

Amphetamine abuse; report of meeting. E. H. Ellinwood and S. Cohen. Science 171: 420-1 Ja 29 '71

Beware the amphetamines: speed kills. W. Cole. il Parents Mag 46:74-5+ N '71

Crackdown on pep pills. Newsweek 77:77 Je 7 '71

Drugs for children; the Omaha program and resulting political involvement. H. Vinnedge. New Repub 164:13-15 Mr 13 '71; Discussion. 164:28-9 Ap 10; 37-8 Ap 17 '71

How speed kills athletic careers. W. B. Furlong. Todays Health 49:30-3+ F '71

Methamphetamine-induced insulin release. E. M. McMahon and others. bibliog il Science 174:66-8 O 1 '71

Panel sanctions amphetamines for hyperkinetic children. R. J. Bazell. Science 171: 1223 Mr 26 '71

Speed: downhill all the way. M. English. il Look 35:88-9 Je 1 '71

He can now add to his working bibliography by making cards for the following articles:

"Amphetamine Abuse: Report of Meeting"

"Beware the Amphetamines: Speed Kills"

"Methamphetamine-Induced Insulin Release"

"Speed: Downhill All the Way"

Then he consults the 1972–1973 volume and finds the following:

AMPHETAMINES

Amphetamine politics on Capitol hill; passage of Comprehensive drug abuse prevention and control act of 1970. J. M. Graham. il Trans-Action 9:14-16+ Ja '72

Amphetamines reconsidered. L. Grinspoon and P. Hedblon. il Sat R 55:33-41+ Jl 8 '72

Society speed; Dr M. Jacobson's treatment of famous patients. il por Time 100:76-7 D 18 '72

Speed and strokes. il Time 99:44 Ja 31 '72

Story of a Dr Feelgood; Dr M. Jacobson's practice. Il pors Newsweek 80:73-5 D 18 '72

He adds these articles to the bibliography:

"Amphetamines Reconsidered"

"Speed and Strokes"

ASSIGNMENT #1: BEGINNING YOUR PRELIMINARY BIBLIOGRAPHY

Find one useful article from a general encyclopedia, one or two books, and at least four articles from *Readers' Guide* on your subject. Be sure to consult the paperback supplements of *Readers' Guide* so that you locate the most current articles on your subject in periodicals. If you are looking for some history and background on your subject, you can skim through bound volumes of the *Readers' Guide* for as many years back as you care to go. Checking your list of examples for bibliography forms, make proper bibliography cards for each of these sources.

NEWSPAPER INDEXES

New York Times Index: The *New York Times Index* is the major newspaper index and most libraries subscribe to the *New York Times* newspaper on microfilm. The index can be helpful to you in three ways.

First, the *New York Times* is the most comprehensive newspaper in the United States; the index, therefore, can direct you to articles on innumerable subjects.

Second, the *New York Times Index* not only lists articles by subject, but also gives short summaries or abstracts for articles of special importance. These summaries will give you a good idea of what the article is about, and you can eliminate some without having to read the articles themselves on microfilm.

Third, the *New York Times* serves as an index to the reporting of events in other newspapers since international, national, state, and even some local news stories are covered on the same day or during the same period of time.

The yearly bound volumes of the *New York Times Index* list articles from January to January of each year. Supplements to the index come out in paperback twice a month, and the index is usually ready six weeks after the issue of the paper itself. Therefore, the *New York Times Index* is one of your best guides for locating current information on a subject.

Excerpts from actual pages of the *New York Times Index* are reproduced below. First the student researching drug abuse looked under "Drugs." This entry referred to "Drug Addiction and Abuse," which was the heading for a long list of articles. A brief excerpt is reproduced below.

> **DRUG Addiction, Abuse and Traffic. Note:** Material here includes narcotics, stimulants, hallucinatory drugs and others deemed socially undesirable
> **See also** Black Panther Party, N 10 in N 3 par. Blood, Jl 7,19,25, Ag 5, S 5 (for addict blood donors). Bombs, Ap 18. Extortion, Mr 31. Football-Professional, Ap 18 (for use of stimulants). Horse Racing — Harness, S 26 (for alleged use of stimulants, depressants or anesthetics). Horse Racing — Thoroughbred, Ky Derby, D 12 (for alleged use of stimulants, depressants or anesthetics). Prisons —

The entry indicates that all the articles in this section are concerned with narcotics, stimulants, hallucinogens and other drugs deemed socially undesirable. Amphetamines will probably be referred to in any article on drug stimulants. Several index pages further on there is a reference to an article of special interest. The *Times Index* helps the researcher by listing its articles of special interest in boldface print, and any article in boldface is generally followed by a summary.

NY Times survey of drug-abuse problem in Sweden; Sweden regarded as having world's most serious amphetamine problem; has 10,000 to 12,000 addicts, more than any country in Eur; 6,000 are in Stockholdm; heroin has not yet caught on but its use is increasing; addicts are chiefly committed to hypodermic injection of Preludin, legally sold in US as a weight-reducing capsule, and Ritalin, legally prescribed in US as an antidepressant; both drugs removed from Sweden's pharmocoepia and their use is illegal; increasing resort to crime by addicts noted; Govt stresses treatment of addicts rather than arrests; Brit and US drug problems compared; effects of amphetamine injection described; Dr N Bejerot, B Klamm and F Hirschfeldt comment; comment on Dr S E Ahstrom, former believer in maintaining addicts on drugs, who has reptdly prescribed 600,000 drug doses to an avg of 82 legitimate patients a mo; illus, Ap 10, 41:1

Although this article at first glance appears to be concerned only with Sweden's amphetamine problem, a look at the summary tells the student that it would be useful to read the whole article on microfilm. He notes that the article refers to the brand names under which amphetamines are legally sold in the United States. He also notes that doctors comment on the effects of amphetamines, and, most important, the article compares the amphetamine problem in the United States and Britain.

The last line of this entry gives specific location information about the article. It is illustrated and it can be found in the April 10 issue of the *New York Times* on page 41, column 1. You will notice that, unlike the citations in the *Readers' Guide,* the year is not given. You must refer to the cover of the *New York Times Index* for the year, which in this case is 1971. You cannot make the complete bibliography card for this article until you actually see it on microfilm because the exact headline is not given in the citation. The space for the title is left blank and filled in when the article is read on microfilm.

Local Newspapers: Nearly every city newspaper has an index of its own. However, instead of indexing articles in a book, the newspaper maintains a room referred to as the **morgue** or the **library** where articles are classified and filed, often in long envelopes, by names and by subject. These files are available to the public for use in the newspaper's library, along with machines for making photocopies of articles. Newspaper employees attempt to keep these files current, within two weeks of the newspaper's publication. The newspaper library also keeps on microfilm copies of all editions of its newspaper.

If you have narrowed your subject to a local aspect of the problem you plan to explore in your research paper, your local newspaper library will be a valuable source of material.

YEARBOOKS

Statistics and miscellaneous facts about various events and agencies are published annually in several sources. These sources are known as **yearbooks.**

Statistical Abstract of the United States: The *Statistical Abstract,* as it is commonly called, is published by the United States Government and it includes a wide range of subjects. The table of contents of the *Statistical Abstract* is very comprehensive, but if you do not find your particular topic listed there, consult the index, which is even more complete. Reproduced below is an excerpt from the index of the 1972 *Statistical Abstract*:

```
Drug violations .......................... 150,151,156,163
      Addicts............................................  81
      Arrests ...........................................  148
```

The student decides that under "Drug violations" he will check out "addicts." Turning to page 81 he finds the chart reproduced below. It is a good example of the type of statistical table you are likely to find in this source.

These charts often have a notation under the heading which bears directly on the figures given in the tables. For example, under the title of table No. 122 the student notes that the figures here are only on those addicts who have been reported to the Bureau of Narcotics and Dangerous Drugs. This means, of course, that the statistics may not be complete. The student also notes that the statistics are current as of December 31, 1970. Because statistics on this subject are always changing, the student should probably find the most recent ones available in current periodicals. Furthermore, the student notes that this table does not list amphetamines, since it refers only to "narcotics addicts," and amphetamines are not classified as narcotics. Because this is the only compilation of statistics about drug addiction in the *Statistical Abstract,* he will now turn to other statistical reference sources.

No. 122. Reported Narcotics Addicts — Summary: 1953 to 1970

["Addict" defined as a person reported to Bureau of Narcotics and Dangerous Drugs by police or hospital authorities as physically addicted to narcotics use. Average age of active addicts as of Dec. 31, 1970, was 30.6 years.]

ITEM	NEW ADDICTS REPORTED									Active addicts, Dec. 31, 1970[1]
	Annual average, 1953–1970	1963	1964	1965	1966	1967	1968	1969	1970	
Addicts, total____	8,170	7,456	10,012	6,012	6,047	6,417	7,219	14,606	12,201	68,864
Reporting agency:										
Federal _____	1,122	815	870	543	509	515	569	1,186	744	5,382
State _____	1,071	1,525	3,415	788	864	572	955	1,789	1,991	11,252
Local _____	5,977	5,116	5,727	4,681	4,674	5,330	5,695	11,631	9,466	52,230
Race:										
White _____	3,949	3,847	5,258	3,562	3,467	3,585	3,785	7,553	6,813	35,275
Negro _____	4,132	3,538	4,720	2,419	2,559	2,817	3,425	7,008	5,345	33,348
Other _____	89	71	34	31	21	15	9	45	43	241
Age:										
Under 21 years __	1,352	1,037	1,358	1,053	1,150	1,361	1,458	3,380	2,923	5,714
21–30 years ____	4,758	4,139	6,085	3,538	3,640	3,775	4,411	8,476	6,874	35,542
31–40 years ____	1,464	1,712	1,970	1,088	993	1,054	1,069	2,095	1,720	19,311
41 years and over	596	568	599	333	264	227	281	655	684	8,297
Sex:										
Male _____	6,630	5,946	7,850	4,954	4,962	5,342	6,136	12,429	10,343	58,445
Female _____	1,540	1,510	2,162	1,058	1,085	1,075	1,083	2,177	1,858	10,419
Drug used:										
Heroin _____	7,540	6,562	9,166	5,430	5,497	6,009	6,824	14,133	11,706	66,040
Morphine _____	201	188	169	117	138	77	98	101	104	697
Opium _____	29	13	9	2	6	16	20	37	83	173
Dilaudid _____	92	128	94	63	63	83	51	59	28	367
Demerol_____	110	149	174	110	112	104	82	70	52	489
Methadone_____	29	14	12	16	6	11	25	46	75	167
Codeine _____	64	110	120	147	107	70	69	69	49	423
Eucodal _____	16	77	56	44	31	10	9	13	7	87
All other_____	89	215	212	83	87	37	41	78	97	421

[1] 20,596 addicts, originally reported during 1953–1965, remained active during the 5-year period, 1966–1970.
Source: U.S. Bureau of Narcotics and Dangerous Drugs, *Drug Abuse and Law Enforcement Statistics.*

World Almanac and Book of Facts: One of the most useful collections of miscellaneous information is the *World Almanac.* It contains statistics on educational, financial, industrial, religious, and social subjects. In addition, it includes lists of historical events and statistics on political organizations and on society in general. An alphabetized index is at the front of each volume. The *Almanac* is considered a reliable source and is kept up to date.

Facts on File: Indexed twice monthly, this reference is cumulated throughout the year. It is a digest of news classified under such headings as World Affairs, National Affairs, Foreign Affairs, Latin American Affairs, Finance, Economy, Arts, Science, Education, Religion, Sports, and Miscellaneous.

Information Please Almanac: This source classifies miscellaneous information with a subject index. Specialists write the articles about books, sports, theater, movies, music, art, and so on. In addition, there are entries with statistical and historical information about various countries of the world as well as sports records and other general information.

Statesman's Year-Book: This manual is a concise, reliable record of descriptive and statistical information about the governments of the world.

The bibliography entry for any of these yearbook sources is prepared in the same manner as an entry from a general encyclopedia. Had the drug abuse researcher found the chart in *Statistical Abstract* useful, his bibliography card would look like this:

"Reported Narcotics Addicts --
Summary: 1953 to 1970,"
*Statistical Abstract of
the United States* (1972),
p. 81.

ESSAY AND GENERAL LITERATURE INDEX

This reference source is an index to essays and articles published in books. Since you cannot find individual essays by subject listed in the card catalog, you must use the *Essay and General Literature Index* to find information in essays collected in books.

Published once every six months, this index is cumulated in a hard cover volume at the end of each calendar year; and every five years the yearly volumes are bound in a single volume. Not all essays published during a year are indexed, however. Only those appear which the editors consider the most important.

The *Essay and General Literature Index* is divided into two parts. The first part indexes the essays by subject, listing the author and the title of the essay and the book in which it appears. Reproduced below is an example of an entry for the subject of drug abuse.

Drug abuse
    See also Drugs and youth
    Study and teaching — United States
Wald, P. A. M. and Abrams, A. Drug education
   In Dealing with drug abuse p123-72

Under "drug abuse" there is a *see also* reference to "drugs and youth."

    United States
Goldberg, P. B. and DeLong, J. V. Federal expenditures on drug-abuse control
   In Dealing with drug abuse p300-28
Wald, P. A. M. and Hutt, P. B. The Drug Abuse Survey Project: summary of findings, conclusions, and recommendations
   In Dealing with drug abuse p3-61
Drug addiction. See Drug abuse; Narcotic habit
Drug addicts. See Narcotic addicts
Drug habit. See Drug abuse
Drugs

    Physiological effects
DeLong, J. V. The drugs and their effects
   In Dealing with drug abuse p62-122
Weil, A. T. Altered states of consciousness
   In Dealing with drug abuse p329-44
Drugs and youth
Wald, P. A. M. and Abrams, A. Drug education
   In Dealing with drug abuse p123-72

Under "drugs" is a subclassification: "physiological effects." Since this is an important aspect of amphetamine abuse, the student researching this topic studies the entry.

What does this entry mean?

DeLong, J. V. is the author of the essay.
The drugs and their effects is the title of the essay.
In Dealing with drug abuse indicates that the name of the book in which this essay will be found is *Dealing With Drug Abuse.*
p. 62–122 is the inclusive page reference for the essay.
Weil, A. T. is the author of a second essay about the physiological effects of drug abuse.
Altered states of consciousness is the title of the article.
In Dealing with drug abuse indicates that this essay will appear in the same book as the DeLong essay.
p. 329–44 is the inclusive page reference for the Weil essay.

The second part of the *Essay and General Literature Index* lists complete information about the books in which the essays appear. Looking now under the title of the book, the student finds this entry.

> *Dealing* with drug abuse; a report
> to the Ford Foundation; fore-
> word by McGeorge Bundy. The
> Drug Abuse Survey Project:
> Patricia M. Wald [and oth-
> ers]. Praeger 1972
> LC 77-189472

What does this entry mean?

Dealing with drug abuse: a report to the Ford Foundation is the complete title of the book. (It also indicates the authorization for the book.)
The foreword is by McGeorge Bundy.
The Drug Abuse Survey Project: Patricia M. Wald [and others] is the group and the individuals who prepared the book.
Praeger is the publisher.
1972 is the date of publication.
LC 77-189472 is the Library of Congress number for this book.

The student will now have to consult the card catalog or the book itself to find the place of publication so that he can make a complete bibliography card. The bibliography card, which is an example of the form for an essay in an edited collection, will look like this:

```
36.2.2
D794d

De Long, J. V. "The Drugs and
their Effects," in Dealing
With Drug Abuse: A Report
To the Ford Foundation, ed.
Patricia M. Wald and others.
New York: Praeger, 1972.
```

SPECIALIZED ENCYCLOPEDIAS

One of the most useful sources for detailed or technical information on a subject is a specialized encyclopedia. A look in the card catalogue under "Encyclopedias" or a walk around the reference room of a library will show you the wide range of encyclopedias on special fields. Just a few of the many specialized encyclopedias you will find are the *Encyclopedia of American Politics,* the *Encyclopedia of Banking and Finance,* the *Encyclopedia of Cybernetics,* the *Encyclopedia of Education,* the *International Encyclopedia of the Social Sciences,* the *Encyclopedia of Oceanography,* and the *Encyclopedia of Religion and Ethics.*

The student researching amphetamine abuse consulted the *McGraw Hill Encyclopedia of Science and Technology.* The Index volume (a portion shown below) directs him to articles on the subject of amphetamines in volumes 2, 6, 9, 11, and 12. He consults the first volume listed, volume 2, page 163, and finds the entry shown on page 290.

choice of units 1 367
field near a current 1 367
magnetic field 8 30–31;
  11 455
right-hand rule 1 367
Ampère's line integral 8 29
Amperometric titration 10 526;
  13 675–676
Amperometry 14 9
Ampharete 12 170
Ampharetidae 12 169–170
Ampharetinae 12 170
Amphechinus 7 164
Amphetamine 2 163; 6 588; 9 6;
  11 84
  effect on sleep stages 12 427
Amphiarthrosis 7 349, 350

Amphibia 1 59, 368–370*, 416;
  3 95, 572; 13 546; 14 359
adrenal gland 1 94
Aistopoda 1 254*
Anthracosauria 1 497*
Anura 1 530–534*
Apoda 1 538*
appendicular muscles
  8 755–756
Apsidospondyli 1 542*
Australian species 14 717
axial skeleton 12 404–405
buccopharyngeal breathing
  11 555–556
cerebellum 9 66
copulatory organ, anatomy of
  11 494

lonite is often almost completely collapsed by compaction and metamorphism. This altered bentonite swells very little and does not have the usual high colloidal properties of bentonite; it is sometimes called metabentonite.

Beds of bentonite show a variable thickness and can range from a fraction of an inch up to as much as 50 ft thick. The color of bentonite is also variable, but perhaps most often it is yellow or yellowish-green. When observed in the weathered outcrop, bentonite tends to develop a characteristic cellular structure. It shrinks upon drying and often shows a characteristic jigsaw-puzzle set of fractures.

Not all beds of ash in the geologic column have altered to bentonite. When present, bentonite is most frequently found in marine beds; thus, it seems certain that alteration from ash to bentonite is favored in sea water.

In the United States, bentonites are mined extensively in Wyoming, Arizona, and Mississippi. England, Germany, Yugoslavia, the Soviet Union, Algeria, Japan, and Argentina also produce large tonnages of bentonite.

[RALPH E. GRIM; FLOYD M. WAHL]

Benzaldehyde

A colorless, liquid aldehyde, C_5H_5CHO, boiling at 179°C and possessing a characteristic aromatic odor resembling that of bitter almonds. It is produced industrially at the rate of about 5,000,000 lb annually. Principal uses of benzaldehyde are as a flavoring agent and as an intermediate in chemical synthesis. For discussions of chemical properties and methods of manufacture see ALDEHYDE.

[HARRY A. STANSBURY, JR.]

Benzedrine

β-Phenylisopropylamine, $C_6H_5CH_2CH(CH_3)NH_2$, also known as amphetamine. Benzedrine is a liquid which has a boiling point of 203–204°C. This amine is slightly soluble in water, but it reacts with acids to form water-soluble salts, such as the sulfate. Several methods of preparation are possible, all of which utilize phenylacetone as an intermediate.

Benzedrine, when administered as the sulfate salt, produces effects similar to those seen when the sympathetic nervous system is activated. General stimulation of the central nervous system is also obtained with this compound. The principal effects of benzedrine are elevated blood pressure, increased heart action, and relaxation of lung and gastrointestinal musculature. In addition it has a stimulating effect on higher centers, such as the respiratory center, thus making it useful in counteracting the depression caused by disease, other drugs, or poisons. Psychic reactions to the drug vary greatly, depending on the prior mental state, the personality of the patient, and the amount and duration of use. The overuse of this drug is due principally to the mild euphoria it induces. The euphoria is marked by a sense of well-being or even exhilaration, lessened fatigue, increased desire to work, and an increased confidence. The pressor activity of benzedrine resembles that of adrenaline and ephedrine. The compound also is used as a vasoconstrictor for local application in rhinology. See AMINE; CENTRAL NERVOUS SYSTEM (VERTEBRATE); SYMPATHETIC NERVOUS SYSTEM.

[MARVIN YELLES]

He does not find the expected heading "Amphetamine." A scan of the page, however, reveals that the *McGraw Hill Encyclopedia of Science and Technology* uses the heading "Benzedrine," the chemical name for amphetamine. This article, although it is short, gives some very specific information about the physiological and psychic effects of the drug. Some "see" references suggest related information. At the end of the "see" reference is the name of the author of the article, Marvin Yelles. Since the author is given, the student will include his name in the bibliography entry for this source.

Yellis, Marvin. "Benzedrine," McGraw-Hill Encyclopedia of Science and Technology, 2 (1971), 163.

THE VERTICAL FILE

You are now familiar with the basic research sources in any library. There is, however, one more source which you will want to know about. This is the **vertical file.** Many college and city libraries keep a filing cabinet which contains folders of newspaper and magazine clippings and pamphlets and bulletins. These materials are arranged by subject. Some libraries keep a separate vertical file for the articles that pertain to their state. Librarians try to keep the vertical file current, particularly on subjects of great general interest. It is a good idea to end your bibliography search with a look at the vertical file.

ASSIGNMENT #2: COMPLETING THE PRELIMINARY BIBLIOGRAPHY

Add to the bibliography cards you already have by consulting *The New York Times Index,* one or more of the yearbooks, the *Essay and General*

Literature Index, and a specialized encyclopedia. Finally, check the vertical file. Obtain any pamphlets and bulletins related to your topic. You may not be able to find information on your topic in all of these sources, but the careful researcher investigates all of them during the preparation of the preliminary bibliography.

REVIEWING YOUR PRELIMINARY BIBLIOGRAPHY

As you look over your preliminary bibliography, you will see that you have obtained your information from two types of reference sources — direct and indirect. Direct reference sources include general and specialized encyclopedias, yearbooks, general and specialized dictionaries, and the vertical file. They are called **direct sources** because you get your information directly from them. **Indirect sources,** such as the card catalog, the periodical indexes *(Readers' Guide* and *The New York Times Index),* and the *Essay and General Literature Index* are called indirect reference sources because they do not contain the information itself but direct the researcher to the books, magazines, and newspapers where he can find the information.

Once you have learned to use these basic reference sources you will be able to use other important indexes for more advanced research. These indexes on specialized subjects will direct you to specialized publications. Some of the indexes are: *Applied Science and Technology Index, Cumulative Index for Nursing Literature, Education Index, Social Sciences and Humanities Index,* and *Business Periodicals Index.*

STAGE 3

ASSEMBLING THE SOURCEBOOK

1. Determining Whether Sources are Authoritative
2. The Systematic Assembly of the Sourcebook

A sourcebook, sometimes called a casebook, is a collection of information on a particular topic. The sourcebook for your research paper is your collection of photocopied articles, clippings from your own newspapers and magazines, bulletins, pamphlets, and any other pertinent material you have found in your research.

STEP 1 **Determining Whether Sources are Authoritative.**   Before selecting the sources you will actually use from your preliminary bibliography, you need to determine whether those sources are authoritative. Simply because something is in print does not necessarily mean that it is true, that it is accurate, or that it is presented objectively. Suppose, for instance, that you had two pamphlets or bulletins about water pollution in a river in your state. Perhaps a major manufacturing company has been guilty of polluting the river and has put out a pamphlet concerning its efforts to assist in correcting the problem. The pamphlet *may* be informative, but you are more likely to get unbiased and completely objective information from a bulletin or pamphlet issued by a neutral investigating agency or commission.

In addition to judging probable objectivity, you will want to check the date of publication of any source to see how old the information is. You might want to use older sources if you are establishing the history or the progress of a problem, but you will also need current information for investigation of an American social problem.

You begin research by checking encyclopedias first not only because you can get a good overview of a subject, but also because the articles in encyclopedias are written by experts in their fields. Sometimes the article is signed at the end; sometimes only the author's initials appear, and you must refer to the list of initials at the beginning of the volume for the author's name. An unsigned article is written by the research staff.

Books published by university presses are often reliable sources because they are written by individuals or groups which have conducted extensive research. Another way of checking the authoritativeness of a book is to find out what the writer has done in the past and what he is currently doing. For instance, *Crime in America* was written by Ramsey Clark, former attorney general of the United States. Dr. Morris Chafetz, who wrote a book about alcoholism in 1962, is now director of the Department of Health, Education and Welfare's National Institute on Alcohol Abuse and Alcoholism. Biographical references such as those found in the *Who's Who* series can help you to determine an author's background and his qualifications to write on a particular subject.

Articles published in technical and professional journals are more scholarly and often more specific and detailed than those published in magazines for wider audiences. However, since you may be using these less technical magazines for your first research project, you should rely on those periodicals that are considered the most accurate and objective.

STEP 2   **The Systematic Assembly of the Sourcebook.** Now, with your preliminary bibliography assembled and with some understanding of what constitutes authoritative material, you can begin to assemble your sourcebook. This can be done just as systematically as you prepared your bibliography.

1. Select the encyclopedia article that you think is the most informative on your topic and then make a photocopy of it. At the top or on the side of the article, write the complete information about the source which you have obtained from the bibliography card.

2. Next, examine the books for which you have made bibliography cards. If a scan of the introduction and the table of contents of a book indicates that the book is of no use to you, return it to the stacks

and remove the card from your set of preliminary bibliography cards. If, however, you find that several pages or perhaps a chapter of a book is useful, make a photocopy of only those pages you are sure you will use. Identify these materials here as you did the encyclopedia article by transferring the information from the bibliography card.

3. Now go to the periodical reading room of the library. Check out the magazine articles for which you have made bibliography cards. Scan each article rapidly to determine whether it contains information that bears on your topic. Copy only those articles which you are sure that you can use. Identify each article by transferring the information from the bibliography card onto the top or side of the first page of the article. If you are undecided about the usefulness of an article, then annotate the bibliography card and set it aside for the time being. Later, if you decide you need this information, a review of your annotated bibliography cards will remind you where to find it. Now add your copies of magazine articles to the sourcebook.

4. After consulting general encyclopedias, the card catalog, and magazines, then consult the other sources. In the case of the *New York Times,* you will have to read the article on microfilm. Some libraries have microfilm copying machines; if your library does not, you will have to take notes directly from the microfilm. If this is the case, then wait until you have had instruction in note taking before you investigate the *New York Times.*

5. Now follow the same procedure for yearbooks and statistical sources, for the *Essay and General Literature Index,* and for the specialized encyclopedias as you did when you investigated the other sources.

6. Finally, add to your sourcebook any pamphlets, bulletins, newspaper and magazine clippings, and other miscellaneous information you have found on your topic. You are now ready to begin taking notes.

STAGE 4

TAKING NOTES

Note taking is the operation by which you extract from your sources the specific information that develops your topic. Notes are theories, facts, illustrations, and examples about your topic. The information on note cards is to the research paper what the list of proof details is to the theme. It is just as important to be systematic in your note taking as it is to be systematic in the preparation of your bibliography. If you follow the steps to efficient note taking, you will enjoy research; and you will save yourself a great deal of time in the preparation of your final paper.

STEP 1 **Making a Note Card.** Notes are written on index cards. These cards can be three by five inches or four by six inches. Some writers prefer to use larger cards for their notes because it is easier to keep them separate from the three by five inch bibliography cards. Some writers feel that using the smaller cards forces them to carefully digest the information from their sources and consequently to take briefer notes. Whatever size you choose, you will need to observe the rules of note taking.

1. *Enter only one type of information on each card.* You may have as many cards as you wish with as many different types of information as you find pertinent to your topic.

296

2. *Make sure that every note card carries a subject heading which classifies the information on that card.* You do this so that when you are ready to write your outline, you can assemble all the note cards in groups according to their subject headings regardless of what source they came from. To organize your themes, you grouped your proof details by classifying them according to what they had in common. You are grouping your note cards in the same way. If you prepare good note cards with properly classified headings according to the subject matter contained on each card, your outline will practically write itself.

3. *Enter on every note card the source and the exact page reference for the information.* The methods for entering the source are explained in detail in Step 2, The Information on the Note Card.

Following these rules will give you some distinct advantages in preparing your research paper:

a. As you arrange your cards by subject headings and put them in the order in which you will present the information in your paper, you will see that the subject headings form a preliminary outline.

b. As you look over your note cards planning ways to arrange them, you will detect gaps in information in the various categories of discussion. With further research you can make additional note cards and add them to the appropriate category.

c. If you should come across new or additional information on your subject, you need only to enter that information on a note card and add the information under its proper classification.

d. If you decide to rearrange major subject headings or proof details for a more effective order, all you need to do is shift your cards as you see fit. Thus, when your note taking is completed, you will be able to arrange and rearrange the note cards simply by shuffling them rather than by writing outline after outline.

e. Because your source and page number are entered on the note card, you can prepare the footnote without returning to the original source material.

STEP 2   **The Information on the Note Card.**   In addition to understanding the purpose of a note card, you need to understand the kinds of information that are put on note cards, the types of notes, and the parts of a note card.

KINDS OF INFORMATION

A student doing research for the first time often has difficulty taking notes from his sources. He must decide what notes to take and how much of the material to quote directly. If you keep in mind the fact that the notes are to your research paper what the list of proof details is to a theme, you will have a better understanding of what kinds of information to extract from your sources. In other words, you will be gathering evidence in the form of facts, theories, opinions, examples, and illustrations that support your topic.

TYPES OF NOTES

There are three ways to transfer information from an original source to a note card:

1. *The paraphrase.* For a paraphrase you read the original material carefully, select those portions that bear on your topic, and restate them in your own words. Most notes are written in the form of a paraphrase.

2. *The direct quotation.* You already know that a research paper is not a series of quotes strung together with a few conjunctions and transitions. Too much direct quoting suggests to the reader that you have not thought through carefully enough the information that you have gathered in your research. However, there are several very good reasons for using direct quotations in a research paper:

   a. Sometimes the wording is so original or the style is so distinctive that to paraphrase it would be to lose its essential impact. If you decide to quote such a passage, be sure that you take it down on your note card in the exact wording of the original, making sure to put quotation marks around it.

   b. Sometimes the material you come across is of such a technical or scientific nature that paraphrasing it would either distort the meaning or make the meaning unclear. In this case it is best to take the material down on the note card directly as it appears in the original — again making sure to put it in quotation marks.

   c. There are times when you will want to quote a word or a phrase because no synonym exists which would give the exact meaning intended by the author.

   d. Direct quotations from an authority on a topic help to give weight to your own conclusions about it.

e. If your research reveals that there are conflicting theories or conflicting information on a subject, then direct qoutes from representatives of both positions will help to clarify the controversy and will also give objectivity to your discussion of the differences.

3. *The combination note card.* The combination note card contains both paraphrase and direct quotes. As you paraphrase material, you may find it necessary to include a word, a phrase, or a sentence of direct quotation for one or more of the reasons given here.

PARTS OF A NOTE CARD

Every note card must have four types of information on it. The experience of competent researchers is that there are built-in safeguards in recording the information on a note card in the following order:

1. The exact source from which the information comes

2. The specific page on which the information was found

3. One type of information

4. The subject heading which classifies that information

In Step 1, Making a Note Card, you learned the reasons for procedures three and four. It is important for you to understand that the first two items of procedure are also essential because you will have to document (identify the sources of your information) in the footnotes to your paper. There are several ways of recording the source information on a note card. The cards illustrate two of the more commonly used forms.

Subject Heading	1	**Source card number** In the upper right hand corner of the note card, the source from which the information comes is represented by a number. The first source from which you start taking notes will be source #1 and the bibliography card which gives the complete information on the source will accordingly be given the number 1.
	Information	
P.___		

The specific page on which the information was found is placed at the bottom of the card after you have recorded the information.

```
Title of Source            Subject Heading
p. ____



            Information
```

Regardless of the method you use, always check your note card to make sure that it carries the source and the specific page reference before you go on to take another note.

STEP 3 **Restricting the Subject Before Taking Notes.** Once you have your working bibliography and your sourcebook assembled, you are ready to start taking notes. From the overview reading of your selected sources, you have general knowledge about your topic. Before you begin note taking, however, you need to decide on a specific limitation of your topic so that you will not spend time taking unnecessary notes. From preliminary reading the drug abuse researcher discovered that there were at least eight possible limitations of the subject: *history* of drug abuse, *kinds* of drug abuse, *reasons* for drug abuse, *sources* of drugs, *cost* of drug abuse, *effects* of drug abuse, *current situation,* and *treatments available* for drug abusers. Once the topic was limited to *kinds of drug abuse* the student found at least five classifications under this topic: *depressants, stimulants, hallucinogens, hard narcotics,* and *intoxicants.*

This student had tentatively decided to limit his topic to hallucinogens or stimulants. When he came across a number of excellent sources about amphetamines while he was gathering his preliminary bibliography, he decided to limit his topic to amphetamine abuse. However, when he thought through this subject in terms of an analysis chart, he realized that a complete discussion of even so limited a subject as amphetamine abuse would involve all eight of the categories listed above — its history, the reasons for amphetamine abuse, the sources, and so on. Since the majority of the articles he came across explored the reasons that speed kills, he decided to limit his topic to the *effects of amphetamine abuse.* Even this topic, however, was too much to handle in a short research paper because the topic would have to include both the psychological and biological effects of amphetamine abuse. Since he was interested in investigating the lethal effects of speed, which is the slang term for methamphetamime, he decided to limit his research topic to *the long term biological effects of methamphetamine abuse.* At this point serious note taking can begin.

STEP 4   The Process of Note Taking.   Looking over his working bibliography, the speed researcher decides to begin his note taking with an article from *Newsweek* entitled "Why Speed Kills." Taking out the bibliography card for this article, he codes the card in the upper right hand corner with the number one, since this is the first source he is taking notes from, and he has decided to use the number coding system for his source (bibliography) cards. Here is the bibliography card:

1	Source card number
"Why Speed Kills," Newsweek, November 16, 1970, p. 121.	Title of article (no author given) Name of publication and date No inclusive page reference because this is a one page article.
Tells about artery disease caused by speed.	Annotation

He now begins to take notes from his copy of the article, which is reprinted here.

"Why Speed Kills"

"Speed kills" has become a favorite shibboleth among those who fear the burgeoning drug culture, and last week, a team of Los Angeles doctors presented shocking new evidence why the slogan should be taken seriously. Methamphetamine, they report in the current issue of the *New England Journal of Medicine,* may cause a serious and potentially lethal disease of the arteries.

The disease is called necrotizing angiitis, and Dr. Phillip B. Citron and his colleagues at the Los Angeles County–University of Southern California Medical Center have diagnosed it in fourteen heavy drug users. Typically, the disorder involves a progressive inflamation of the medium and small arteries throughout the body, and a common result is permanent damage to the kidneys, intestines, liver, and pancreas. In five cases the disease proved fatal.

Most of the patients, who included six women and eight men, had used a wide range of drugs, from hashish to LSD, but methamphetamine appeared to be a common denominator and the most likely cause of angiitis.

In view of the rising use of methamphetamine, the California investigators fear that speed-induced angiitis may become a national health problem among drug users. Indeed, new cases are turning up at Los Angeles County Hospital, Citron notes, at the rate of one a week.

From the article "Why Speed Kills" the student took these notes.

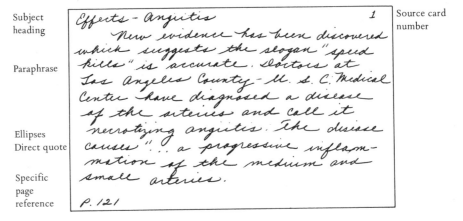

An omission within a direct quote is indicated by ellipses (three spaced periods). For complete information about ellipses, see page 392.

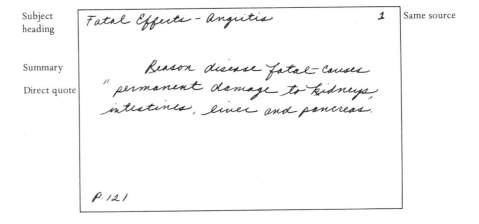

Notes can be taken in abbreviated or shortened forms because full sentences can be developed when writing the paper. The main point is that notes should be accurate and complete enough so that you can make sense of them when you are ready to write.

The organs affected are stated in direct quotation because there is no way to effectively paraphrase this medical information.

New subject heading — *Statistics - Angiitis* — 1 — Same source

Summary — 14 heavy drug users diagnosed L. A. County Hosp. - 5 died.

Citing the authority — One new case a week turns up at L. A. County Hospital, according to Dr. Philip B. Citron, spokesman for the research team.

P. 121

New subtopic heading — *Statistics - future angiitis* — 1 — Same source

Direct quote / Ellipses — "In view of the rising use of meth-amphetamine . . . speed-induced angiitis may become a national health problem among drug users.

(note: these figures are from only one study at one County hospital, and Calif. is a trend setter.)

P. 121

At the bottom of his note, the student reminds himself to elaborate on the possibility of a national health problem. (1) These facts are likely to be represented in other areas of the nation. (2) He may want to check further — perhaps at a large city hospital in his own area.

Having transferred to his note cards the essential information from his first source, the speed researcher now moves to another source. He keys the bibliography card to his note card with the number 2 since this is the second source from which he is taking notes. Here is his second source card:

2	Source card number
Black, Jonathan. "Speed' That Kills -- or Worse," New York Times Magazine, June 20, 1970, pp. 14-28.	Author's name Title of article Name of publication Publication date Inclusive page reference
Explains hepatitis, amphet. psychosis, metabolic cannibalism	Annotation

One page of the article " 'Speed' That Kills . . . or Worse" is reprinted on page 305.

Because the student had his own photocopy of this article, he was able to annotate its contents in the margins. This kind of analytical reading can save you from taking more notes than necessary. Before beginning note taking, however, you should understand what plagiarism is and how to avoid it.

PLAGIARISM

Often the student who is taking notes for the first time from original material tends to borrow heavily from the sources. When a writer uses another person's writings without rewording the information, that is plagiarizing. Student researchers may do this unintentionally because they lack experience in note taking. Sometimes the plagiarized material is evident because the researcher lifted the original material almost in its entirety. In other cases, the plagiarized material is more subtle because the researcher changed the order of sentences and kept only a few of the original phrases.

(Continued from Page 18)
state of intense irritability or despair. To avoid it, the speeder may take some "downs" in an effort to sleep — or take more speed. This solution can lead to typical runs of from several days on up to one or two weeks. During that period it is impossible to sleep or eat — food literally cannot be swallowed — and speed's cannibalism of the body begins: "I knew I was dying," one speeder recalls. "My tongue was shredded, my lips were cracked, the whole inside of my mouth was eaten out. My skin was itching all over, my fingernails were flaking off, and my hair and teeth seemed to be falling out."

"Speed is a hundred times more dangerous than heroin," says one amphetamine researcher at Rockefeller Uni-

"Speed is still not a ghetto drug and probably will never be. Heroin makes the junkie oblivious to rats and roaches and garbage; speed only makes him acutely aware of his surroundings."

versity. "A lifetime intravenous drip of pure heroin would produce no medical damage." But speed knocks out the body's defenses by pushing it beyond the limits of endurance with hyperactivity while depriving it of rest and nourishment. Common speed damage includes colds, infections, muscle tremors, cardiac problems, nausea, cramps, respiratory difficulties and hepatitis — the last not only a frequent result of using unsterile needles but probably stemming in part from the toxicity of Methedrine itself. Malnutrition symptoms appear without exception, and there is a high incidence of minor accidents: cuts, scratches, sprains and bruises.

Besides the physical destruction, there is the psychic damage. Although amphetamines provide a brief glow of potency and confidence, the other end of the seesaw is nothingness:

"I make lots of plans, but I don't ever carry any of them out," says one speed freak. "I get into this megalomaniac bag about five hours into speed, and I'll build these mountainous castles in my mind, all the far-out things I'm going to do, and all the money I'm going to make. I'll be driving a Rolls-Royce and have two speed labs going at once, a heroin refining plant, my own private two-engine plane. I'll be running the Mafia. And when I start to come down I realize that none of it is going to exist and it's like someone pulled the bottom out of your brain. I feel empty and suicidal in about four or five hours."

HEAVY speeding invariably produces two psychic nightmares: hallucinations and paranoia. The hallucinations go beyond gentle spiritual probes

Notice the differences in the paraphrased note card on page 307 and the two plagiarized note cards which appear below. The original material comes from page 22 of the article " 'Speed' That Kills — or Worse" reprinted on page 305.

OBVIOUS PLAGIARISM

> Met. Cannibalism, Cont.   2
>
> The speeder takes some "downs" so that he can sleep. Sometimes this leads to typical runs from several days to one or two weeks, and in this period the speeder finds it impossible to sleep or eat and literally impossible to swallow food.
>
> p. 22

Here the student follows nearly the same phrasing and the exact sentence structure of the original material. He eliminates a word here and there and substitutes the phrase "literally impossible to swallow food" for the original "food literally cannot be swallowed." Although he will footnote the information, he has still been trapped into the act of plagiarism because he has not expressed the information in his own words.

Now look at this note card:

> Met. Cannibalism, Cont.   2
>
> A run of from several days to one or two weeks follows the speeder's effort to get some sleep. He also finds that the speed's cannibalism of the body begins, for he finds it difficult to swallow his food, thus impossible to eat. He also finds it difficult to sleep and in an effort to sleep he may take some "downs."
>
> p. 22

Although the student did not follow the sentence structure of the original, he has plagiarized because he has used the same phrasing as the original. All the student has done is to rearrange the material; he has not reworded it. Compare the original text with this note card. Phrases such as "a run of from several days . . . to one or two weeks," "effort . . . to sleep," "speed's cannibalism of the body," "impossible to . . . eat," and "may take some 'downs'" are still the exact wording of author Jonathan Black.

A good practice for you to follow while you are taking notes is to read the original material carefully and then to look away from that material when you write your note card. In this way there is less chance of plagiarizing. However, if you wish to use the exact phrasing, then you must enclose that material in quotation marks so that you will remember to do so when you use the information from that note card in your own paper.

SUITABLE NOTE CARDS

Observe how the student using the same material avoids plagiarism. Here are the notes this student took from the second source. Notice that the information about metabolic cannibalism runs over to a second note card. If you have a long note, it is better to continue it on a second card rather than to write on the back of a card. When you use the cards to write the final paper, you will find that flipping cards over is awkward, and it is also possible to omit information that is on the other side.

New subject heading	*Effects – Metabolic Cannibalism* 2	Source card number
	Rockefeller Univ. researcher made startling comment. "Speed is a hundred times more lethal than heroin. A lifetime intravenous drip of pure heroin would produce no medical damage."	
Direct quote		
	(use in intro.?)	
Specific page reference	p. 22	

Subject heading continued	*Met. Cannibalism, cont'd* 2
Paraphrase	*A speed run, which lasts from several days to two weeks, speeds up the body's metabolism.*
Quote	*A speeder doesn't eat or sleep so his system is pushed "beyond the limits of endurance with hyperactivity."*
	p. 22

The term "metabolic cannibalism" was used on an earlier page in this article. The student now picks up the term and explains its process from the information found on page 22. Notice that only part of a quotation is used, but no ellipses are necessary because the quotation completes an integral part of the writer's sentence.

	Effects – suicide 2
	1) Occasional suicide from deep depression while "crashing." (p. 22)
Brackets to indicate writer's addition within quote	*2) "They [speed freaks] do commit suicide." Amphetamine-induced psychosis drives them to bizarre and distructive behavior.*
	(p. 18)
	pp. 18, 22

Suicide from "crash" depression and amphetamine-induced psychosis is discussed on several pages of this article. The student combines the information into one note with the same subject heading, at the same time noting the several page references.

These are the note cards from the first two sources the amphetamine researcher studied. However, as the student worked through his bibliography cards he found articles which discussed still other lethal effects of speed. One article described a speed-induced syndrome which resembled insulin shock and another article discussed the relationship between speed and strokes. This student already has the major inference for his thesis statement: *Speed kills*. With the additional information he has gathered after he completes note taking, he can complete his thesis.

STEP 5   **Stating the Preliminary Thesis.**   Using the information he has found during his note taking, the student can now complete his analysis chart and state the thesis. If he put the chart on paper, it would look like this:

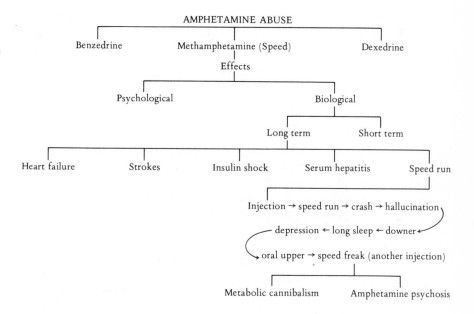

Thesis statement: The long term use of injected methamphetamine is lethal because it can cause heart failure, strokes, insulin shock, and serum hepatitis. It also induces a "speed cycle" which results in metabolic cannibalism and in amphetamine psychosis which may even trigger suicide.

STEP 6   **Setting up the Preliminary Outline.**   The researcher is now ready to set up a preliminary outline. In a short paper this outline is constructed directly from the minor inferences of the thesis. In a longer paper, such as this research paper, you will find that there may be several types of information you would like to present to your reader before you develop the minor inferences of the thesis. For example, you may feel that the reader needs a good working definition of your topic or of several key terms connected with the topic. You may decide that a brief history of the problem you are discussing would be relevant. You may also decide that you want to impress the reader with the seriousness of your topic as an American social problem by a discussion of the extent of the problem. Certainly you will want to conclude the paper with some possible solutions to the problem — those suggested by experts and those you propose from your own conclusions based on your research. Here is the way the researcher set up his preliminary outline:

```
(Temporary title) SPEED KILLS

Thesis statement: The long term use of injected
methamphetamine is lethal because it can cause
heart failure, strokes, insulin shock, and serum
hepatitis.  It also induces a "speed cycle"
which results in metabolic cannibalism and in
amphetamine psychosis which may even trigger
suicide.

    I. Extended definition of methamphetamine
       abuse
       (Discuss difference between amphetamines
       and methamphetamines, their chemical
       makeup, generic and trade names, slang
       terms, physiological vs. psychological
       dependency, etc.)
   II. Extent of problem
       (Discuss who abuses the drug -- their sex,
       age, occupation; the sources -- legitimate
       and street markets; problem in U.S.
       compared to that in other countries;
       estimates of number of people involved in
       abuse.)

  III. Heart failure

   IV. Strokes

    V. Insulin Shock
```

```
   VI. Serum hepatitis

  VII. Metabolic cannibalism

 VIII. Amphetamine psychosis -- suicide
```

Concluding statement: The slogan "speed kills" is not to be discounted as a mere scare tactic on the part of those who wage campaigns against drug abuse.

EXERCISE 4-1: PRACTICING NOTE TAKING

Unemployment in many fields continues to be a problem in the United States. In spite of strict government restrictions, discrimination because of age contributes to the problem. Assume that you are writing your research paper on age discrimination in employment and that you are taking notes from your first source, which is an article about job prospects for those over age forty-five. The article is reprinted here.

Fort Lauderdale News and Sun-Sentinel, Sunday, March 24, 1974 16E

45-Year-Olds' Job Prospects Looking Bleak

By JACK HOUSTON
Chicago Tribune

After devoting 32 years to the company, George Johnson, 52, was asked to resign. For more than a year he has been job hunting.

Some interviewers claim he is "overqualified." Most say, bluntly, that he is too old.

The outlook remains bleak, as it does for the thousands over 45 left unemployed each year. Some, like Johnson, have years of business-oriented experience; others, only the desire to work.

Yet, despite strict government restrictions against age discrimination, older workers continually are confronted with the same bias: they are too old to do an employer any good.

Last year the Department of Labor found 1,836 employers, employment agencies, and unions violating the Age Discrimination in Employment Act of 1967 in their help wanted advertisements.

In addition, nearly 15,000 workers aged 40 through 65 were victimized by illegal hiring, firing, job referral, and other prohibitions of the Act.

Not everyone is convinced, though, that age discrimination is much of a problem today. Lon D. Barton, president of Cadillac Associates, an employment agency specializing in executive placement, calls such bias, "almost a thing of the past."

"Though most companies actually never practiced age discrimination, they have placed heavy weight on youth in making a hiring decision. That's changed now," Barton said.

"It used to be that the sure way to fill a position was to send an eager 25-year-old out for an interview. Today companies seem to be looking for a mature 40-year-old."

Johnson wishes he could tell a similar story.

George Johnson is not his real name. He contacted this reporter late last year after reading another story about how it feels to be unemployed.

"The subject has occupied all of my time, effort, and attention for the last 12 months," he said.

"I sincerely believe that I contributed more to divisional growth and profitability than any single individual. Then I was asked to resign. I no longer satisfied the youthful image the company was attempting to forge.

"I, and many others, fell victim to indecisive management — a management that was unable to relate to business problems other than by a change of personnel."

Johnson admits he lacks sufficient evidence that there was a program to remove middle-management that no longer fit the youthful image. Neither does he care to quarrel with such a concept.

"I do deplore, however, the despicable practice of dismissing long-term employes at an age where it is almost impossible to relocate and with nothing more than a measly amount, sufficient only to keep one off the unemployment rolls."

Barton said his agency is continually finding companies that will consider 50-year-old executives for top jobs — an admitted change from previous practice.

"It used to be almost impossible to place men or women in their late 40s or 50s — even though many of them were willing to take cuts in pay," he said.

Barton explained the change this way: During the last recession many firms cut back heavily. One of the first things to go were training programs. Instead, companies temporarily ignored building for the future and concentrated on the present.

As a result, a genuine shortage of young executive talent developed.

"This shortage will continue because many training programs haven't been reinstituted," Barton said. "Companies want proven performers rather than potential superstars." Therefore, they are hiring more experienced — and older — executives.

Barton added that one big reason firms avoided older executives has been discarded: the old approach was to hire a young person you could count on for a 30-year career rather than someone with only a decade left.

"Fortunately, companies have realized that executive mobility is not a passing fad. No company is going to keep their young executives for 30 years — four or five is more like it.

A. Make a proper bibliography card for this article and key it as source #1. Complete the first three note cards with information which relates to the subject heading on each card and which corresponds to the type of note specified.

B. Now you are on your own. Finish taking notes from the article by completing the next four blank note cards, making sure that each carries the four essential parts of a note card. Under each card, indicate the type of note you have taken (paraphrase, direct quote, or combination).

Exercise 4-1A: Practicing Note Taking

Note card (Paraphrase)

Statistics--Help wanted ads
violation

Note Card (Combination: Quote and Paraphrase)

Statistics--Victimized Workers

Bibliography Card

Note Card (Direct Quote)

Contrary Opinion

Exercise 4-1B

Type of note:

Type of note:

Type of note:

Type of note:

STAGE 5

PREPARATION: TAKING AND USING YOUR OWN NOTES

1. Correct Footnote Form
2. Preliminary Writing

You are now ready to take notes from your own sources. In order to better understand the relation between your note taking and the actual writing of your paper, three very short papers will be written as your note taking continues. The papers will be drawn from different types of sources and will make use of different types of development for expository writing. This advance preparation has several distinct advantages:

1. You will understand how a writer comes to eliminate some notes, how related notes are combined, and how the wording of the notes is often changed as the paper is written.

2. You will gain practice in the preparation of the various forms of footnotes which give credit to your sources.

3. You will have an opportunity to review the several types of expository development and to see how they are combined and used in a longer paper.

4. You will also see whether there are any gaps in your note taking. If there are, this will be the time to review the cards you had set aside from your preliminary bibliography. If you cannot use any of the sources listed on these cards, then you will need to get other sources, add them to your working bibliography, and do further note taking.

These short papers will not necessarily be used in the order you write them, nor will they be used in their entirety. However, you will certainly be able to transfer a great deal of this writing to the developmental paragraphs of your final paper.

STEP 1   **Correct Footnote Style.**   Acceptable footnote styles for the bibliography entries on pages 261–5 are shown below.

FOOTNOTE FORMS

Notice that a footnote for a book differs from the bibliography form in six ways:

1. Footnote form for a book with one author:

[1]Ramsey Clark, *Crime in America* (New York: Simon and Schuster, 1970), p. 33.

Bibliography form for this book:

Clark, Ramsey. *Crime in America.* New York: Simon and Schuster, 1970.

The differences:

FOOTNOTE FORM	BIBLIOGRAPHY FORM
1. The footnote is indented five spaces from the margin. If the footnote runs beyond one line, other lines are flush with the left margin.	1. The bibliography entry begins flush with the left margin. If the entry runs beyond one line, other lines are indented five spaces.
2. The footnote carries an Arabic numeral, called an index number or superscript number. It corresponds with the footnote number in the text of the paper.	2. The bibliography entry, which appears alphabetically on the bibliography page, carries no index numeral.
3. The author's first name is first.	3. The author's last name comes first.
4. A comma follows the author's name. No punctuation follows the title of the book because the next item is enclosed in parentheses.	4. A period follows the author's name. A period follows the title of the book.
5. Publication information is enclosed within parentheses.	5. Publication information is not enclosed within parentheses.
6. The page reference in the footnote indicates the page(s) where the information was found.	6. The bibliography entry for a book does not give the page references.

2. A book with two authors

[2] Morris E. Chafetz, M.D., and Harold Devone, Jr., *Alcoholism and Society,* 4th ed. (New York: Oxford University Press, Inc., 1962), p. 112.

3. A book with three authors

[3] Robert Lee Sutherland, Julian Woodward, and Milton A. Maxwell, *Introductory Sociology,* 6th ed. (Chicago: Lippincott, 1961), p. 72.

4. An edited book

[4] Leo Hamalian and Frederick R. Karl, eds., *The Radical Vision: Essays for the Seventies* (New York: Thomas Y. Crowell Company, 1970), p. xii.

The page reference in lower case Roman numerals indicates that the writer is citing material from the introduction.

5. A book with corporate authorship

[5] National Institute on Amphetamine Abuse, *Amphetamine Abuse,* ed. J. Robert Russo (Springfield, Ill.: Thomas, 1968), p. 66.

6. An essay in an edited collection

[6] Lynn White, Jr., "The Historical Roots of Our Ecologic Crisis," in *The Radical Vision: Essays for the Seventies,* ed. Leo Hamalian and Frederick R. Karl (New York: Thomas Y. Crowell Company, 1970), p. 456.

7. A translated book

[7] Jean Francois Revel, *Without Marx or Jesus: The New American Revolution Has Begun,* trans. J. F. Bernard (Garden City, N.Y.: Doubleday, 1971), p. 31.

8. A work of several volumes

[8] Arthur Wallace Calhoun, *A Social History of the American Family* (New York: Barnes and Noble, 1960), II, 221–222.

The writer is citing the second volume of a three volume work. Because the volume number is given, the pp. for "pages" is dropped.

9. A book that is one of several volumes in a series

[9] Robert H. Ferrell, *George C. Marshall,* in *The American Secretaries of State and Their Diplomacy,* ed. Robert H. Ferrell, XV (New York: Cooper Square Publishers, 1966), 127.

In this series, the first ten volumes were edited by Samuel Flagg Bemis, as indicated in the bibliography entry for this source. Subsequent volumes were edited by Ferrell. Since the volumes were published in different years, the volume number precedes the facts of publication.

10. The Bible

[10] Corinthians: ii. 14.

ENCYCLOPEDIAS AND YEARBOOKS

11. A signed encyclopedia article

[11] Mary S. Calderone, "Sex Education," *Encyclopedia Americana,* 24 (1969), 629–629b.

12. An unsigned encyclopedia article

[12] "Early Childhood Education: Overview," *The Encyclopedia of Education,* 3 (1971), 146.

13. Statistical Abstract

[13] "Marital Status by Sex and Age," *Statistical Abstract of the United States,* 92 (1971), 32.

14. Yearbooks

[14] "The Energy Crisis: Gasoline Shortage," *Facts on File,* 1974, p. 122.

PERIODICALS

15. An unsigned magazine article

[15] "Cities Suffocating in Trash: Crisis in Five Years," *Conservation News,* 38 (July 1973), 2.

The volume number is given and the monthly publication date is enclosed

*in parentheses followed by a comma and specific page reference without p.
for "page."*

¹⁵ "New Weapons Against Shoplifting," *U. S. News and World
Report,* February 14, 1972, p. 71.

*The volume number is omitted for weekly periodicals, and p. for "page"
precedes the specific page reference.*

16. A signed magazine article

¹⁶ Glenda Daniel, "Child Abusers: Parents Anonymous,"
PTA Magazine, 68 (September 1973), 34.

17. An unsigned newspaper article

¹⁷ "Radioactive Waste Storage Is Nuclear Age Problem,"
Miami Herald, December 3, 1973, sec. C, p. 1.

18. A signed newspaper article

¹⁸ Sandra Blakeslee, "Study Doubts That Smoking Causes
Smaller Babies," *New York Times,* January 15, 1972, sec. 7,
p. 15.

The author's name is followed by a comma.
The title of the article is followed by a comma.

MISCELLANEOUS SOURCES

19. Public documents

¹⁹ U.S. Department of Transportation, *Transportation Noise
and Its Control* (Washington, D.C.: U.S. Government Printing
Office, June 1972), p. 32.

20. Bulletins

²⁰ National   Tuberculosis   and   Respiratory   Association,"
NTRDA Bulletin (New York, 1972), p. 2.

21. Pamphlets

²¹ Committee on Aging: Council on Medical Service, *Health
Aspects of Aging,* The American Medical Association (Chicago,
[n.d.]), p. 17.

22. **Interviews**

[22] James Davis, Chairman, Oriole County Housing Authority, Gaston, Georgia, Personal Interview on Housing for the Aged, December 29, 1973.

or

[22] Interview with James Davis, Chairman, Oriole County Housing Authority, Gaston, Georgia, December 29, 1973.

23. **Television or radio program**

[23] "The Scene Tonight," ABC telecast on the problems of the aged, April 30, 1974: "Momma Lives on Miami Beach." Narrator, Clarence Jones.

These are the basic footnote forms. You will need to know five other particulars about footnotes before you begin to write them: (1) what to footnote, (2) how to number footnotes, (3) how to place and space footnotes, (4) how to footnote a source when you have already given full information about it in a previous footnote, (5) other kinds of footnotes.

1. WHAT TO FOOTNOTE

Understanding why you footnote is the first step in understanding what to footnote. There are two primary reasons for footnoting. The first is to give full credit to your sources — to let the reader know that the information you have presented was not original with you. The second reason is to give your reader an opportunity to follow up your sources if he wishes to find out more about your topic. If you use another person's ideas, information, or wording without giving credit, you are plagiarizing. The following types of information must be documented with footnotes:

a. Direct quotations
b. Paraphrases of opinions, facts, and conclusions that belong to others
c. Statistics
d. Charts, photographs, diagrams, tables, and other graphic devices prepared by others as well as any graphic illustrations you have prepared from information provided by others
e. Information obtained through interviews or letters

You do not need to give credit for information that is considered general knowledge. Beginning researchers are often uncertain about what can be considered general knowledge. Consider whether your reader would be likely to know a particular kind of information if you are in doubt about whether to footnote it. Would the reader have known it from general education, from observation, or from the media? If so, do not footnote it. If you are in doubt, it is wise to footnote the information. Another guideline is, did you know this information prior to researching your topic? If not, you would do best to footnote it. However, if a piece of information occurs again and again in your sources, you can assume that it is common or general knowledge even though you may not have known it at the beginning of your project. For example, if you were researching the subject of child abuse, you would find that it was originally given the name "the child battering syndrome." You may not have known this, but most articles and books on the subject mention it, and a mature reader is likely to know it. Hence, this is general knowledge and need not be footnoted. It is also fairly well known that the abused child is most often under three years of age. You may decide that one fact which is not common knowledge and which surprises many people is that those who have themselves been abused as children often become abusing parents. This fact you would footnote.

2. HOW TO NUMBER FOOTNOTES

a. In the text

Use Arabic numerals sequentially throughout the text of your paper.

Raise the numeral one-half line.

Place the footnote number after the final punctuation in a sentence.

b. The footnotes

Number the footnotes themselves sequentially to correspond to the footnote numbers in the text.

3. HOW TO PLACE AND SPACE FOOTNOTES

a. You can place footnotes at the bottom of each page of the text of your paper. If a page has three footnote index numerals, then the three footnotes which document the information will appear at the bottom of that page. Do not carry a footnote over from one page to the other.

If you place footnotes at the bottom of the page, separate them from the text by an eight to fifteen space bar line one double space below the last line of your text, beginning at the left margin.

Begin the first footnote a double space below this bar line.

Single space within each footnote but double space between footnotes.

(b.) You can collect your footnotes in numerical order and place them on a separate page at the end of your paper just before the bibliography page.

Use the raised index numeral and space the footnotes in the same manner as if you were placing them at the bottom of each page. Many writers prefer this method as it simplifies the typing of the paper.

4. HOW TO FOOTNOTE SOURCES PREVIOUSLY CITED IN FULL

Once you have provided full reference information for a source, subsequent footnotes referring to that source may be shortened. Modern documentation practice favors the use of the author's last name followed by a comma and the specific page reference. In the absence of an author, you can use an abbreviated or shortened title followed by the specific page reference. These subsequent citation forms are used instead of the Latin abbreviation *Ibid.* (in the same place), *op. cit.* (in the work cited), and *loc. cit.* (in the place cited). Here is an example of a complete initial reference and a subsequent citation of the same work:

[1] Jim Davis, "Teacher, Students: A Redefined Liaison," *Fort Lauderdale News,* April 24, 1974, p. 1C.

[2] Davis, p. 7C.

If you have more than one book or article by the same author, then add a shortened version of the title after the author's last name. The student using these citations was drawing from a series of articles written by Mr. Davis. The second article was footnoted as follows:

[3] Jim Davis, "How Students See Teachers," *Fort Lauderdale News,* April 25, 1974, p. 4B.

[4] Davis, "Students See Teachers, p. 1B.

If you have material from two authors with the same last name, then in the shortened citations you would give the first initial and the author's last name — for example, J. Davis and M. Davis.

5. OTHER KINDS OF FOOTNOTES

The footnotes discussed above are known as **reference** footnotes. There is another kind of footnote, however, known as an **explanatory** or **content** footnote. You may find that the occasion arises where you have material which is related but not directly pertinent to a point being discussed. If you think the reader would profit by having this additional information, you can discuss it in a brief explanatory footnote. Here is an example:

---

[6] The *clinical teaching* approach to remediating learning disabilities has been developed by Myklebust and Johnson over a period of fifteen years at the Institute for Language Disorders at Northwestern University.

Now examine the student model research paper "Indian Education" on pages 326–327 to see how this student handled footnotes in her paper.

STEP 2   Preliminary Writing.   You are now ready to begin to take notes and to write the short papers which will be the basis of your research paper.

PRELIMINARY WRITING ASSIGNMENT 1: DEFINING YOUR TOPIC

Review Extended Definition (Part I, Stage 8). From your sourcebook, select the articles you have photocopied from the general and specialized encyclopedias. Take notes from these sources.

After you have taken notes, write a short paper of extended definition on your topic. In some cases a topic will be only one word — "Alcoholism," "Dyslexia," "Recession." More often than not, the topic for a social problem will be more than one word. Examples of such topics are "Invasion of Privacy," "Migrant Housing," "Women's Liberation," "Learning Disabilities," "The Problem Drinker."

Work out a formal sentence definition of your term, and then extend the definition in as many ways as you think necessary so that your reader will fully understand the term.

Document this short paper with appropriate footnotes. Following is an example of one student's extended definition. Her topic is "Euthanasia."

EUTHANASIA: THE GENTLE DEATH

The subject of euthanasia has been controversial throughout history. Euthanasia is the act of putting to death any person suffering an agonizing, incurable disease or condition. The word comes from two Greek words, eu meaning "well" and thanatos, meaning "death." The concept of euthanasia came about because while death is usually feared by most people, when circumstances become intolerable, a painless death is sometimes preferable to a life filled with useless suffering and continual physical deterioration. Euthanasia is regarded as a crime in the United States; however, in other times and in other countries, it was not regarded as a crime. In ancient Greece, Plato in his Republic and Aristotle in his Politics endorsed euthanasia, or mercy killing as it is more commonly known today.

Distortions of the pure motivation for euthanasia -- to eliminate suffering -- appeared almost as soon as the concept of euthanasia. For example, infanticide was widely practiced in Sparta as a method of eliminating defective children who would impede the efficient operation of the state.[1] Societies soon began to eliminate old people when they became infirm and could no longer be productive citizens and care for themselves. In ancient Sardinia, for instance, old men were clubbed to death by their own sons, and in India it was common to throw old people in the Ganges. In the twentieth century, Adolph Hitler's Third Reich established compulsory euthanasia clinics where government appointed examining boards determined who would live and who would die. Under this compulsory euthanasia program, hundreds of thousands of people alleged to be suffering from incurable diseases were put to death because they were unable to lead productive lives.[2] More accurately, they were unable to fit into the Third Reich program.

----

[1] Carl E. Wasmuth, M. D., "Euthanasia," Encyclopedia Americana, 10 (1974), 712.

[2] "Euthanasia," Americana, p. 712.

Although the motivation for euthanasia is a merciful one, the practice raises complicated ethical, medical, and legal objections. Most Christian religions hold that a death other than a natural one is a violation of the Sixth Commandment, which prohibits murder. St. Thomas Aquinas described euthanasia as a "usurpation of the Creator's power over life and death."[3] Many medical men feel that "social surgery" is a violation of the Hippocratic Oath, which holds that the physician's duty is to relieve suffering and prolong and protect life. With the founding of the Voluntary Euthanasia Legislation Society in England by C. Killick Millard, an organized movement for legalization began in 1932.[4] There are now a number of euthanasia societies in this country as well; they too are working to legalize euthanasia. Although all proposals contain direct provisions for safeguarding against murder, legislators have failed to pass any of the proposed bills.[5] Thus, it is clearly apparent why this "gentle death" is so controversial; for while life can become intolerable, no one can guarantee that abuses will not occur or that death holds a better alternative.

---

[3] H. J. Rose, "Euthanasia," Encyclopedia of Religion and Ethics, 5 (1960), 600.

[4] "Euthanasia," Encyclopaedia Britannica, VIII (1964), 894

[5] "Euthanasia," Black's Medical Dictionary, 1971, p. 334.

Notice the statements in this short paper that do not need foot-notes:

1. The etymology, which can be checked in any dictionary.

2. The mention of euthanasia by Plato and Aristotle, which most articles on the subject mention and which is known by most educated people.

3. The prohibition against murder in the Sixth Commandment, which is general knowledge.

4. The main idea of the Hippocratic Oath, which is also general knowledge.

Notice that while the information for footnote 1 and footnote 2 comes from the same source and the same page, it cannot be cited in one footnote because the writer's own comment about the elimination of the aged and infirm comes in between. If this comment had not intervened and the student had given two or three pieces of information in successive sentences from the same source, one footnote would suffice.

PRELIMINARY WRITING ASSIGNMENT 2: ENUMERATING DATA

Select from your sourcebook your statistical and yearbook sources and take notes on them. Statistics indicate just how widespread a particular problem is. For example, both child abuse and rape are found in almost every community and among every class of Americans. Statistics answer the questions who, where, when, how, why, under what conditions, and to what extent.

Write a paragraph enumerating statistics about your topic. If the statistical and yearbook sources you have selected do not give you sufficient information, scan your magazine and newspaper articles for statistics. If you still do not have enough "hard data" to answer the questions who, where, when, how, why, under what conditions and to what extent, then you know that you will have to do some more research. It is much better to find this out now than on the day you are writing your first draft for the paper.

Document this paper with appropriate footnotes. Following is an example of a student's enumeration paragraph. Her topic is "Indian Education."

INDIAN EDUCATION

The rate of illiteracy among the American Indians is appalling. Nearly 60 percent of all Indians have less than an eighth grade education. Ten percent of the Indians over age fourteen have had no schooling whatsoever. Although approximately 90 percent of all Indian children are enrolled in school, they do not usually remain in school. Forty-two percent of these children drop out of school before reaching the twelfth grade. This figure is almost double the national average drop out

rate.[1]   Even when the children do remain in
school, their level of achievement drops
progressively lower with each succeeding year
than that of white children. Achievement test
scores indicate that in the first grade an
Indian child is, on the average, only 2 percent
behind a white child in nonverbal skills;
however, he is 10 percent behind the white child
in verbal skills. By the time an Indian child
reaches the twelfth grade, he has fallen almost
10 percent behind in nonverbal skills and 17
percent behind in verbal skills. His reading
scores are 15 percent lower than those of a
white child, and his mathematics scores are 11
percent lower.[2] With achievement levels
consistently behind those of a white child,
few Indian Americans attend colleges and
universities. Indians comprise only 0.6
percent of the total number of students from
minority groups.[3] The question now arises,
why do these conditions exist?

---

[1] "American Indian," The New York Times Encyclopedic
Almanac, 1972, p. 237.

[2] "Achievement Tests: Median Scores for Students by
Race or Ethnic Groups," Statistical Abstract of the United
States, 92 (1971), 119.

[3] "School Enrollment and Indian Children," Statistical
Abstract, p. 128.

PRELIMINARY WRITING ASSIGNMENT 3: ANALYZING CAUSES AND EFFECTS

Vital to any kind of research is an analysis of the causes and
effects of a particular problem. Without such analysis, no re-
mediation and no solutions are possible.

Review Cause and Effect Analysis (Part I, Stage 11, page
233). Complete note taking from all of your sources. Write a
short paper about the causes and effects of your topic. Document this paper with appropriate footnotes. Following is one student's cause and effect analysis. His topic is "Migrant Housing."

MIGRANT HOUSING

America's large corps of migrant workers
harvests the fresh fruits and vegetables that
Americans enjoy. But these workers are among
the most underprivileged of the nation's
minority groups. One of the most serious of the
many problems these people face is the appalling
condition of their housing. Some live in
converted chicken coops, some live in abandoned
truck trailers whose cabs have been removed and
hauled elsewhere. Other migrants live in
hastily erected buildings that begin to fall
apart almost as quickly as they are
constructed. More than half of all migrant
families -- sometimes ten or more people -- live
in one room. Why is migrant housing so poor?
There are four basic reasons for this situation.

First, the farmers and growers who provide
the housing for these seasonal workers do not
want to spend money on building new housing or
on improving the old. They say that the
migrants are at each location only several weeks
or at most several months of the year, and the
growers have more pressing expenditures in the
form of land, machinery, and operating capital,
leaving very little money for housing.[1] Then
too, the growers claim that the migrants do not
know how to care for the housing and that they
damage it or tear it up in a few weeks.[2] As a
result, many of the shacks have wide cracks in
the walls and foundations which invite rodents
and insects. Some of the housing has no
windows, no sanitary facilities, and wiring so
inadequate that it constitutes fire hazards.
Other migrant housing has no indoor cooking
equipment, so the workers must set up outdoor
facilities to prepare the hot meals they
have.[3]

---

[1] Truman Moore, The Slaves We Rent (New York: Random
House, 1965), p. 48.

[2] Moore, p. 49.

[3] These conditions were observed by the writer on an
inspection of Northern Illinois migrant camps with a member
of the Wheeling Migrant Council.

While some migrant housing is provided with
government funds, especially in those camps
which the workers inhabit up to six months of
the year, a second reason the housing is so poor
is that public health agencies consistently have
to operate with inadequate budgets. Even when
it is built under government auspices, the
housing is often too cramped or obsolete by the
time it is built.[4] Furthermore, government
agencies in charge of inspecting migrant
facilities are lax in enforcing the laws which
would make the growers improve the housing; many
violations of health and housing are overlooked
as a result.[5]

A third reason for the condition of migrant
housing is the migrant himself. He is isolated
from the rest of the world, and the growers and
labor camp operators keep him that way. He is
not accustomed to planning beyond his immediate
needs, he tends to accept conditions as they
are, and he is uneducated in the care and
maintenance of property. Although health
agencies do attempt to put into effect some
programs to assist the migrant, their methods
appear to alienate rather than benefit the
migrant. Worse yet, most migrants do not know
how to go about getting help from the programs
that do exist.[6]

A fourth reason for the problem is general
public apathy. If an incident about a migrant
camp does reach the news, people hear about it
and forget about it in a few days. If it does
not touch their lives personally, people find
that it is easier simply not to think about it.

With farmers, growers, and labor camp
operators reluctant to cooperate with government
agencies, with government agencies
insufficiently funded and staffed, with the
migrants themselves mostly powerless to help
themselves, and with a public that is generally
apathetic, the condition of migrant housing
continues to be a national disgrace.

---

[4] R. H. Browning and T. J. Northcutt, Jr., On the Season
(Monograph No. 2, Florida State Board of Health, n.d.), p. 45.

[5] Browning and Northcutt, p. 46.

[6] Dennis Holder, "Programs Not Reaching Migrants," The
Miami Herald, March 19, 1972, p. 13BR.

STAGE 6

BEGINNING THE PAPER

1. Writing the Introductory Paragraph

Having completed note taking and preliminary writing and having gained some experience with footnoting, you are now ready to begin writing your final paper.

STEP 1 **Writing the Introductory Paragraph.** In the short essay the lead-in statement is usually only a few sentences. These sentences, followed by the thesis statement, make up the introductory paragraph. In the longer paper you will be able to write a more extended introductory paragraph. When you are taking notes from your sources, you will inevitably get some good ideas for your introductory paragraph. You can include one or several of the following in this paragraph: a significant quotation, startling statistics, description, narration of an incident, a series of questions to be answered, a formal definition, a very brief history.

Here are some introductory paragraphs written by students for their research papers. The first is by the student researching amphetamine abuse. The thesis statement in each model is underlined.

EXAMPLE #1.

"UP" IS ALL THE WAY DOWN

"Speed is every bit as lethal as heroin although its toll may not show up as directly as in the weekend body counts of heroin overdoses."[1] This startling observation was made

---

[1] Jonathan Black, " 'Speed' That Kills -- or Worse," <u>New York Times Magazine</u>, June 21, 1970, p. 22.

by an amphetamine researcher at Rockefeller University. In some countries amphetamine abuse is the number one drug problem. In the United States it is epidemic, particularly among college students. Because much misinformation about drugs has been circulated by so-called official sources during the past several years, many young people have come to ignore or to scoff at the warnings and slogans about drug abuse. However, an increasing body of evidence supports the validity of the slogan "speed kills." The long term use of injected methamphetamine is lethal because it can cause heart failure, strokes, insulin shock, and serum hepatitis. It also induces a "speed cycle" which results in metabolic cannibalism and in amphetamine psychosis which may even trigger suicide.

EXAMPLE #2.

POLLUTION IN NEW RIVER

Fort Lauderdale, Florida, with its 270 miles of scenic waterways, is known as the Venice of America. One of the major waterways is New River, which winds through the downtown part of the city and on through the residential areas. A trip up the dreamy New River with its ever-changing scenery is a real tropical experience. Along the banks of the river are rare trees and flowering plants and exotic birds such as flamingos and macaws. The thick green lawns of the waterfront homes meet the river's edge. Once, the only pollution of this river was a gull's wing. Today, New River is seriously contaminated. The causes of this pollution are three: plant distribution of chemically treated effluent, dumping of raw sewage, and intrusion of salt water. The effects of this unfortunate pollution are unsanitary water for recreation, poisoned marine life, and unsafe water for irrigation.

EXAMPLE #3.

THE NEW LARCENY

A sixteen-year old girl sits in the security office of a large department store crying and wondering what will happen to her. Both the police and her parents have been summoned. As she was leaving the department store clad in a fashionable pants suit, she was apprehended by a store detective who had noticed that when she entered the dressing room of the junior sports clothing department, she was wearing only shorts and a halter. This girl had just committed a serious form of larceny -- one which is on the increase in America. This larceny is shoplifting. Although the apprehension of shoplifters is a common occurrence in many stores, there are still more shoplifters who are successful than those who are caught. Shoplifting affects merchants, who lose millions of dollars a year in merchandise; and it affects the consumer, who must pay higher prices for the goods he buys. In order for the public to better understand the extent of this problem, some basic questions must be answered: How much does this illegal practice cost the parties involved? Who are the shoplifters? What are their reasons for shoplifting? How can shoplifting be prevented?

EXAMPLE #4.

PARADISE LOST -- AMERICAN STYLE

Nothing in all history had ever succeeded like America, and every American knew it. Nowhere else on the globe had nature been at once so rich and so generous, and her riches were available to all who

had the enterprise to take them and the fortune to
be white. As nature and experience justified
optimism, America was incurably optimistic.[1]

Commenting on the optimism of Americans about
their "boundless" natural resources, historian
Henry Steele Commager observes that in
transforming their geographical assets to wealth
and power, Americans have become notoriously
shortsighted. They have discovered that their
resources were not unlimited after all, and they
have been consuming them at a rate faster than
they can replace them. One of the natural
resources in greatest danger is the forest;
America has fewer than one million acres of
virgin forests left.[2] Our forests are being
cut faster than they can be replanted, due
largely to a harvesting practice known as
clearcutting. Clearcutting is a method of
harvesting trees whereby every tree in a given
portion of the forest is cut regardless of age
or size. So serious had the problem of
clearcutting become that by 1960 Congress
enacted the Multiple Use and Sustained Yield
Law, which contained a provision to control
timber cutting.[3] In spite of this
legislation, 60 percent of all timber harvested
in the National Parks is clearcut, and
commercial loggers intend to increase
clearcutting 30 percent.[4] In addition to
endangering our timber supply, clearcutting is
damaging to our forests because it destroys the
land aesthetically, it disrupts watersheds,
causing the fouling of streams and rivers, and
it threatens the wildlife.

---

[1] Henry Steele Commager, The American Mind (New Haven:
Yale University Press, 1950), p. 5.

[2] Nancy Wood, "Clearcut," American West, 22 (November
1971), 12.

[3] Michael Frome, "Clearcutting the National Forests,"
Field and Stream, 67 (July 1971), 32.

[4] "Timber Management: Improvement Implies New Land-Use
Policies," Science, December 25, 1970, p. 1390.

EXAMPLE #5.

SINGLE PARENT ADOPTION

"Future shock" is already here. One of the most rapidly changing of American institutions is the family. Among the many alternate lifestyles to be observed on the current scene is that of the single parent. Obviously, some parents are single by reasons of death or divorce of a spouse. Then there are others, never married, who wish to be parents. Grace Simpson is a thirty-eight-year old woman who has never been married or pregnant and who has adopted a biracial girl.[1] In 1970, Ms. Marjorie Margolis, after two and a half years of waiting, was able to adopt a Korean orphan girl. Ms. Margolis is single.[2] In 1971 the Vancouver, Washington, Court of Appeals upheld the decision of bachelor R. Sturedwart, Jr., to adopt his two young cousins whose parents had died.[3] These are but three examples of single people who felt that they could be good parents and offer children the advantage of family life. There are, however, differing points of view as to the validity of these views on the part of single people. The controversy has created some hurdles for the individual who may wish to become a single parent. The problems faced by the single person wishing to adopt a child include the availability of children for adoption, the adopting agency's concern about the overall health, character, and previous child raising experience of the single applicant, and the agency's concern about the single applicant's ability to provide for the physical, emotional, and special needs of the child.

---

[1] J. C. Hefley, "One Parent . . . Better than None," Today's Health, 59 (March 1971), 33.

[2] Marjorie Margolis, "Adopting a Child If You're Single," Mademoiselle, 76 (December 1972), 136.

[3] "Bachelor R. Sturedwart, Jr., 19, Wins Court Approval to Adopt 2 Children," New York Times, April 15, 1971, p. 20.

EXAMPLE #6.

```
        REHABILITATING THE AMERICAN JUNKIE

    Heroin addiction was once a problem of the
poor.  Its victims were primarily the blacks,
the Puerto Ricans, and other socially
disadvantaged minority groups.  They lived with
the horror of heroin every day, yet little was
done to help the addicts.  In recent years
heroin addiction has crept across the United
States like a plague.  The "junkie" now comes in
all colors and from all social backgrounds.  Yet
even with this rising rate of addiction, there
has been a generally discouraging record of
attempts to rehabilitate addicts.  However,
there is hope in that attempts are being made to
find ways to rehabilitate these people.  The
task of rehabilitation is not an easy one, for
no one method works in all cases.  Some methods
now in use or being investigated in the United
States are the British method, narcotic
antagonists, methadone treatment, and
therapeutic communities.
```

WRITING ASSIGNMENT 1: THE EXTENDED INTRODUCTORY PARAGRAPH

Using one or several of the methods for extended introductory paragraphs listed on page 330, write the introductory paragraph for your own paper. Conclude the paragraph with your thesis statement.

WRITING ASSIGNMENT 2: PREPARING THE OUTLINE

You know that by the time you form your thesis statement you already have a preliminary outline. Now group your cards according to the major subject headings. These subject headings correspond to the minor inferences in your thesis and when developed will form the major sections of your paper. Within each group of subject headings, arrange the cards according to the order in which you want the proof details to appear.

If you discover that you have cards that you cannot use because they contain duplicate information or irrelevant information, set them aside. Do not discard them because some instructors like to see unused note cards and unused bibliography cards so they can follow your process of selection and limitation.

Once you have decided on the final order of your notecards, number them on the bottom. These numbers will correspond to the footnote numbers in your paper. A bonus to numbering the note cards is that if they should get out of order you can quickly reassemble them.

Now review the form for the standard topic outline (Part I; Stage 7, page 141). Also study carefully the outline for the model research paper on "Indian Education" on page 347. Then write your own outline.

STAGE 7

WRITING THE ROUGH DRAFT

    1. Using the Note Cards
    2. Checking the Rough Draft

STEP 1   **Using the Note Cards.**   With a detailed outline and a complete set of note cards arranged to correspond to the outline, you will have little trouble writing the first draft of your paper. Using the outline as a structural guide and the note cards to supply the supporting details, you can begin to write. Since you have already written the introduction, you can begin the first draft with your first developmental paragraph.

    Writing is a very personal process. Some people like to rough out the whole paper rapidly, waiting for revision to check grammar, sentence structure, punctuation, and general style. Others prefer to develop one section of the paper at a time, polishing and revising each section before going on to another section. Whichever method you use, you will find that following a few hints for rough draft procedure will make the writing go smoother.

    1. Watch the development of your paragraphs carefully. Make sure that you have a topic sentence for each which contains a controlling inference. Work in the raw material from your notes in a smoothly flowing and unified way. The following pages illustrate how the student researcher on "Indian Education" worked her note cards into her paper. The second page of her research paper is reproduced on page 340. Opposite this page are the note cards she worked with.

    Attached are the original note cards taken by the student as she was researching her subject. Notice how this information was incorporated in the paper.

language barrier

"Educational achievement by Indian children is still far below that of white children of the same age or grade, not for lack of native intelligence but because of insufficient knowledge of English when they enter school."

1

Although the orignial note was a direct quote, the student chose to paraphrase the information for her paper.

school statistics
(English)

2/3 of All Indian children entering BIA schools speak little or no English.

p.15-16

4

Here the note is a paraphrase of the original material, but the information and reworded her own note.

school statistics
(language skills)

more than 1/2 of the Indian children between ages of six and eighteen speak in own native language.

p.56

4

Notice how the student incorporated the facts from this card, reducing the information to a phrase.

Indian language

The Indian languages are radically different in structure and under-lying thought patterns from any Indo-European language.

p.57

5

Here the student has expanded the information from her note card with general knowledge.

poor education - Causes
(language)

Use of Indian language is strictly forbidden in school. Use of native tongue incurs corporal punishment.

p.110

4

Once again the student rewrites her original note in order to achieve unity. In every case, the student user her notes to good advantage.

p.55

not adapted to the needs of the children;
fourth, the treatment of the Indian children in
the schools is deplorable.

A massive barrier stands between Indian
children and educational achievement.   That
barrier is language.[5]   Two-thirds of the Indian
children entering BIA schools (schools which are
controlled and maintained by the Bureau of
Indian Affairs) speak little or no English.[6]   Of
the Indian youth between the ages of six and
eighteen, over half speak in their native
language.[7]   Thus, learning in school becomes a
twofold problem for the Indian child; he must
not only attempt to grasp new concepts, but he
also must hear the explanation of these concepts
in a tongue which is foreign to him, a tongue
which is radically different from his own in
structure and in thought patterns.[8]   The
language problem is augmented, rather than
lessened, by rules which strictly forbid the use
of Indian dialects in school.[9]   Therefore, it is
obvious that special programs for teaching
English are needed in the schools.   Such
programs, TESL (Teaching English as a Second
Language) for example, do exist and have been
found to be quite beneficial in raising the
achievement level of Indian children.

---

[5] "Indians, American," Encyclopedia Americana, 15
(1969), 15, 16.

[6] E, Fuchs, "Time to Redeem an Old Promise," Saturday
Review, 53 (January 24, 1970), 56.

[7] Fuchs, p. 57.

[8] Donald A. Erickson, "Failure in Navaho Schooling,"
Parents' Magazine, 45 (September 1970), 110.

[9] Fuchs, p. 55.

2. Write on one side of the paper only, and write on every other
line or every third line. Give yourself wide margins. Then you will have
plenty of room to add details you may have omitted and to revise your
sentence structure.

3. Some people prefer to prepare each footnote as they go. Others prefer to enter the footnote numeral on the rough draft and then prepare the footnotes later by referring back to the note and the complete source information on the bibliography card. In any case a good idea when you write the rough draft is to circle every footnote numeral in the body of the text with a pencil or a colored pen so that when you type the final paper you will not overlook any footnote numerals.

4. Check direct quotes very carefully to make sure that you are quoting the original exactly. If a quotation does not appear to be accurate on your note card, or if you are uncertain whether you have paraphrased or directly quoted in a particular instance, then check your notes against the source.

Use appropriate words to introduce your direct quotes. You can find words more vigorous and explicit than "says" and "states." Try "predicts," "warns," "estimates," "argues," "thinks," "discovered," "hopes," and other words appropriate to the sense of your quotation.

When you introduce a quotation, mention the name and the title or function of the person responsible for it if possible.

Check the Mechanics Guide, page 396 for the proper punctuation for introducing quotations.

5. After you finish the body of the paper with all of the major sections developed, then add the introductory paragraph to the beginning.

6. Now write the conclusion of the paper. This will be one or several paragraphs in which you discuss what steps are currently being taken to correct the social problem you have investigated, what solutions have been proposed by experts on the subject, and what your own conclusions and ideas are about the topic.

STEP 2   **Checking the Rough Draft.**   Look at the checklist on page 341 of this book. It is a review of the format for your paper and the conventions of documentation, and it can help you in two ways. First, if you check this list against your rough draft, you will prevent unnecessary changes in your final copy. Second, a paper which is accurate in these respects stands a better chance of getting a good grade than one which is not. Obviously, these criteria are not the only ones which will be used in the evaluation of your paper, but correct form and documentation are primary basic requirements for this research paper.

After you have checked the format and documentation of your paper, go over it for corrections in grammar, sentence structure, spelling, and punctuation. It is often helpful to read through the paper once for general sense and continuity and again for the mechanics. Some students find it helpful to read the paper aloud or to have a friend read it over in order to catch sentence structure problems.

CHECKLIST FOR RESEARCH PAPERS

1. Title page

   Does the title page carry, properly spaced, the title, your name, the name, number, and section of the course, the instructor's name, the date of presentation?   _____

2. Outline

   a. Is the outline written in standard topic form?   _____
   b. Is it paged with lower case Roman numerals?   _____
   c. Is the outline correctly punctuated and capitalized?   _____
   d. Have you double spaced between Roman numerals?   _____
   e. Are parallel topics grammatically constructed?   _____

3. First page of text

   a. Is the title repeated?   _____
   b. Are your margins set according to manuscript form?   _____

4. Succeeding pages

   a. Are all of the following pages numbered?   _____
   b. If your footnotes are on a separate page, is that sheet paginated consecutively with the text?   _____
   c. Is your bibliography sheet paginated?   _____

5. Quotations
   a. Has each direct quotation of four lines or fewer been put
      in quotation marks?   _____
   b. Has each quotation longer than four lines been indented
      and set off by single spacing, without quotation marks?   _____
   c. Have double and single quotation marks, italics, ellipses,
      and brackets been used consistently, according to accepted
      practice? (See Mechanics Guide, page 387.)   _____
   d. Has each quotation been smoothly introduced with an ap-
      propriate verb and proper punctuation? (See Mechanics
      Guide, page 372.)   _____
   e. Has each quotation been properly acknowledged with a
      footnote?   _____

6. Footnotes
   a. Does the raised numeral in the text correspond in each
      case with the number of the footnote that acknowledges
      the source reference?   _____
   b. Is the footnote clearly separated from the text?   _____
   c. Are the footnote numbers indented five spaces from the
      left margin and raised one half space?   _____
   d. Are the footnotes single spaced within and double spaced
      between?   _____
   e. Are the footnotes numbered consecutively?   _____
   f. Are the authors' first names given first?   _____
   g. Are the footnotes punctuated according to correct usage?   _____
   h. Have you acknowledged in a footnote *all* material that was
      quoted directly or paraphrased or was not original with
      you?   _____

7. Note cards
   a. In addition to the information on the card, does each note
      card carry a subject heading, the source identification, and
      a specific page reference?   _____
   b. Have you attached a note card for every footnote in your
      paper?   _____
   c. Are the note cards numbered sequentially as you have
      used them, corresponding with the footnote numbers in
      your paper?   _____
   d. Have you bound or attached the notecards in the manner
      requested by your instructor?   _____

8. Bibliography

   a. Does the bibliography conclude your paper? _____

   b. Are the references alphabetized by author's last name, or in the absence of a name, by the first important word of the title of the article? _____

   c. Is the first line of every bibliography entry flush with the left margin? _____

   d. Are second and following lines of each entry indented five spaces? _____

   e. Is a seven space line used in place of an author's name for the second and successive items by that author? _____

   f. Have you given *all* the necessary bibliographical data in the order and with the punctuation and spacing shown in the bibliography examples on page 261? _____

   g. Have you titled the page WORKS CITED or SELECTED BIBLIOGRAPHY? _____

   h. Have you included in the bibliography only those works which you cited in your paper? _____

9. Minimum sources

   a. Have you satisfied the minimum source requirements for this paper? _____

   b. Have you drawn from the variety of sources recommended by your instructor? _____

10. Binding the paper

   Have you assembled all the pages in their proper order and bound or fastened them together in the manner requested by the instructor? _____

Order:
a. Title page
b. Outline
c. Text of paper
d. Footnote page if separate
e. Bibliography

The Title Page carries the title of the paper in capital letters, properly spaced; the student's name, the name, number, and section of the course; the instructor's name; and the date of presentation.

INDIAN EDUCATION

Debbie Ledford

English 101.016

Ms. Benjamin

December 8, 1972

The title is repeated on the outline page.

The format of the outline follows the general principles of standard outline form (see Part I, Stage 7, page 143). The outline begins with the thesis statement.

The outline is very complete, carrying five stages of classified information. Your outline may not be five stages, but to be adequate it should be at least a three stage outline.

INDIAN EDUCATION

Thesis statement: The education of Indian
Americans is far below standard. There are four
basic reasons for this: first, a language
barrier exists between the children and their
teachers; second, the system under which the
schools operate is faulty; third, the schools
are not adapted to the needs of the children;
fourth, the treatment of Indian children is
deplorable.

I. Language barrier

   A. Cause of low achievement level
      1. Insufficient skills in using English
         a. Little or no English spoken by
           two-thirds entering BIA schools
         b. No English spoken by one-half
           between ages six to eighteen
      2. Difficulty in learning English
         a. Indian dialects different in
           structure
         b. Indian dialects different in
           thought patterns
      3. Use of native dialects forbidden in
         schools

   B. Programs for teaching English
      1. TESL (Teaching English as a Second
         Language)
         a. Cause for better achievement in
           school
         b. Prevention of widespread use by
           lack of funds
      2. NBEA (National Bilingual Education
         Act)
         a. $7.5 million appropriated for
           NBEA in 1970
         b. $300,000 used for 772 children

II. Educational system   ii

   A. Funds
      1. Over half of BIA budget given to
         education
      2. $18 per year per child allowed by BIA
         while $40 allowed by the federal
         government

   B. Teachers
      1. Lack understanding and appreciation
         of Indian culture
      2. Have poor attitude
         a. Have vindictive attitude toward
            Indian religions and values
         b. 25 percent prefer not to teach
            Indians
      3. Need to update education and methods
         of teaching

   C. Indian noninvolvement
      1. Responsibility of education to BIA
         officials
      2. Authority on education kept from
         Indians
      3. Interaction between school and
         community

III. Conventional schools

   A. Curriculum
      1. No different than for white child
         except TESL program
      2. No studying of Indian History,
         current problems

   B. Attitude
      1. Ignore Indian culture
      2. Fit white man's mold
         a. Lose "Indianness"
         b. Adopt "Great White Way"

The page numbers of the outline are written in lower case Roman numerals — ii, iii, iv. Since this outline is three pages, the second page is numbered ii, and the third, iii.

The outline ends with the concluding statement.

                                                                iii
    C. Textbooks
       1. Ability of child to relate to them
       2. Portrayal of Indians in them
          a. "Savages" used to refer to Indians
          b. "Victory" and "massacre" used as
             bias words

IV. Treatment of the Indian child

    A. Manner of treatment
       1. Sent to boarding schools
       2. Boarded out to white families during
          vacations
       3. Regimented to strict schedule
       4. Provided with recreational program
          a. Forms of recreation
             (1) Polishing floors
             (2) Washing bed frames
          b. Funds for recreational equipment

    B. Effect on children
       1. Poor attitude
       2. Unruly behavior
       3. Poor self-image
       4. Drunkenness and alcoholism
       5. Disorientation
       6. Suicide

Concluding statement: There is no legitimate
reason for such conditions to exist. The
Indians themselves want a better education, and
the causes of poor Indian education are not
insuperable.

TITLE

The title is centered and typed in capital letters about one fourth of the way down from the top of the page. There are three spaces between the title and the first line of the text.

PARAGRAPHS

Each paragraph is indented five spaces. There are two letter spaces after all terminal punctuation, but a single letter space after other marks.

THE INTRODUCTORY PARAGRAPH

In the introductory paragraph the student has sifted information from her short data enumeration paper (see page 326). The thesis statement is two sentences.

PAGING

The first page need not be numbered. If it is, the number is usually centered at the bottom of the page.

FOOTNOTES

Footnotes may be separated from the text by a short solid black line (about 15 spaces) or by a triple space between text and footnotes without the line. Your instructor will indicate which method to use. Footnotes 1 and 2: The first time a source is cited all of the necessary information is given. Footnotes 3 and 4 are subsequent references, and an abbreviated form is used.

INDIAN EDUCATION

The rate of illiteracy among American Indians is appalling. Nearly 60 percent of all Indians have less than an eighth grade education. Ten percent of the Indians over age fourteen have had no schooling whatsoever.[1] Although approximately 90 percent of all Indian children are enrolled in schools, they do not usually remain in school.[2] Forty-two percent of these children drop out of school before reaching the twelfth grade.[3] Even when the children do remain in school, their level of achievement drops progressively lower than that of white children with each succeeding year. Achievement test scores indicate that the twelfth grade Indian student is, on the average, 13 percent behind the white student in the same grade level.[4] Clearly, the education of Indian Americans is far below standard. There are four reasons for this: first, a language barrier exists between the children and their teachers; second, the system under which the schools operate is faulty; third, the schools are

---

[1] "Indian," The New York Times Encyclopedic Almanac, 1972, p. 237.

[2] "Indians," Statistical Abstract of the United States, 92 (1971), 119.

[3] "Indian," N.Y. Times Encyclopedic Almanac, p. 237.

[4] "Achievement Tests: Median Scores for students by Race or Ethnic Groups," Statistical Abstract of the United States, 92 (1971), 119.

The page number of all succeeding pages is typed two spaces above the first line of the text at the right hand margin.

Notice that the footnote number in the text is placed after the punctuation mark and raised slightly above the line (one-half space). Notice also that the footnote numbers are consecutive.

The second paragraph begins with a discussion of the first cause: the language barrier. Here, the writer sifts in statistics that apply to this cause. (See page 339 in Rough Draft Procedure for a demonstration of how information from her note cards was used to write this part of the paper.)

Footnote 5 lists both pages 15 and 16 because the material began on one page and continued on the next. In a bibliography the dash between page numbers indicates inclusive page references for an article; in the footnote the comma is used to indicate a carry over.

The footnotes in this paper are placed at the bottom of each page rather than collected on a separate page at the end of the paper.

This student made good use of a variety of sources indicating thorough research. If she had used only one source for supporting details, she would have been presenting only one opinion.

2

not adapted to the needs of the children;
fourth, the treatment of the Indian children in
the schools is deplorable.

A massive barrier stands between Indian
children and educational achievement.   That
barrier is language.[5]   Two-thirds of the Indian
children entering BIA schools (schools which are
controlled and maintained by the Bureau of
Indian Affairs) speak little or no English.[6]   Of
the Indian youth between the ages of six and
eighteen, over half speak in their native
language.[7]   Thus, learning in school becomes a
twofold problem for the Indian child; he must
not only attempt to grasp new concepts, but he
also must hear the explanation of these concepts
in a tongue which is foreign to him, a tongue
which is radically different from his own in
structure and in thought patterns.[8]   The
language problem is augmented rather than
lessened by rules which strictly forbid the use
of Indian dialects in school.[9]   Therefore, it is
obvious that special programs for teaching
English are needed in the schools.   Such
programs, TESL (Teaching English as a Second
Language) for example, do exist and have been
found to be quite beneficial in raising the
achievement level of Indian students; however,
federal cutbacks in appropriations prevent the
widespread implementation of these helpful

---

[5] "Indians, American," Encyclopedia Americana, 15
(1969), 15, 16.

[6] E. Fuchs, "Time to Redeem an Old Promise," Saturday
Review, 53 (January 24, 1970), 56.

[7] Fuchs, p. 57.

[8] Donald A. Erickson, "Failure in Navaho Schooling,"
Parent's Magazine, 45 (September 1970), 110.

[9] Fuchs, p. 55.

In this paragraph the student begins with transition: "Language programs are not the only area that suffers from a lack of funds; . . ." She then begins to discuss the next cause — an insufficient budget. Thus, this first sentence serves both as transition between the first two developmental paragraphs and as the topic sentence for the second developmental paragraph.

Notice that the student has used four different sources for this page. Two sources had been previously cited, and two are sources that are being cited for the first time.

3

programs.[10]   Furthermore, money appropriated
for such programs does not always reach the
Indian.   For instance, of the $7.5 million
appropriated in 1970 for the National Bilingual
Education Act, only $300,000 was spent on Indian
programs benefiting 773 children.[11]

Language programs are not the only area that
suffers from a lack of funds; the entire Indian
school system operates on an insufficient
budget.[12]   By 1966 over half of the BIA budget
was spent on education.[13]   Even at this rate,
the BIA was able to spend only $18 per year per
student for textbooks and supplies; at this
time, the federal government was spending $40
per year for each child attending public
schools.[14]   A second fault in the education
system lies with the teachers.   There is no
school which prepares teachers for the special
problems involved in teaching a group of
children who are culturally different from
average Americans.   Consequently, the teachers
are ill-equipped by their own background,
knowledge, and disposition.[15]   Not only do most

---

[10] Erickson, p. 110.

[11] Fuchs, p. 56.

[12] "Indian Education: A National Disgrace," Today's
Education, 59 (March 1970), p. 27.

[13] "Indians, American," p. 16.

[14] Edward M. Kennedy, "Let the Indians Run Indian
Policy," Look, 34 (June 2, 1970), p. 36.

[15] Erickson, p. 109.

In the paragraph that begins "Because the schools tend . . ." the student begins by drawing her own conclusions from facts she has researched. She then adds support from her sources.

4

teachers not have any understanding or appreciation for Indian culture,[16] but many teachers even have a vindictive attitude toward the Indian religions and sets of values.[17] Approximately 25 percent of the teachers of Indian children actually admit that they would prefer not to teach Indians.[18]   Furthermore, a large number of teachers need to update their own education and methods of teaching.[19]   In addition to having meager funds and ill-equipped teachers, the system is undesirable in that there is little Indian involvement in controlling the schools.   In nearly all cases the educational staff is responsible to BIA officials rather than to the Indian parents. Authority in educational matters is rarely given to the Indians,[20] and there is, therefore, little interaction between the school and the community that it serves.

Because the schools tend to be isolated from the communities that they serve, a third problem arises; the schools themselves are much too conventional; they are not adapted to the needs of the children who attend them.   Other than the TESL program, the curriculum for the Indian student is the same as the one for any other

---

[16] Fuchs, p. 74.

[17] "Indians, American," p. 16.

[18] "Voice for Indians in Educational Decisions," School and Society, 98 (Summer 1970), 303.

[19] Robert D. Alley and Ronald G. Davison, "Educating the American Indian," Clearing House, 46 (February 1972), 349.

[20] Fuchs, p. 74.

A quotation of more than four lines is indented five spaces from the left margin and is single spaced. Any indented quotation is not enclosed with quotation marks.

The ellipses at the beginning of the indented quote indicate that some of the material has been omitted. Since the quotation begins in the middle of a sentence, the first word is not capitalized.

Notice that the word introducing the quote, *that,* is not followed by a punctuation mark because the quotation is an integral part of the sentence structure.

Within the quotation the verb *is* appears in brackets because the writer used her own word for better continuity.

The single quotation marks indicate that those words were already within quotation marks in the original passage.

5

student. Indian history, current Indian
problems and other classes which would be
especially relevant to the Indian child are not
offered by the schools.[21] Instead, the schools
attempt to eradicate the cultural heritage of
their students.[22] As Senator Walter F. Mondale
of Minnesota stated, the educational system
tries to force the Indian child to " 'lose his
Indianness' " and teaches him " 'to disregard his
family's teachings and adopt the Great White Way
of doing things.' "[23] Just as the curricula and
attitudes of the schools are unsuited to the
students, so also are the textbooks that are
used.[24] At a workshop session conducted by Will
Antell, Director of Indian Education in
Minnesota, a participant noted that

> . . . history books are biased through the
> eyes of the conqueror. 'When the whites won
> it was called a massacre.' Minnesota, Star
> of the North . . .[is] a particularly
> offensive book in that the word 'savage' is
> used more often than the word 'Indian.'[25]

Mona McCormick, teacher at the St. Francis
Mission in South Dakota, observed, "Most of
their [Indian children's] textbooks, consciously
or unconsciously, actually teach them that they
are ruthless savages and 'unpersons.' "[26]
    Not only are Indian children degraded in
their textbooks, but they are also ill-treated

---

[21] Fuchs, p. 57.

[22] Fuchs, p. 74.

[23] "Voice for Indians," p. 303.

[24] "Indian Education," p. 27.

[25] "Voice for Indians," p. 303.

[26] Mona McCormick, "American Indians Must Not Stop
Running," New York Times, July 29, 1971, p. 33.

Since this indented quotation began at a paragraph, the student had to indent three additional spaces.

The four spaced periods for the ellipses indicate that the material omitted came at the end of the original sentence. The fourth period is for the terminal punctuation.

in other ways. Of the Indian children who
attend school, 31 percent are sent long
distances to boarding schools.[27] In the case of
some children who live very far from school, the
children may not even be allowed to go home
during vacation times but are boarded out to
white families living in the same area.[28] The
more fortunate children who are able to see
their parents on weekends must still face the
drudgery of the long school week. While living
at school, the children are strictly regimented
according to a specific time schedule. The
schoolwork itself is highly regimented.

> Many other aspects of the youngsters'
> lives were regimented. The children filed to
> meals in groups of thirty or forty spaced at
> precise intervals. While one group was
> scraping plates and [other groups] returning
> to the dormitories, still others were moving
> briskly through the chow line and eating at
> assigned seats. Another group was doing
> calisthenics on the sidewalk . . . . Going
> to bed, getting up, recuperating from
> illness, bathing, buying candy from a
> dispenser, going to classes -- virtually
> everything was subject to unvarying
> routine.[29]

They play at a certain time. Their play, if it
can be called that, is sometimes such forms of
amusement as polishing floors and washing the
steel frames of bunk beds. With meager funds
the schools have little time to spend on
recreational equipment. Growing up under such
poor treatment greatly affects the lives and
attitudes of Indian children. In the classrooms
the children are withdrawn, somber, or angry.
They misbehave in class and pay very little
attention to their studies.[30] They come to have

---

[27] "School Enrollment of Indian Children," Statistical
Abstract, p. 119.

[28] Fuchs, p. 55.

[29] Erickson, pp. 67, 68.

[30] Erickson, p. 68.

Since the conclusion is the student's own comment, it is not footnoted except for the quotation by Velma Shing.

7

a very poor self-image, and their expectation of
failure becomes self-fulfilling. Moreover,
drinking and alcoholism are common among
students even in elementary school.[31] Caught
between tribal teaching and white culturization,
the children lose their identity and begin to
wonder, "Who am I?"[32] For some children, the
ultimate result of this unhappy childhood is
suicide.[33]

There is no legitimate reason why such a
condition should exist. The Indians themselves
want a better education. They realize what a
good education means to them. As Velma Shing,
Hopi Follow Through director, said, "I know from
experience that education is a way off the
reservation. Education is also a wy to stay, to
create new jobs, a better living, and keep the
things we love."[34] Moreover, the problems which
are the causes of poor Indian education --
language barrier, faulty educational system,
conventional schools, and ill-treatment of
children -- are not insuperable. With more
money, new leadership in the school system,
maximum involvement of Indian parents, and a
change of attitude on the part of the white
majority, these problems could be alleviated to
some degree, if not fully eradicated.

---

[31] McCormick, p. 33.

[32] Story Moorefield, "To Keep the Things We Love,"
American Education, 6 (August-September 1970), 6.

[33] McCormick, p. 33.

[34] Moorefield, p. 8.

This page carries pagination because the "Works Cited" page is considered part of the research paper.

For a short paper the student has used the number and types of sources specified by her instructor. She has listed only those works actually cited in the paper; therefore, she titles her bibliography "Works Cited."

8

WORKS CITED

"Achievement Tests: Median Scores for Students
by Race or Ethnic Groups," <u>Statistical
Abstract</u> <u>of</u> <u>the</u> <u>United</u> <u>States</u>, 92 (1971),
119.

Alley, Robert D., and Ronald G. Davison.
"Educating the American Indian," <u>Clearing
House</u>, 46 (February 1972), 347–351.

Erickson, Donald A. "Failure in Navaho
Schooling," <u>Parents'</u> <u>Magazine</u>, 45
(September 1970), 66–68+.

Fuchs, E. "Time to Redeem an Old Promise,"
<u>Saturday</u> <u>Review</u>, January 24, 1970,
pp. 54–57+.

"Indian," <u>The</u> <u>New</u> <u>York</u> <u>Times</u> <u>Encyclopedic
Almanac</u>, 1972, p. 237.

"Indians," <u>Statistical</u> <u>Abstract</u> <u>of</u> <u>the</u> <u>United</u>
<u>States</u>, 92 (1971), 119.

"Indians, American," <u>Encyclopedia</u> <u>Americana</u>, 15
(1969), 16.

"Indian Education: A National Disgrace," <u>Today's
Education</u>, 59 (March 1970), 24–27.

Kennedy, Edward M. "Let the Indians Run Indian
Policy," <u>Look</u>, June 2, 1970, pp.36–38.

McCormick, Mona, "American Indians Must Not Stop
Running," <u>New</u> <u>York</u> <u>Times</u>, July 29, 1971, p.
33.

Moorefield, Story. "To Keep the Things We Love,"
<u>American</u> <u>Education</u>, 6 (August–September
1970), 6–8.

"School Enrollment of Indian Children,"
<u>Statistical</u> <u>Abstract</u> <u>of</u> <u>the</u> <u>United</u> <u>States</u>,
92 (1971), 119.

"Voice for Indians in Educational Decisions,"
<u>School</u> <u>and</u> <u>Society</u>, 98 (Summer 1970), 303.

STAGE 8

WRITING AND SUBMITTING

THE FINAL PAPER

1. Preparing the Final Revision
2. Proofreading
3. Assembling the Research Packet

Before beginning the final version of your paper, study again the student model of the research paper, "Indian Education," which begins on page 345. Observe the form of the title sheet, the outline, the first page of the text, the handling of footnotes, and the bibliography. Read the annotations.

STEP 1 **Preparing the Final Revision.** First assemble the materials you will need. This seems obvious, but many students attempt to produce the paper without the tools, and the result is an unprofessional looking paper. Use a good grade of standard bond paper, or the heavier grade of erasable bond. Keep on hand one of the type correction products. Use a new typewriter ribbon if the old one is producing faded type, and be sure to clean the type keys before beginning.

Get out your detailed outline, your notecards assembled in order, and your polished rough draft. Set your typewriter margins so that you will have one and a half inch margins at the top and on the left, and about one inch at the bottom and on the right. Begin the first page with the title in all capital letters, about one-fourth of the way down the page. If you are planning to place your footnotes at the bottom of each page, determine how many footnotes will fall on each page and leave the necessary space at the bottom of the page.

When the paper itself has been typed, prepare the title page, giving the title of your paper, your name, the name, number, and section of your course, the instructor's name, and the date.

Retype the outline neatly. It is wise to leave the final typing of the outline until last because even in the typing of the final version you may decide to change the order of an item or two in your paper.

Prepare the footnote page if it is to be separate from the text of your paper.

Last, prepare the bibliography page. If it is a list only of the sources actually used in your paper (those which you documented with footnotes), then the bibliography will be titled "Works Cited" or "List of Works Cited." If it includes one or several works which you used as background material but did not actually cite in your paper, then the bibliography will be titled "Selected Bibliography" or "Selected References."

STEP 2   Proofreading.   Proofreading is a vital step in submitting an acceptable paper, and it is a step that many students either ignore or fail to devote sufficient time to. It is best to leave some time gaps in the preparation of your paper — at least a day between the writing of the rough draft and the final revision and another day between the writing of the final paper and the proofreading. Start your proofreading when you are fresh; go over every word in every sentence. This is the time to get out the checklist again and check the final paper against each item on it.

If you find an error or two on a page, correct them neatly in ink. It is much better to have neatly made corrections than to submit a paper with obvious errors. If the corrections make an untidy appearing paper, it is best to type that page over again.

STEP 3   Assembling the Research Packet.   When your research packet is ready to submit, it will look like the one in the photograph on page 254. Use a plain two pocket folder. Write the title of your paper and your name on the front. Then assemble it in the following order (from top to bottom): on the left side put the note cards and bibliography cards; unused note and bibliography cards; clippings, pamphlets, and copies of sources. On the right put the complete paper; the extended introduction; the cause and effect paper; your data enumeration paragraph; the extended definition; and a rough draft if one is requested.

These, then, are the stages and steps to successful expository communication, and by working through them you have discovered that you *can* write.

Part 3

A Brief Guide to Mechanics and Style

MANUSCRIPT FORM

Typed Papers. Use standard size 8½ by 11 inch paper.
Double space, using black ribbon and clean type.
Type on only one side of each sheet of paper.

Hand Written Papers. Use standard size 8½ by 11 inch paper with lines about a half inch apart.
Write legibly, using black or blue ink.
Write on only one side of each sheet of paper.

Margins. Leave about an inch and a half at the left and at the top, an inch at the right and bottom.

Indentation. Indent paragraphs about one inch at the left for handwritten manuscripts.
Indent five spaces in typewritten copy.

Paging. The first page is sometimes not numbered. If it is numbered, place the number centered at the bottom of the page.
Use Arabic numerals in the upper right hand corner to mark all pages after the first.

Title. Write the title in capital letters.
Center the title on the page about an inch and a half from the top for typed manuscripts; for handwritten manuscripts, place the title on the first ruled line.
For typed manuscripts, leave three spaces before beginning the paper.
For handwritten manuscripts, leave the line after the title blank.
Do not put quotation marks around the title or underline it.
Do not put a period after the title.

Abbreviations
1. Avoid the use of abbreviations in formal writing.
2. Use only acceptable abbreviations such as Mr., Dr., B.C., A.D., etc.
3. The titles *reverend* and *honorable* must not be used with surnames only; those words should be followed by the first name or the initials.

4. In ordinary writing, except in footnotes, bibliographies, addresses, tabulations, *spell out:*
   a. Names of countries, states, and cities
   b. Names of days and months
   c. Words such as chapter, page, avenue, street, manufacturing company, mountain, Christmas, volume, number
   d. Personal names

Numbers
1. Spell out numbers that can be expressed in two words.
2. Use figures
   a. For numbers not easily written out
   b. For several numbers occurring in the same passage
   c. For street numbers
   d. For room numbers
   e. For page numbers
   f. For chapter numbers
   g. Decimals and percentages
   h. Statistics or tabulations
   i. Hours of the day with A.M. or P.M.
3. Use figures for dates, but do not use *st, nd, rd,* or *th* with the day of the month.
4. Do not begin a sentence with a number.
5. In expository writing, do not express a sum in both words and figures.
6. Use o'clock following the hour written in words.

Syllabication
1. Do not divide proper nouns.
2. Do not divide words of one syllable.
3. Do not separate a name and the initials, titles, or abbreviations of degrees that go with the name.
4. In typescript and manuscript do not divide short words of two syllables. Only divide words that are more than six letters.
5. Do not divide the last word of a paragraph on a page.
6. Divide between syllables (consult a dictionary if necessary).
7. Divide double consonant words between the two consonants.
8. Divide compound words on the hyphen.
9. In words with prefixes, divide, if possible, on the prefix if it has three or more letters.
10. In words with suffixes, divide on the suffix if it has three or more letters.
11. When dividing, carry over three or more letters if possible.

CAPITALIZATION

Capitalized (cap)   Not Capitalized (lc)

GENERAL RULES

1. The first word of a sentence
2. The first word of each item
   in an outline
   I. Colonial tokens
      A. Authorized by
         British
         1. Rosa Americana
         2. Hibernia coppers
      B. Designed by colonists
3. The first word in each item of
   a list
   Our investigation showed the
   following:
      1. Inadequate lighting
      2. Unpaved streets
      3. Broken walkways

ADDRESSES

1. Specific street names
   4230 Fig Tree Lane

1. Not specific
   The second avenue after the
   first traffic light
2. The second word in a compound
   number
   5620 Fifty-third Street

ABBREVIATIONS

1. For degrees:
   B.A., M.S., Ph.D.
2. For B.C., A.D., A.M.,
   P.M.:
   in 24 B.C.
   1604 A.D.
   at 7:42 A.M.
   at 9:30 P.M.

Capitalized (cap)	Not Capitalized (lc)

BRAND NAMES

1. Only the brand name,
   not the product:
   Venus pens
   Ford trucks
   Gala paper napkins

COURSES OF STUDY

1. Names of specific courses:
   English 101
   Chemistry 202
   American History 311

   1. Studies other than languages:
      chemistry
      typing
      American history
      biology

CALENDAR EVENTS

1. All days of the week

2. All months of the year

3. All holidays:

   Fourth of July
   Christmas Eve
   Veterans' Day

   1. Seasons of the year:
      spring
      summer
      fall
      winter

DEGREES AND TITLES AFTER A NAME

1. John Lawton, Ph.D.

2. Titles of Distinction:
   Harvey Cohen, Mayor
   Thomas R. Henry, Jr.
   Stephen P Warfield, Sr.

   1. Ordinary titles used in
      a general sense:
      Tom is a junior officer on board
      his ship.
      Harvey Cohen was elected
      mayor last week.

DIALOG

1. The first word of the sentence
   following expressions such as
   continued, said, explained, replied:
   The professor continued, "We
   must show that we have grown
   intellectually and that we can
   tolerate others."

   1. Expressions like *he said, replied,*
      continued, and others
      introducing the second part of
      a sentence:
      "We must show," continued the
      professor, "that we have grown
      intellectually and that we can
      tolerate others."

Capitalized (cap)	Not Capitalized (lc)

DIRECT QUOTATION

1. All words capitalized
   by an author:
   Miss Anderson wrote, "Captain
   Wharton was a Saint among the
   members of his crew."

INSTITUTIONS

1. Specific names:
   Northwest Medical Center
   The Senior Class of
   Bucknell University
   Leigh Valley High School

1. Used in a general sense:
   A medical center usually has
   visiting hours from 4 P.M.
   to 8 P.M.

LETTERS

1. Adjectives following the first noun
   in a complimentary closing:
   Very truly yours,
   Your loving niece,

2. The word *dear* when it follows *my*
   in a salutation:
   My dear Dean Harding:

MOVEMENTS, EVENTS, PERIODS IN HISTORY

1. The Anglo-Saxon Period
   The Romantic Movement
   The War Between the States
   World War II
   Declaration of Independence

1. Name of a century not thought of
   as a movement:
   We live in the twentieth century.

ORGANIZATIONS

1. Special interest groups:
   Democratic party
   Republican party
   American Historical Society
   Lions Club

2. Names of companies:
   Mutual Insurance Company
   Lifelite Corporation

Capitalized (cap)	Not Capitalized (lc)

POINTS OF A COMPASS

1. Sections of the country:
   We moved to the Midwest eight years ago, but he remained in the East.

1. Directions:
   The mountains are six miles south of Bryson City, North Carolina.

PROPER NAMES

1. Political divisions:
   Arlington Heights, Illinois
   Switzerland
   Westmoreland County
   Lake Placid

1. earth, sun, moon:
   The best place on earth to watch the sun rising is here on this mountain top.

2. Constellations:
   Orion
   Big Dipper

3. Planets:
   Mars
   Jupiter
   Earth (if listed as a planet)

4. Streets, parks, buildings, hotels:
   Main Street
   Wrigley Building
   Yellowstone Park

5. Adjectives derived from proper nouns:
   Southern
   Canadian
   Indian

1. Proper nouns which have become common:
   a china cup
   a moroccan leather wallet

6. Names of ships, planes and trains (also italics):
   the *Seaward*
   the *Caroline*
   the *Hiawatha*

7. All names of races and nationalities:
   Greeks
   Indians
   French

Capitalized (cap)	Not Capitalized (lc)

RELIGION

1. Words designating the deity:
   Lord
   Savior
   Master
   Allah
   Buddah
   Yahweh

1. Not the word god or goddess referring to a pagan god unless it is a title:
   the Greek gods
   the Goddess of Liberty

2. Pronouns referring to the deity:
   We are sure He loves us.

2. The pronoun *whom* may or may not be capitalized in reference to the deity:
   Praise God from whom all blessings flow.

3. Sacred books:
   Old Testament
   Bible
   Koran

4. Names of religious groups:
   Baptists
   Catholics
   Jews
   Buddhists

TITLES OF ESSAYS, BOOKS, POEMS

1. First, last, and important words:
   "The Shape of Peace"
   From Here to Eternity

1. Prepositions, conjunctions, and articles:
   "The Death of the Hired Man"

2. Prepositions of five letters or more:
   "The Stage Without a Curtain"

TITLES WITH A NAME

1. Preceding a name:
   President Johnson
   the late President Truman
   Captain Ellington
   Aunt Ruth
   Professor Wolff

1. The name of a worker in a particular field:
   Barron is a television technician for the Rayo Corporation.

Capitalized (cap)   Not Capitalized (lc)

2. Substituted for a name:
The President of the United
States
The President will arrive with
the Secretary of State

2. Officers of organizations:
The president of the Elks Club
called the meeting to order.

3. Used in place of a name
Tell me, Doctor, when will he
be released from the hospital?

3. Family relationships preceded
by a possessive:
My father is a football fan.

4. Family relationships not preceded
by a possessive or used as a
substitute for a name:
The family held a reunion for
Grandmother's eighty-fifth
birthday.

4. Titles used in a general sense:
The old dean looked at his
students without saying a
word.

GRAMMAR PROBLEMS

Rule   Example

A. Pronoun-Antecedent

1. Pronouns agree with their
antecedent in person,
gender, and number.
2. Use *who, whom,* when
referring to persons.
3. Use *that* or *which* when
referring to things.
4. Use *that* or *which* when
referring to both persons
or things.
5. In formal writing, do not
use *you, they,* or *it* in
the indefinite sense.

1. *Each* of us must do *his* share.
All of the people in the
room raised *their* hands.
2. The *girl who* is standing
near the door is my cousin.
3. May I have my *pen which*
you have in your hand?
4. Let us not forget the *men*
and their *machines* upon
which we are dependent.
5. *Incorrect:* They do not want
you to talk in the library.
Correct: The librarians do
not like to have students
talk in the library.

Rule   Example

B. Subject-Verb

1. Verbs agree in number and person with the subject.
2. Intervening phrases between the subject and the verb do not affect the verb.
3. Use a singular verb with nouns that are plural in form but singular in number.
4. In *there is* or *there are* sentences, the verb will agree with the subject that follows it.
5. The relative pronoun *who* may be plural or singular, depending on the antecedent, and the verb will be selected accordingly.

1. *Each one* of the candidates *is* worthy of the office.
2. *Jane,* as well as her mother, *has returned.*
3. The *news is reported* each evening at six o'clock.
4. There *are* six *chairs* in the hall.
5. He is one of those modern *writers who* have attempted to make science fiction popular. (Who refers to writers.)

ILLOGICAL COMPARISONS (comp)

1. Avoid a misleading comparison

Original:
His face is like a movie actor.
Correction:
His face is like that of a movie actor.
Original:
Joan Baez is more popular than any folk singer.
Correction:
Joan Baez is more popular than any other folk singer.

2. Complete all comparisons

Original:
I like him more than my mother.
Correction:
I like him more than my mother does.

Rule	Example
3. Tandem comparisons: Complete the first comparison before adding on the second.	*Original:* He looks as strong, if not stronger than his brother. *Correction:* He looks as strong as his brother, if not stronger. *Original:* The salaries earned by construction workers are at times as high or if not higher, than the salaries earned by college graduates. *Correction:* At times the salaries earned by construction workers are as high as those earned by college graduates, if not higher.

MODIFIER PROBLEMS

Rule	Example
1. **Misplaced modifiers or misplaced parts:** (mis pt) Modifiers should be placed as near as possible to the word they modify.	*Original:* Every passenger will have long hair, male or female. *Correction:* Every male or female passenger will have long hair.
2. **Squinting modifiers:** (mod) This is a modifier that can possibly modify two different words in the sentence. *Original:* I only read four books this year. *Correction:* Only I read four books this year. or I read only four books this year.	*Original:* After we had stopped at the Information Desk with the help of the boys we found our location on the museum's map *Correction:* With the help of the boys we found our location . . . or After we had stopped at the Information Desk with the help of the boys, . . .

Rule	Example
3. Dangling Modifiers: (dgl) There is no word in the sentence to which the modifier can refer.	*Original:* When writing a research paper, certain rules must be followed. *Correction:* When a student writes a research paper, he has to follow certain rules. *Original:* Riding down a country road, a mailbox covered with flower designs can be seen. *Correction:* Riding down a country road, we saw a mailbox covered with flowers.

REFERENCE PROBLEMS (ref)

Rule	Example
1. **Vague pronoun reference:** (ref)	*Original:* After the boys made camp, they remembered that they had forgotten their flashlights, but that didn't bother them. *Correction:* After the boys made camp, they remembered that they had forgotten their flashlights, but that oversight didn't bother them.
2. **Indefinite use of pronoun:** (ref)	*Original:* It says in the newspaper that the number of child abuse cases has risen. *Correction:* The newspaper reports that the number of child abuse cases has risen.
3. **Ambiguous pronoun reference:** (ambig)	*Original:* When Terry met John he told him that he had just been selected as Student Government president.

Rule	Example

Correction:
Terry told John, "You have just been selected Student Government president."
or
Terry told John, "I have just been selected as Student Government president."

4. **No antecedent for pronoun:** (ant)

Original:
We enjoyed our stay in Italy. They are friendly and hospitable people.
Correction:
We enjoyed our stay in Italy. The Italians are friendly and hospitable people.

SENTENCE STRUCTURE (ss)

1. Make your sentence complete when you use *so, too, such:*

Original:
They were so tired.
Correction:
They were so tired that they went to bed immediately.
Original:
The boy was too young.
Correction:
The boy was too young to join the Boy Scouts.
Original:
That is such a rare coin.
Correction:
That is such a rare coin that you should place it in a museum.

Rule	Example
2. Be sure that a word calls for the same form of a verb and preposition in tandem constructions. If not, write the correct form before the second construction.	*Original:* The ixora bushes were clipped and the lawn mowed on Saturday. *Correction:* The ixora bushes were clipped and the lawn was mowed on Saturday.
3. Do not write sentences that are awkward or difficult to understand: (awk or k)	*Original:* At the moment of King Henry the Eighth's death, Elizabeth became queen, although many formalities and traditions had to be gone through. *Correction:* At the moment of King Henry the Eighth's death, Elizabeth became queen. However, because of tradition, Elizabeth had to go through several formalities before assuming the throne.
4. Do not write sentences that are obscure: (nc)	*Original:* The wedding announcement was made in the form of a miniature newspaper with stories and pictures of the couple accompanied with a light buffet. *Correction:* The wedding announcement was made at a small reception where a light buffet was served to guests. The announcement was made in the form of a miniature newspaper with stories and pictures of the couple's courtship.

Rule	Example
5. Avoid mixed figures of speech: (fig sp)	*Original:* The young candidate for Congress is rapidly gaining a foothold in the public's mind. *Correction:* The young candidate for Congress is rapidly gaining a place in the public's mind.
6. Express parallel thoughts in parallel form: (// or paral)	*Original:* Two things I would like to know how to do well are to play the piano and water ski. *Correction:* Two things I would like to know how to do are to play the piano and to water ski.
7. Use the correlatives (//) both . . . and not only . . . but also neither . . . nor either . . . or whether . . . or only before the sentence elements that are parallel in form:	*Original:* He neither likes beets nor spinach. *Correction:* He likes neither beets nor spinach. *Original:* I don't know whether to call my neighbor or if I should call the service station for help. *Correction:* I don't know whether to call my neighbor or the service station for help. *Original:* You either begin to set the table or start dinner. *Correction:* You begin either to set the table or start dinner.

Rule	Example
8. Do not split constructions: (ss)	*Original:* I want to quickly finish my term paper. *Correction:* I want to finish my term paper quickly. *Original:* The house has, although none of the tourists would think so, been visited by ten thousand people. *Correction:* Although none of the tourists would think so, the house has been visited by ten thousand people.

SHIFTS (shift)

Avoid unnecessary shifts in:

Rule	Example
1. **Tense**	*Original:* He sent his manuscript to the publisher, but it is returned to him. *Correction:* He sent his manuscript to the publisher, but it was returned to him.
2. **Person**	*Original:* For the inexperienced boatman, it is advisable to moor your boat before attempting to raise the sails. *Correction:* For the inexperienced boatman, it is advisable to moor the boat before attempting to raise the sails.
3. **Mood**	*Original:* We all wished the game was over. *Correction:* We all wished the game were over.

Rule	Example

4. Relative pronoun

Original:
She refused to buy the machine that had no cover and which had plastic parts.
Correction:
She refused to buy the machine that had plastic parts and that had no cover.

5. Voice

Original:
As a camp counselor I taught the boys how to make tea from pine needles and how to scale a fish; also, they were taught how to make camp.
Correction:
As a camp counselor I taught the boys how to make camp, how to scale a fish, and how to make tea from pine needles.

PUNCTUATION GUIDE (p)

APOSTROPHE

1. **Used to show possession:**
   Stephen and Susan's bicycle *(joint ownership)*
   Stephen's and Susan's bicycles *(individual ownership)*
   his brother-in-law's car *(compound word)*
   a nickel's worth of candy
   a month's pay
   the girls' apartment
   the children's playground
   Charles Dickens's novels

2. **Used to show plurals of letters, words, and numbers:**
   a. Dot your *i*'s, cross your *t*'s, an don't use so many *and*'s.
   b. Your answer should have three 9's in it.

3. **Used for omission of numbers or letters:**
   a. The class of '49 is having a reunion June 14 at one o'clock.
   b. Who's the one to investigate this haunted house.

BRACKETS

1. **To enclose a parenthesis within a parenthesis:**
   If he attends the college of his choice (Dixon University [the largest one in the state]), his parents refuse to help with expenses.
2. **To enclose material a writer has inserted within a quotation to explain it or correct it:**
   The detective wrote, "The motive [for the betrayal of his producer] had not yet been determined."
3. **To enclose the word *sic* in a quotation to indicate that an error in spelling appeared in the original quote:**
   "The robbed [*sic*] faculty members were the first in the graduation procession," reported the *Daily News*.

COLON

1. **Before formal appositives:**
   On the sign was written one word: *love*.
2. **Before quotations introduced formally:**
   These words from the late President J. F. Kennedy's Inaugural Speech will be long remembered: "Ask not what your country can do for you, but what you can do for your country."
3. **Before statements introduced formally:**
   Our objections to the building of condominiums on the golf club grounds are several: our homes would depreciate in value, our view would be hampered, our roads could not support the burden of a minimum of 1,200 new cars in the area, and our children would be deprived of the park they now enjoy.
4. **Before a series introduced with words like the following, as follows, are these:**
   Among the suggestions for world peace were these: total disarmament and the withdrawal of all troops.
5. **Between independent clauses when the second clause explains or amplifies the first:**
   a. Woodrow Wilson said, "Often the fate of a word is fortuitous: it falls on evil or good days by accident."
   b. The popular media, too, has been caught up in the occult revival: horror movies are more popular than ever.
6. **In certain formal uses:**
   a. Hours:minutes: 7:45 P.M.
   b. Salutation of a business letter: Gentlemen:, Dear Sir:
   c. City:publisher: St. Louis: Conrad Publishers
   d Act:scene: Act IV: 3

e. Bible chapter:verse: John 2:4
f. Title of book:subtitle: *The Principles of Writing: A Handbook and a Workbook*
g. Newspaper page:column: p. 14A:6

COMMA

1. **To separate coordinate clauses joined by <u>and</u>, <u>or</u>, <u>for</u>, <u>nor</u>, <u>yet</u>, and <u>but</u> except when clauses are very short and closely related in meaning:**
A letter of application may get you an interview, but you may still not be accepted for the job.

2. **To separate words, phrases, and clauses in a series:**
   a. The bowl was filled with oranges, grapes, bananas, and apples.
   b. The products at the Chicago Home Show were from Japan, from New Zealand, from Portugal, and from Italy.
   c. The weather was clear, the sun was shining, and the humidity was low.

3. **To separate coordinate adjectives not joined by a conjunction:**
The Anglo-Saxons spent days in the Mead Hall listening to loud, boastful promises.

4. **To set off a long introductory subordinate phrase or clause:**
   a. *Phrase:* With all chapters of the novel completed, Sarah was ready to submit it to the staff for final editing.
   b. *Clause:* Although Americans are admired for their industrious spirit, they are criticized by Europeans for this same characteristic.

5. **To set off nonrestrictive elements:**
   a. *Nonrestrictive elements:*
      (1) John Ellington, in a gray flannel suit, looks like a typical young American executive of the 1950s.
      (2) Hair styling for men, which is always expensive, costs less in this town.
   b. *Restrictive elements:*
      (1) The boy who walked in late is my roommate.
      (2) The man in the gray flannel suit looks like a typical young American executive of the 1950s.
   c. *Read either way:*
      (1) The coin which was made of silver was valued at one thousand dollars. (Several coins are on the table.)
      (2) The coin, which was made of silver, was valued at one thousand dollars. (Only one coin was on the table.)

6. **To set off modifiers or elements out of the normal word order:**
   Tired and hungry, the hunters returned to their camp without having found any game.

7. **To set off transitional conjunctions (conjunctive adverbs) like however, nevertheless:**
   a. They agreed, however, not to file suit against the dog's owner.
   b. I wish to travel in Europe this summer; on the other hand, my husband prefers to visit Japan.

8. **To set off yes, no, and mild interjections (oh):**
   a. Oh, I forgot to lock the patio doors when I left.
   b. No, this is not the time to squander money on luxuries.

9. **To prevent misreading:**
   Beyond, the road suddenly curved to the right without warning, and we had to be careful to avoid driving our car over the cliff.

10. **To set off appositives:**
    The final assignment, the Cause and Effect Theme, will need both footnotes and a bibliography.

11. **To set off a direct address:**
    We agree, Ronald, that you should jog at least one hour a day.

12. **To separate verbs of saying such as says, responded, asked:**
    When Kay was asked how old she was she answered, "Plenty nine."

13. **Between parts of an address, dates, name and degree, name and title of distinction:**
    a. Ray Fletcher lives at 4722 Woodmont Avenue, Arnold, Pennsylvania. He was born on June 22, 1954.
    b. David L. Tillman, B.A., M.A., Ph.D.
       Linda Foster, Director of Community Services
       Brian Cohee, Ambassador from Ireland

14. **For contrast and for emphasis:**
    The coach was forced to use the smaller practice field for his first game, not the stadium designed especially for league games.

15. **For omission of a word:**
    My older sister lives in Milwaukee, Wisconsin; my brother, in Wheaton, Maryland.

16. **To add a short question:**
    It is safe to swim in this canal, isn't it?

17. **To set off an absolute phrase which modifies the sentence as a whole:**
    Our world trip over, we finally settled in Arlington Heights, Illinois.

18. **Salutation of a friendly letter:**
    Dear Jane,

DO NOT USE COMMAS

1. **To separate the subject and its verb:**
   a. Only the students who pre-registered for the Occult Seminar, were permitted to attend.
   b. In the 1970s horror movies such as *Sixth Sense* and *Night Gallery*, captured the evening viewers, and *Dark Shadows*, chilled the watchers of daytime television.

2. **To separate a verb from its complement:**
   His favorite sports are, fishing, hunting, and scuba diving.

3. **Between an adjective and the noun it modifies and between adjectives that are not coordinating:**
   The pretty, little, mountain, village near Mt. Etna in Sicily caters to tourists who wish to ski on the slopes.

4. **After a coordinating conjunction:**
   No one can teach you how to become a financially successful writer but, a good teacher can help you to learn to write well-organized, well-structured papers.

5. **Before coordinating conjunctions joining two words or two phrases:**
   The room was decorated with original paintings done by her children, and with those she had purchased from an artist she had met in Europe.

6. **After the verb of <u>saying</u> in an indirect quotation:**
   Lara McFarland said, that there would be a large voter turn out for the next election.

7. **With an appositive that is felt to be part of a single proper name, such as William the Conqueror:**
   Was it Mary, Queen of Scots, who was beheaded?

8. **Before a parenthesis, only after:**
   [1]Hans Holzer, *Ghosts of the Golden West,* (New York: Ace Books, 1973), p. 24.

9. **After a short, essential introductory adverbial clause or phrase:**
   Last night, I met a former classmate of mine who is now listed in *Who's Who in America.*

10. **After a short prepositional phrase which introduces the sentence:**
    After today, I will quite smoking.

11. **To separate a restrictive element from the sentence:**
    Georgia is a girl, who enjoys reading science fiction novels.

12. **Between the main clause and a dependent adverbial clause which follows it:**
    There would be fewer problems for students in foreign language classes, if they knew English grammar better.

DASH

1. **To indicate hesitation or uncertainty in speech or speech that is broken off abruptly:**
   You turn three blocks to the right — or is it only two blocks — before coming to City Hall.
2. **To indicate sudden breaks in thought:**
   Did you realize that John — well, I won't even discuss his misfortune.
3. **To indicate a break in sentence structure:**
   a. To separate a long appositive that is a series with internal punctuation:
      The dogs — poodles, shepherds, terriers, and retrievers — will be judged later this week.
   b. To separate an explanatory or parenthetical phrase or clause:
      Your mother and I were pleased — proud, we should say — when you received the Bausch and Lomb Science Award.
   c. For special or dramatic emphasis:
      If you should miss the plane — heaven forbid! — you will not be able to charter another one for three months.
   d. Before an author's name when the name appears at the end of a quotation:
      "Wisdom denotes the pursuing of the best ends by the best means." — Francis Hutcheson.
   e. To indicate the omission of words or letters:
      Are you familiar with the writer Grant Allen (1848–1899)?
      Lt. William C— has been a subject of controversy since his arrest.

ELLIPSES

1. **Use three spaced periods within a sentence to show an omission:**
   "Yet despite strict government restrictions . . . older workers are confronted continually with the same bias: they are too old to do an employer any good."
2. **If the omission is at the end of a sentence, use four spaced periods:**
   In 1973 "the Department of Labor found 1,836 employers, employment agencies, and unions violating the Age Discrimination in Employment Act of 1967 . . . ."

3. **Use a full line of spaced periods if a paragraph of quoted material has been omitted:**
Not everyone is convinced, though, that age discrimination is much of a problem today. Lon D. Barton, President of Cadillac Associates, an employment agency specializing in executive placement, calls such bias, 'almost a thing of the past.'

. . . .

'It used to be that the sure way to fill a position was to send an eager 25-year-old out for an interview. Today companies seem to be looking for a mature 40-year-old.'[1]

[1] Copyright *Fort Lauderdale News,* 1974, reprinted by permission.

END PUNCTUATION

1. **Period**
   a. *After all abbreviations commonly used in writing:*
      Mrs., Ms., Dr., St. (You may omit the periods after some organizations and agencies, such as CBS, AFL, NBC, CIA, TWA.)
   b. *Inside all quotation marks:*
      He sang a song from the 1940s, "Blue Moon."
   c. *Outside parentheses when the parenthetical statement, figure, or word is part of the preceding statement:*
      He paid thirty dollars ($30.00).
   d. *Only one period if the sentence ends with an abbreviation:*
      He is a registered C.P.A.
2. **Exclamation mark:**
   a. *Use infrequently*
   b. *To follow an expression of strong feeling that is a complete sentence:*
      Wrong: Look before you cross the railroad tracks!
      Right: Look out! The train is coming.
   c. *Never use more than one:*
      I'll never date him again!!! Only one exclamation mark is necessary: I'll never date him again!
   d. *Use at end of the sentence even when words such as* oh, no, yes, *introduce the sentence:*
      Oh no, I didn't win the million dollar lottery!
3. **Question mark:**
   a. *Enclosed within parentheses after a doubtful date or figure:*
      The Reverend James Brameton (1694?–1744) wrote in *Art of Politics:*

What's not destroyed by Time's devouring hands?
Where's Troy, and where's the Maypole in the Strand?

b. *To follow separate questions within a single interrogative sentence:*
The investigator asked several questions: How old are you? What is your home state? How long have you lived in the apartment? How long do you plan to remain here?

c. *With quotation marks:*
1. Did you answer question 10, "Comment on Hardy's selection of the name Father Time for Jude's son"?
2. Answer only the first question, "How does Clarisse influence Guy Montag in *Fahrenheit 451?*"

d. *Incorrect:*
The comedy (?) is to be presented again at the Forest View Theater on Saturday at 8:00 P.M.

HYPHEN

1. **With two or more words forming a compound adjective:**
This was a never-to-be-forgotten vacation.

2. **With compound numbers from twenty-one to ninety-nine:**
If you count carefully, you will find that there are twenty-seven boxes in the stock room.

3. **At the end of a line to mark a division in a word when the remainder of the word is carried over to the next line:**
Not since the Civil War have so many men pro-
tested the war policies of their government.

4. **Never put a hyphen at the beginning of a line:**
Incorrect:
Behind the Amnesty debate lies the sta
-tistics of the United States involvement in the Vietnam War.

PARENTHESES

1. **To enclose material that is supplementary, explanatory, or interpretive:**
A growing minority is willing to substitute service in such groups as the Peace Corps or VISTA (Volunteers in Service to America) for imprisonment for draft evaders.

2. **General rule to distinguish difference in use of comma, dash, and parentheses:**
a. *Commas* set off material close to the thought of the sentence.
There we met Jerry Frey, who directed us to the department for film editing.

b. *Dashes* set off material that is loosely connected to the thought of the sentence.

Bruce Davenport — he's very handsome — is campaigning for Student Government president.

c. *Parentheses* set off material to indicate the most distant relation to the thought of the sentence.

Amnesty groups argue that the Vietnam War (lasting eleven years and one month) was illegal because the United States government never officially declared war.

Note: Do not use parentheses to cancel any part of your writing.

Incorrect:

The psychological impact of today's movies (effect) affect great numbers of viewers, especially those between the ages of thirteen and thirty.

Correct:

The psychological impact of today's movies   great numbers. . . .

SEMICOLON

1. **Between the clauses of a compound sentence when independent clauses are not joined by one of the coordinating conjunctions:**

   The dog stopped and sniffed; a rabbit was running swiftly through the hollow log nearby.

2. **Before a coordinating conjunction when the independent clauses contain other punctuation:**

   When the university opened its law school, 450 applicants requested admission; but the Dean of Law reported that there were only 170 places available that year.

3. **Between clauses (occasionally between phrases) to indicate balance or contrast or to give a more definite separation than a comma would:**

   When the crowd became quiet again, he said, "There will be no sermon; no lecture; no condemnations. We wish only to exchange ideas."

4. **Before a conjunctive adverb** *(therefore, however, hence, accordingly, then, thus, still, moreover, subsequently)* **that is used to separate two independent clauses:**

   The psychiatrist considered shock movies such as *The Exorcist* to be full of fear and confusion; nevertheless, fans were willing to stand in line for hours just to view the movie.

5. **To separate a series that has internal punctuation:**
The following officers were elected at the last meeting: Tom Harvey, president; Judy Shank, vice-president; Mitchell Turner, secretary; and Barbara Heinz, treasurer.

QUOTATION MARKS

1. **Double quotation marks ("):**
    a. *For a single sentence, to enclose a direct quotation:*
    When asked what he would buy if he could have anything in the department store, three-year-old Billy answered, "The toy department."
    b. *For several sentences, only at the beginning and at the end of the entire quotation*
    c. *For several paragraphs:*
       1. Begin each paragraph with quotation marks, but place them at the end of the last paragraph only.
       2. In a typed manuscript indent and single space quotations which are more than five lines long.
       Do not use quotation marks with material indented in this manner (see pages 360–363).
    d. *For dialog:*
       1. Use a separate paragraph for every change of speaker.
       2. Enclose short descriptive, explanatory, or narrative passages with dialogue if they are placed between sentences of dialogue spoken by the same person:
       "No," he said, "I have not hurt myself." However, he leaned against the wall, closed his eyes, sucked in his breath, and bit his bottom lip.
       "Mr. Nye," the boy shouted, "stay where you are, and I will go for help." He had noticed that while Mr. Nye was leaning there, drops of blood began trickling down the side of his face.
    e. *For titles:*
       1. Essays, articles, short stories, chapters, short poems, or any subdivision of a periodical or book:
       The title of the essay is "Clearcutting: A Devastation of Our Forests."
       Perhaps the article "Fungus Enzyme Changes Wastes Into Sugar" can be used for your research paper.
       Read "That Only a Mother" from the science fiction anthology *Speculations.*